THE SOCIALIST REGISTER

D1296877

THE COMMUNIST MANIFESTO NOW

SOCIALIST REGISTER 1998

Edited by LEO PANITCH and COLIN LEYS

MERLIN PRESS UK
MONTHLY REVIEW PRESS NEW YORK
FERNWOOD PUBLISHING HALIFAX

First published in 1998
by The Merlin Press Ltd
2 Rendlesham Mews, Rendlesham
Nr. Woodbridge, Suffolk
IP12 2SZ

© The Merlin Press 1998

Published in the US by:
 Monthly Review Press
 122 West 27 Street
 New York
 NY 10001

Published in Canada by:
 Fernwood Publishing Co.
 P.O. Box 9409
 Station A
 Halifax
 Nova Scotia
 B3K 5S3

British Library Cataloguing in Publication Data

The Socialist Register. — 1998
  1. Socialism — 1998
  I. Panitch, Leo
  355'.005

Typesetting by
Creative Print and Design, Harmondsworth, Middlesex

Printed in Finland by WSOY

TABLE OF CONTENTS

PREFACE

For the thirty-fourth volume of *The Socialist Register*, published in February 1998, *not* to have focussed on the *Communist Manifesto*, published in February 1848, would have been hard to justify. The fact that this 150th anniversary falls within less than a decade of the collapse of Communism with a capital 'C', and of the parties associated with it, in no way diminishes the appeal and necessity of a cooperative, democratic and egalitarian social order. This is what might be called communism with a small 'c', and it poses and will always pose a threat to capitalism. For this reason it is a privilege as well as a pleasure to be able to celebrate 'the single most influential text written in the nineteenth century' (as Peter Osborne, in his essay in this volume, rightly calls it). Our theme, in other words, is anything but antiquarian. We are interested in the Manifesto *now*, to see both why it was such a uniquely influential text, and what light it can still throw on our situation today.

The Manifesto was a radically new kind of political document, breaking entirely new ground rhetorically as well as analytically, and in its conception of the relation between theory and practice; but it was also a product of much more than the genius of one man (or two, counting Engels). Its subsequent fame and influence have tended to obscure the fact that it was very much the product of a political movement, at the time far from strong or even popular. Seeing how it tried to respond to the problems faced by the activists of the Communist League – 'de-reifying' the Manifesto, as Rob Beamish puts it in his evocative discussion of how it came to be written – brings out its contemporary relevance in a new way.

Marx and his fellow activists had been living through a period of reaction, as we are; the defiant language of the Manifesto bears no

vii

relation to the actual strength of the social forces they sought to mobilise and represent. What it does testify to is their determination not to be intimidated by the strength of the forces ranged against them, their capacity to look beyond that strength to the contradictions undermining it, and – above all – their acceptance of responsibility for trying to bring about change. As Boris Kagarlitsky remarks, in a striking essay cited in our own contribution to this volume: 'People have either to organise themselves to carry out joint actions or to reconcile themselves to their fates'. No document has ever made this clearer than the Manifesto. Re-reading it today, in the context so vividly brought to life in the essays by Bernard Moss and Paul Thomas published here, is to be reminded forcibly of this truth.

As for the light that the Manifesto throws on contemporary problems, two things stand out most strikingly from the other essays in this volume. One is how much of the global expansion of capitalism, now reaching something of a climax, is not merely foreshadowed, but analysed with phenomenal precision in the Manifesto. So far from Marx being a 'dead dog' (as he himself in his postcsript to *Capital* complained people were making Hegel out to be) he is very much alive and biting. Not to avow oneself a pupil of Marx, in the same sense that he avowed himself 'the pupil' of Hegel – i.e. to distance oneself clearly from the condescensions of 'post-Marxism'- would be petty and absurd. (For the same reason, we too have even 'here and there coquetted with the mode of expression peculiar to him', as he said he did with Hegel – for which we hope to be forgiven). On the other hand, what also stands out is how, even where the Manifesto was wrong, or left problems unresolved, or where contemporary problems fall outside its scope, its *way* of approaching problems has stood the test of time, as is demonstrated in the powerful essays published here by David Harvey, Sam Gindin, John Bellamy Foster, Peter Gowan, Sheila Cohen and Kim Moody.

Last but not least, the Manifesto still retains its power to inspire in a different way, as is demonstrated by Sheila Rowbotham's remarkable 'letter from a socialist feminist'- a lively, yet also profound and even moving critique of the Manifesto's failure to do justice to the goals or the achievements of the socialist feminists of its time. Marx, one hopes, would have endorsed this criticism were he living today, rather than drowning the critic in a torrent of counter-argument as the author of the letter fears.

Readers will note that Colin Leys has joined Leo Panitch as co-editor, thus reestablishing the Register's tradition of co-editorship interrupted by Ralph Miliband's untimely death. Our Manchester and Toronto editorial collectives remain as active and important as ever, for which the co-editors are very grateful, as we also are to our corresponding editors in Athens, Berlin, Boston and Hong Kong, who are now joined by Patrick Bond in Johannesburg and Barbara Epstein in San Francisco. A further welcome sign of the continued international standing of the *Socialist Register* is the publication in New Delhi of a separate Indian edition by J.P. Bagchi; and a new publication in Greek, consisting of a selection of articles from the 1996 and 1997 volumes of the *Register*, is due to appear in Athens in 1998.

Readers will notice, and we hope also endorse, a change in the format and font size of this year's *Socialist Register*, which we think makes it more attractive and easier to read, and for which we owe our publisher, Martin Eve, grateful thanks. A change in our future plans should also be mentioned here. We are bringing forward the publication date of future volumes of the *Socialist Register*. The present volume is the last that will appear at the beginning of the year whose date it carries. Subsequent volumes will appear in the autumn of the preceding year, beginning with the 1999 volume which will be published in autumn 1998 on the central theme of 'globalisation and democracy': it will include important essays by, among others, Atilio Boron, David Coates, Joachim Hirsch, Birgit Mahnkopf and Konstantinos Tsoukalas. Various considerations have led to this change, chief among them being the disadvantages that arise when for one reason or another publication of a volume is held up so that it does not reach bookshops until well into the year.

The change coincides with new arrangements that we are also putting in place to make it easier, and as far as possible usual, for people to subscribe regularly to the *Register*. Readers can obtain information on how to do so by writing to the publishers whose addresses are printed elsewhere in this volume, or by joining our electronic mail discussion forum, socialist-register@yorku.ca or visiting the Socialist Register website.

This year's contributors are located as follows. Sheila Rowbotham is at the Department of Sociology at the University of Manchester and David Harvey is Professor of Geography at Johns Hopkins University in Baltimore. Sam Gindin is Assistant to the President of the Canadian Automobile Workers (CAW) in Toronto; Sheila Cohen is associated with Trade Union Forum in London, and Kim Moody is director of Labour Notes, a Detroit-based independemt labour magazine. Peter Gowan is Principal Lecturer in European Politics at the University of

North London and Bernard Moss is associated with the Institute for European Studies in London. John Bellamy Foster is in the Department of Sociology at the University of Oregon; and Peter Osborne is at the Centre for Research in Modern European Philosophy at Middlesex University in London. Paul Thomas teaches political science at the University of California, Berkeley; and Rob Beamish teaches the sociology of sport at Queen's University in Kingston, Ontario.

In conclusion we would like to thank all our contributors for the effort they put into their essays for this volume, and Paul Cammack for originally suggesting the theme. As usual we should remind our readers that neither our contributors nor the editors necessarily agree with everything that appears in the volume. Special thanks are also due to Alan Zuege for his editorial help; to Dave Timms for his initiatives on promotion; and finally to Martin Eve, both for the exceptional professional expertise he always brings to the production of the *Register*, and for his insistence on the value of including the *Manifesto* itself in this volume.

January 1998   L.P.
                                                                C.L.

DEAR DR MARX
A LETTER FROM A SOCIALIST FEMINIST

Sheila Rowbotham

"12 John Street,
Toronto ,
Upper Canada.
December 29th, 1851

Dear Dr Marx,*
I am woefully behind the times. I plead revolution, exile, the laundry
of the Wisconsin Phalanx, an American women's rights convention
and two young children. Philosophy has been quite swept away and I
have only just read your rousing Manifesto. I chanced upon it in the
most extraordinary circumstances – you will, I am sure, agree that the
'frightful hobgoblin'[1] made its most unusual entry yet when I tell you
my tale.

I would have read you and Mr Engels in Paris back in '48 if I had
not been running from the barricades to the office of *Voix des Femmes*
and then to the women's clubs. After the horror of the June days I
was working so hard in our associated house and creche that I read
very little apart from the women's newspapers we kept starting. You
probably know the circumstances which forced me to flee from
France in 1850 after the police raided us in the home of Mme
Deroin at the end of May. She and Pauline Roland were held for trial
with Femme Nicaud and imprisoned for their part in the federation

---

*The author of this imaginary letter, Annette Devereux, is a fictional character, along
with her husband, Victor, the Chartist typographer and M and Mme Ducrocq.
However all the other characters mentioned are historical figures and information
about them is provided in the order in which they appear at the end of the letter. The
arguments and demands presented , the political events described, the journals and the
Fourierist Phalanx at Wisconsin are all based on historical reality.

of associations. My husband Victor had been in correspondence with the American Associationists for several years. It was thus that I arrived in Wisconsin.

The Wisconsin Phalanx was breaking up in squabbles and recriminations just as we arrived. You will be interested to hear however, that, unlike some of the Eastern communities, our Wisconsin Phalansterians were economically sucessful. Utopias you see come in differing shapes and forms. Our Wisconsin Associationists knew about farming and we had a surplus to take to market.

To be frank, though, I believe we could have been happier in the East. Among the farmers we were always to be outsiders. Victor and I would wander among the reeds by the lake nearby and conjure the cobbled streets of Saint Germain. Paris is not the place to prepare you for nature whatever M. Fourier says about the virtues of country air for passional harmony and well-being. I prefer on the whole to visit nature rather than to dwell in it.

Victor was able to pursue his trade – they enjoyed smoking the cigars he made in the evenings – but the conversation was mainly about agriculture. I was compelled to spend long hours in the laundry with the women who spoke only of domestic matters. My attempts to do more fulfilling work came to nothing. The Americans did not consider that my English was sufficiently fluent for school teaching. I have found a certain prejudice here against those whose mother tongue is not English, which I resent. I know I could have improved the school greatly. The children were still learning mainly by rote and the passional abilities so valued by Associationists were completely neglected. My pleas for music, dancing and painting were disregarded. There was democracy there of a sort, but if you were not a stockholder your voice counted for little.

But I am straying from my promise to tell you of the curious and amusing manner in which the *Manifesto* found its way to Wisconsin. One consequence of the Phalanx's success was viewed with a lack of enthusiasm by the women members; our prosperity attracted visitors and visitors resulted in more laundry. Before you condemn us I beg you to try the steam yourself for eight hours. Baskets and baskets of dirty linen do not incline you to welcome their wearers. Personally I was prepared to regard the philosophical and literary minded visitors with *some* favour for they brought news of the world. But lecturers on such topics were not fond of going so far West, so sadly we were inclined to attract economists and I found their conversation too dry to compensate for the extra drudgery.

You must have guessed by now! I am proud to announce that I rescued your *Manifesto* from drowning. There it was in a shirt pocket covered with washing – a copy of *The Red Republican* all the way from London with Miss Macfarlane's translation of your work. I was concerned for its welfare amidst the steam and promptly sought out its absent-minded owner, a young typographer and former Chartist who was shaking off the disappointments of the old world. We engaged in the most animated conversation about the ideals and failures of '48. This brief interval was one of my happiest memories of Wisconsin, for there were few people who understood what that year had meant in Europe. The opportunity to communicate with one who had known similar defeat was a salve for the pent-up anguish I had brought unaware to America. In that chance meeting I felt fully alive again. He insisted I kept the journal as a gift when he continued his journey further West. I should really have given it to the Phalanx library, but it was such a treasured possession.

Mr Dana passed through later (he favoured us because of his passion for horticulture) and was greatly amused when I showed him *The Red Republican*. You are no doubt familiar with the newspaper he edits, the *New York Daily Tribune*. He said he had heard that it was Mrs Marx who encouraged you to collaborate with the working men of the Communist League. I can imagine her noticing the discomfort of workers amidst philosophers who can sometimes act with an unintended scholarly arrogance, assuming familiarity with terms and ideas alien to those who have had to educate themselves. Working people are then inclined to suspect that an aristocracy of scholars is to replace an aristocracy of money. I believe that we socialist women are similarly able to detect democratic dictators within our own ranks, so I can appreciate Mrs Marx's insight most heartfully.

We left the Phalanx amidst discord six months ago. It had become the victim of its own success, serving for some as a stepping stone to becoming capitalists. But it is an ill wind that blows nobody any good, after a brief spell in Akron we moved here at the suggestion of M. and Mme Ducrocq who have established a school based on associationist ideals of an integral education. I am able to teach once more and delight in how the children flourish through the exercise of the body and the senses as well as the intellect. We encourage them to learn from experience as well as from books, and our school, which is attended by the children of artisans and teachers alike, is a little palace of social harmony. Instead of rote learning and harsh punishments our pupils discover knowledge for themselves in a spirit of cooperation and democracy. I believe that education should be, as far as possible, a joyful affair. I have fond memories to this day of Mrs Marx's delightful recitations. Tell her the children are already able to give dramatic renderings of Goethe and Shelley. How I wish you could hear their voices across the Atlantic.

My husband is able to practise his trade independently – but I assure you my honest Victor is not at all the bourgeois. He is at present studying the conditions of working people in Toronto and talking with other men in his trade about association. Thus, while so many of our great hopes have been dashed, here we can still do something. I continue to miss France and especially my beloved Paris but I am beginning to recognise a spirit of liberty and a readiness to break down the divisions which prevail in the old world which I value greatly. The real enemy of association here is greed rather than an aristocracy of birth.

So we have been busy, but at last this month, amidst heavy snow, I have had time for reflection in the evenings and could finally read your Manifesto. I went straight through in one rush with mounting excitement. My first impression was the drama and the vigour of the language – so different from the dry style of most political economy. I could see what efforts you had made to break with a purely philo-sophic style. This was not just a matter of words – the workers are there in the centre of the stage striving for their emancipation. It reminded me of the epics of old, as tremendous forces gather and engage in combat – but this was about the here and now – the harsh devouring system of society which has been breaking every custom, shattering all we had assumed and making the very earth seem to tremble under our feet. I marvelled at your ability to reach through to the very bedrock of society and to present such a broad vision of history with such admirable clarity.

As I read I was back in the Rue Vanneau. How you would pound the table! Mr Ruge would explain that it was necessary, as the socialist principle must be 'ruthless criticism of all that exists'.[2] Nonetheless Mrs Marx cast many an anxious eye at the crockery. Talk was all we knew of socialism in those days. So much has happened in the eight years since then that it seems like another era. How could we have imagined the barricades, the betrayals or the present despotism in France? Our political world has turned full circle and been shaken inside out. Was it some inner intimation which led you to write 'All that is solid melts into air'?[3] I know you would reproach me, if we were back in Saint Germain, for entertaining notions of the fantastic. But you were writing as a revolution simmered beneath the surface and the Manifesto is prescient of some great conflagration. But what are we to make of it all now? If we knew the outcome of our endeavours, would we act with greater wisdom or freeze in dread before capricious circumstance? I cannot feel as certain as you about our inevitable triumph. Over here in the new world I can see few signs of any historical movement towards association – quite the reverse. It seems we have to proceed piecemeal.

I have now read the *Manifesto* several times in a more critical spirit and would be interested to know whether you have reconsidered some of the points you make in the light of the terrible defeats we have witnessed since 1848. And – though I would dearly love to hear your opinions in person – I suspect an epistle is going to favour me, for you are inclined to drown objections in a torrent of oratory. As you are a man of great power and considerable learning it is not easy to stand one's ground in opposition to your views face to face, so it is perhaps as well that we have the Atlantic between us.

I concurred with your criticisms of 'reactionary conservative Socialists'.[4] Many members of the Wisconsin Phalanx did indeed become more interested in their stock than in spreading Association. Still I thought you were over harsh in your dismissal of the Associationist cause. Communities varied greatly. Ours, as I said, was strong on economy and weak on conviviality, however I think a better mix might have been possible in other circumstances. When we moved on I felt regret that we were abandoning Association as a way of life and in looking back I have garnered my happier memories – shelling peas in the summer time or singing with the other women as we worked. I could not help but wonder whether your brief and unhappy attempt at associated living might have prejudiced your judgement somewhat. Mrs Ruge had many virtues but she and Mrs Marx had little in common. If a community is large and diverse it should be more possible to seek out those whose company is pleasing and rewarding.

Before you accuse me of seeking the ideal let me say that it has been a valuable – if sobering – experience to see the theories we debated so enthusiastically in Paris put into practice. My time at the Wisconsin Phalanx taught me how great the gap can be between an idea and its realisation. The best of concepts can become so messy and muddied when it is applied and this is true of revolutions and Phalanx laundries alike. The effort to live out our beliefs may, as you say, contain folly – but it is a great instructor. And surely what we have learned must contribute to the question of how we are to alter our habits, which will surely arise when we make the wider social revolution which you envisage. I know you would say that such circumstances will be entirely different, but the proletarians will have lived in the old ways before and this could cause obstacles to be placed in the way of the 'free development'[5] of some – particularly I suspect if they are women.

I have, over the last decade or so, been so thoroughly immersed in women's debates about social regeneration that I speak with a profound conviction when I say that the section on women and the family was a great disappointment. It had the same abstract quality as M. Cabet's writing on the question, as if you were both content with second-hand opinions. I realise this will make you angry, as you abhor the Icarians, but the truth is that like him you ignore the ideas and the participation of women themselves. The richness and complexity of *our* thinking is not present at all in the manifesto of the proletarians. It is as if in your eyes there is no place for us amidst the striving and the struggles. You offer us the protection that you think fit and deny our own voices. Do we not have a world to win too?

I agree of course that women have indeed been regarded as 'instruments of production'[6]. I have been impressed by the way in which women in North America have flocked to the anti-slavery cause and I suspect that this is not only because of religious and democratic ideals about the equality of all souls, but because they have a capacity to imagine being used in body and spirit. But you and Mr Engels make no mention of the means by which we *women* might change our present circumstances. Are we really to wait for the 'abolition of the present system'?[7] What of the mean time?

While I can understand that you were forced to compress your thoughts in the *Manifesto*, the exclusion of all reference to women's part in our own emancipation presents us as all weakness and working men as all strength. You thus deny the efforts women have made through association to put equality and democracy into practice in Europe, and by omission set back the cause for the abolition of all privileges of sex, race, birth, caste and wealth for which we too have sacrificed so much. While there is little enthusiasm over here for democratic socialism, the movement for women's emancipation is developing apace. The 'dissolution of the old ideas'[8] and 'conditions of existence'[9] are occurring among women and I am convinced that the consequences will be as significant as the emancipation of the slaves and the struggles of the proletariat.

You, who have such a suspicion of the ideal as opposed to the actual, might have been wary of assuming that in real politics women can afford to rely for their emancipation upon men. I do not mean to suggest that individuals cannot rise above the prejudices of their sex, but there are so many instances of men in general acting in protection of the narrow interests of the masculine sex that the weight of history is against the assumption that freedom will be easily given. Even among our proletarian brothers injustice and an anti-democratic spirit can prevail. Have they not refused to defend our claims to political equality, denied women equal pay and excluded women from their associations? M. Delbrouk even insisted that Mme Deroin should deny her part in devising the scheme for federation of our workers' associations in Paris, on the grounds that her connection with the cause of women's rights would bring disrepute to the Union of Associations and to socialism. In her trial she denied her right to speak for the associations in order not to reveal the bitter discord among us to our adversaries.

Our voices, silenced and reviled in Europe, have reached across the Atlantic. While in Akron I was privileged to attend the women's rights convention and helped Mrs Mott in securing and translating the inspiring letter composed by my dear sisters and fellow associationists, Jeanne Deroin and Pauline Roland, from their French

prison. They regard this new movement for women's rights in
America as hope burgeoning from despair, and consider that the
denial of democracy to one half of humanity helped stifle liberty:
'The darkness of reaction has obscured the sun of 1848, which
seemed to rise so radiantly. Why? Because the revolutionary tempest
in overturning at the same time the throne and the scaffold, in
breaking the chain of the black slave, forgot to break the chain of the
most oppressed of all the pariahs of humanity.'[10]

There are certainly some differences between our approach as socialist
women and the American women's movement for emancipation.
They stress their rights to equality and liberty on the basis of their
revolution's constitution, though I have heard that the working
women are forming their own associations to improve their conditions of labour. And there was also a most singular address at the
Akron convention by a former slave who goes by the name of
Sojourner Truth. She pointed out that she had 'plowed and sowed
and chopped and mowed'[11] as well as any man.

Such claims for equality and emancipation, rooted as they are in
experience, are surely 'actual relations springing from an existing class
struggle, from a historical movement going on under our very eyes.'[12]
Women's expression of the relations you describe frequently differs
from men's, for the circumstances of our subjugation are not entirely
the same. For this reason Désirée Gay argued that women workers in
the national workshops should have their own meetings and also
attend meetings with the men. I believe a combination of autonomy
and solidarity is necessary if real democracy is to be achieved.

At the Akron convention the American women agreed the following
resolution:
'We deny the right of any portion of the species to decide for another
portion . . . what is and what is not their "proper sphere"'.[13]
I am not in complete agreement with this declaration in *all* circumstances, as I fear it may undermine the genuine bonds of solidarity
that I have known through association. On the other hand surely this
idea that women must act for their own emancipation is in accord
with your insistence that 'the proletarians have nothing to lose but
their chains'.[14] We socialist women in France believed that the cause
of women and the cause of the workers would march in union
despite cases of prejudice and hostility. But we knew also that if we

were to overcome scorn and injustice we must combine as *women* and act autonomously from men. I consider that the social emancipation of all will be based on the self–emancipation of all the *pariahs* of society.

At Akron I was disturbed to find that such connections are not assumed in this new women's movement and I find myself stranded. Between the Americans who stress women's independence rather than the union of the working classes, and you and Mr Engels, who follow the course of democratic movements so closely, yet have somehow contrived to eradicate our thought and action, where are we socialist women to place ourselves? I was reminded of the words of Louise Otto: 'The history of all ages, especially that of the present, teaches us that those who forget to think of themselves will be forgotten . . . In the midst of the great revolutions in which we find ourselves, women will find themselves forgotten, if they forget to think of themselves.'[15]

As I am assailed on all sides and the only weapon I have is my pen I intend to give you my account of our ideas and debates, for the revolution we lived through was a great teacher and I am concerned that so much thought should not 'melt into air'. It may enable you to consider a wider span of opinion and action in your future work.

We were greatly inspired by the women of the early '30s. Pauline Roland, Desiree Veret, Suzanne Voilquin and Claire Demar (to name but a few) showed us that women must indeed search within themselves if they are to achieve emancipation. From these brave women, and from Flora Tristan, we learned that the woman who does not become her own woman owns nothing. However having established the need to act on our own behalf we did not forget that our cause was connected to that of the working class. Indeed I was surprised to see no mention in your Manifesto of Flora Tristan's proposal for a Workers' Union in 1843 and her recognition that the emancipation of the working man was impossible when women remained oppressed in the family.

We certainly did not 'oppose all political action'.[16] In the dedication of her *London Journey* to the 'Men and women of the working classes', Flora Tristan said '. . . do not lose sight of your *political rights*'[17], adding that these were the 'means' of challenging 'abuses . . .

in the social order'.[18] She warned however that 'It is the social system, the base of the structure, which must concern you, not political power, which is but an illusion, supreme one day and overthrown the next, restored in a new form only to be overturned the next.' [19] I think you and Mr Engels might have acknowledged this great woman.

We '48-ers (as the Americans call us) have surely done much that would make you modify some of the assertions in the *Manifesto*. For example in the women's club of the *Voix des Femmes* we claimed that as the people were sovereign we too constituted 'the people'. Jeanne Deroin presented herself as a candidate in 1849 but the only group to treat her with respect were the Democratic Socialists. We turned to association not because of any disregard for politics but out of necessity. How else were we to secure employment or raise our pay? Believing that 'to associate is to prevail' we set about linking associations with the aim of overcoming isolation. After Jeanne Deroin proposed the Association Solidaire et Fraternelle de Toutes les Associations Reunis in *L'Opinion des Femmes*, the delegates of a hundred and four associations united without distinction of sex. When the police raided our meeting and took us away to jail they accused us of conspiring to overthrow the government by force, but violence was not our intention.

The idea of a federation of associations came about through the experience we gained in '48 and '49, when seamstresses, midwives, silk workers and laundry workers were all forming associations. Because we had direct experience of the problems they faced in obtaining capital, determining needs and marketing their produce, we were able to envisage the advantages and foresee the likely difficulties in a more extensive form of cooperative production. Untrained in abstract political economy, many of us nonetheless understood the economies of our own households. The result was a most developed plan for a cooperative system of production, distribution and exchange, which did not spring from the head of a theorist who knew nothing of workers' lives. Concerned always with what was possible, our aim was a Federation balancing the needs of producers and consumers and fixing a just price for commodities. We also considered creating financial institutions which would be sympathetic to poor women and be run on the lines of mutuality and democracy. Such aspirations were to be crushed by the tyranny which drove us into exile or destroyed us in prison. All the more reason for remembering what we accomplished. For surely the better organisation of society which we all desire will require some thought and preparation.

Otherwise I wonder what are we to draw upon as we move from one system of social organisation to another? You write of the elements of a new society within the old. But how are we to sort out what to keep and what to throw away? I see myself sitting in a kind of political lumber room, salvaging objects which carry precious memories. You are inclined to use broad brush strokes and not trouble yourself with details. But it is the details that we live amidst and which constitute a commodious life. Philosophers, you see, can benefit from the skills of housewifery!

In America, as I said, the claim for women's rights is usually made on the grounds of an inalienable right to equality but Jeanne Deroin believes that women's experience of mothering gives us a special understanding of cooperation and love. She argues that women would bring such qualities into the social sphere. I am aware of your suspicion of feeling in discussions of social change, yet I am sure you will concede that human feeling has a part to play. Is it not possible then to see in the valuing of the capacities developed by women as mothers a form of resistance to being reduced to 'mere instruments of production'? I can see that in demanding our rights as mothers we might box ourselves in and lose our foothold in the terrain of equals. On the other hand a purely abstract equality conceived according to masculine reasoning can eclipse the experiences unique to women as a sex. This dilemma has been hotly debated now by socialist women for two decades and yet you make no mention of it. It has a bearing too on the more general question of how the oppressed are to prevail. If they have no understandings to bring to the great project of social regeneration, how will they prevent people in possession of privilege, opportunities and knowledge from once more gaining the ascendency?

Are you familiar with Claire Démar's little book, *Ma Loi d'Avenir,* published by Suzanne Voilquin in 1834, the year after Claire's tragic suicide? Claire's was a lonely voice. Distrustful of fixed ideas of woman's nature, while claiming freedom of expression for women's needs, inclinations and desires, she was impatient with M. Enfantin's decrees which gave the Saint-Simonian woman the emotions and man the world. I was too young then to understand her conflict with Suzanne Voilquin and the other Saint Simonian women, but now I can appreciate her rebellion against their conception of 'woman' as moral redeemer, which she believed would impose a new set of regulations on women. Instead she believed that even as we define '. . . our own nature, our own desire, we proclaim that each nature, each desire is sacred and demands satisfaction.'[20]

Her life remains the subject of scandal because she defended '. . . a physical trial of flesh by flesh'[21] but there is considerable hypocrisy in the outcry because young men do as much with a nod and a wink from their elders. How can we say there is to be one morality for man and another for woman? She questioned fidelity based on fear and she and her young lover paid a terrible price in taking their own lives.

The real danger for the free woman, in my opinion, is the extreme difficulty in challenging prejudice on so many fronts. This can be destructive and lead to great suffering. For this reason I can sympathise with your and Mrs Marx's dislike of the abuses which can result from some versions of 'free love'. I am sure there were excesses in the early '30s, for people felt that the known world was collapsing all around them. There are always certain socialist men too (I remember Mr Herwegh's insult to Mrs Marx) who will interpret freedom as licence. Then there is the question of children of course. I do not like Claire Démar's proposal to deny the biological parents the right to rear their children and I think Pauline Roland's contention that paternity is of no importance places too great a responsibility upon the woman. Pauline Roland and Jeanne Deroin have advocated celibacy, but neither of them stood by this for long. And why should women sacrifice love and maternity for an idea of freedom? For what is left of freedom when life passes us by and we are alone?

I was no more satisfied, however, with your pronouncement that we must wait for the abolition of the present system for the resolution of these questions. I fear we will all be too old and grey to care much by then. I am sure you are right – the ideas and forms of the present day will change with the future organisation of society. But how are we to go on in the mean time? And once we become aware of oppression, how can we continue to live in a condition of unhappiness and subordination? What of the woman defended by Claire Demar in the loveless marriage bed? Surely as democrats we can agree with

Jeanne Deroin that motherhood should be voluntary and respect Pauline Roland's rejection of marriage because of the inferior position of the wife? As for Communism, did not Flora Tristan argue most convincingly that inequality in the families of the working classes was the cause of much violence and cruelty? Your account of the family does not consider the question that has greatly concerned socialist women – the link between men's mastery in the home and their assumption of superiority in politics and in the workplace. We have sought since the early '30s to challenge inequality and despotism in all spheres of existence and many of us have suffered most severely as a result. You have not done us justice. You have given the Communists' cause a Manifesto in which it is as if all this had never been.

I know you are sceptical of 'castles in the air'[22] so I am concluding with a list of the proposals we have developed through action:–
- Women's equal civil and political rights.
- Equal participation of women on workers' committees.
- Equal pay, an end to women's low pay, long hours and exclusion from certain trades.
- Payment of homeworkers at the same rate as workers in the workshops.
- The sharing of work in times of unemployment.
- Alternative employment for prostitutes.
- Restaurants and creches in all workplaces.
- Training centres for women, including midwives.
- Centres for domestic servants to meet and organise.
- The development of associations among women and men workers through the power of union in order to provide capital.
- Good conditions of employment.
- The means of exchanging labour for produce and protection in times of need – including a literary and artistic association to help women workers in these fields and to spread interest in art, and an association also for unemployed women.
- Large airy houses with gardens providing cheap communal meals and living quarters for families with children and single parents.
- Public restaurants, wash houses, meeting rooms, libraries and creches. Public space for recreation.
- Free public education and training for all children including girls.
- A system of social welfare which would not insult poor mothers to be.

- Free medical service and the payment of midwives by the state.
- A social fund to provide for women so they do not have to be dependent on men.
- Voluntary motherhood.

My experience of phalanx life has convinced me that these reforms are best secured not by withdrawing, but by agitating in working class neighbourhoods. I intend to raise the cry for women's rights in Toronto and to set about securing the social rights which I believe would enable the women of the working classes to make their own choices about their lives. Our defeats have been hard to bear but we have the courage to confront them and ideas and proposals to contribute to future generations. Our cause truly is international. I take heart from the letter of Pauline Roland and Jeanne Deroin to the American women's convention last summer: 'Sisters of America! your socialist sisters of France are united with you in the vindication of the right of women to civil and political equality. We have, moreover, the profound conviction that only by the power of association based on solidarity – by the union of the working-classes of both sexes to organise labor – can be acquired, completely and pacifically, the civil and political equality of women, and the social right of all.'[23]

Yours truly in the struggle for Freedom,
Annette Devereux."

Guide to historical figures

Jeanne Deroin was a dressmaker who became a self-educated teacher. A republican, influenced by Saint-Simonian ideas, she was involved in the women's newspapers *Voix des Femmes* and then in *Politique des Femmes*. She married an engineer and had three children. After her arrest she went into exile in Britain and published an *Almanach des femmes* in French and English. Towards the end of her life she was in contact with William Morris' Socialist League. **Pauline Roland** was a teacher and lived among the Saint Simonians in Paris in the early 1830s. In 1848 she organised the Fraternal Association of Socialist Male and Female Teachers and Professors. She had a child from an early relationship and three more in a free union with another man. By

1848 she regretted the responsibilities and lack of security which single parenting involved. However she refused to deny her views on marriage after her arrest in 1850. In December 1851, after Louis Napoleon's coup d'etat, she was arrested again and sent to a penal colony in Algeria. She died while returning to France. **Femme Nicaud** was the leader of the Laundresses' Association. **Charles Fourier** was an early theorist of socialism who advocated small cooperative communities which he called 'phalanxes'. His ideas were taken to America in the 1830s by Albert Brisbane and several communities were established there. **Helen Macfarlane** translated the *Communist Manifesto* in the *Red Republican*. **Charles Anderson Dana** was an American theorist of Fourierism and editor of the *New York Daily Tribune*. He visited Marx in Cologne with Brisbane in the summer of 1848 and in 1852 was to invite Marx to write a regular column in the paper. **Jenny Marx** was living in Paris with her new husband in 1843, where they moved into a communal house with **Arnold Ruge** and his wife, but Jenny did not get on with **Mrs Ruge**. She preferred Emma Herwegh, whose husband, the poet **Georg Herwegh**, was a friend of Marx's. Jenny Marx disapproved of the bohemian poet's affairs, rejected his attempt to seduce her and was appalled by the discussion of free unions in Paris. In 1847 Jenny Marx encouraged Marx to work with the Communist League and copied out the *Communist Manifesto* while preparing for a Christmas party of the German Workers Union in Brussels, where she gave one of her dramatic recitations. In 1845 when the Marxes were in exile in Brussels, Helene Demuth a young woman of 25, had joined them as a servant. In 1851 she became pregnant with Karl Marx's son, who was to be called Freddy Demuth. He was brought up by a working class couple in Hackney, London. **Etienne Cabet** was the author of *Voyage en Icarie* and a well known advocate of communism in France during the 1840s. His followers were known as 'Icarians'. In 1841 in *La Femme dans la société actuelle et dans la communauté* he refuted the idea that socialism meant the end of marriage and the family. He later formed a utopian community in Texas. **Lucretia Mott** was an anti-slavery campaigner and supporter of women's rights who made links with the French socialist women. **Sojourner Truth**, a former slave and itinerant preacher, joined the Northampton (Massachusetts) Association in 1843–44 where she was influenced by William Lloyd Garrison and Frederick Douglass. She dictated a narrative of her life in 1850 and attended the women's rights convention in Akron, Ohio in 1851. **Louise Otto** advocated women's education in Germany (including science and gymnastics) in 1847.

She founded a women's newspaper during the German revolution of 1848, *Frauen-Zeitung*, which continued until 1852. She believed in woman's special mission in politics and wanted poor working women to contribute to her paper. **Désirée Veret (later Gay)**, a milliner influenced by the Saint Simonians, was involved in *La Femme Libre* in 1832. She went to London, making contact with the Owenites and marrying Jules Gay, an Owenite, in 1837. She was particularly interested in the democratisation of the workplace and in 1848 led the protest against women's inequality in the National Workshops. She also helped organise an association of linen seamstresses. After Louis Napoleon took power she went into exile in Switzerland and then in Belgium. **Suzanne Voilquin** was involved in the Saint Simonian movement and believed that women had essentially different qualities to men. She thought socialists had to introduce a new morality. In 1848 she organised the United Midwives, an association which demanded equal pay and training with male obstreticians. She went to live in a community in the United States. **Claire Démar** wrote *A Woman's Call to the People for the Enfranchisement of Women* in 1832. Her *Ma Loi d' Avenir* was published posthumously by Suzanne Voilquin despite their intense disagreements. Isolated from the Saint-Simonian women, Claire Démar committed suicide with her lover, a younger man. **Flora Tristan** worked as a colourist in a lithographic shop and was pressurised into an unhappy marriage with her employer. She fled four years later, pregnant and with two sons. Unable to look after her children she worked as a maid and travelling companion. She was active in socialist circles in France in the 1830s, made contact with Owenites and Chartists, and, in the 1840s, wrote and lectured extensively on workers' conditions, advocating the creation of the Workers' Union in 1843. She died on a discouraging organising tour in 1844. **Prosper Enfantin**, a Saint Simonian leader and theorist who argued for the need of a Woman Messiah, challenged conventional morality but sought to impose his own authoritarian views on the women in the Saint Simonian circle.

NOTES

Apart from the books and articles in the endnotes I have also drawn on Werner Blumenberg, *Karl Marx* NLB, London 1972. Maire Cross and Tim Gray, *The Feminism of Flora Tristan*, Berg, Oxford, 1992. Carl J. Guarneri, *The Utopian Alternative. Foruierism in Nineteenth-Century America*, Cornell University press, Ithaca, 1991. Claire Goldberg Moses, *French Feminism in the 19th Century*, State University of New York, Albany, 1984. H.F. Peters, *Red Jenny. A Life with Karl Marx*, Allen and

Unwin, London, 1986. Joan Wallach Scott, *Gender and the Politics of Hstory,* Columbia University Press, New York, 1988.

1. Helen Macfarlane translated 'spectre' as 'frightful hobgoblin' in the shortened version of the *Manifesto of the Communist Party* which was serialised in *The Red Republican*, November 9, 1850. A reprint was issued with an introduction by John Saville and published by Merlin Press, London, 1966. The 'frightful hobgoblin' appears on p. 161. All subsequent references are to Karl Marx and Frederick Engels, *Manifesto of the Communist Party*, Lawrence and Wishart, London, 1968.
2. Karl Marx to Arnold Ruge, September 1843, Marx/Engels *Collected Works*, Volume 3, Lawrence and Wishart, London, 1975, p. 142
3. Marx and Engels, *Manifesto of the Communist Party*, p. 38
4. Ibid p. 61
5. Ibid p. 53
6. Ibid p. 50
7. Ibid
8. Ibid p. 51
9. Ibid
10. Jeanne Deroin and Pauline Roland, Letter to the Convention of the Women of America, 15 June, 1851, in eds. Susan Groag Bell and Karen M.Offen, *Women, the Family and Freedom. The Debate in Documents,* Volume One, 1750–1880, Stanford University Press, Stanford, California, 1983, pp. 287–8
11. Sojourner Truth quoted in Nell Irvin Painter, Sojourner Truth's Defense of the Rights of Women (as reported in 1851; rewritten in 1863) in ed Linda K. Kerber, Jane Sherron De Hart, *Women's America* Fourth Edition,Oxford University Press, New York, 1995
12. Marx and Engels, *The Manifesto of the Communist Party*, pp. 46–47
13. Quoted in Ellen DuBois, *Feminism and Suffrage: The Emergence of an Independent Women's Movement in America,1848–1869*, p. 36
14. Marx and Engels, *The Manifesto of the Communist Party*, p. 63
15. Louise Otto, Program, Frauen-Zeitung, Ein Organ fur die hoheren weiblichen Interessen, no 1 (21 April 1849) in eds Bell and Offen, *Women,the Family and Freedom,* p. 263
16. Marx and Engels, *Manifesto of the Communist Party,* p. 61
17. Flora Tristan,*The London Journal of Flora Tristan,* 1842, Translated, annotated and introduced by Jean Hawkes, Virago, London, 1982
18. Ibid p. 3
19. Ibid
20. Claire Demar quoted in Eleni Varikas, 'A Supremely Rebellious Word'. Claire Demar: A Saint-Simonian Heretic, *Argument Sonderband,* AS 185, p. 98
21. Ibid p. 99
22. Marx and Engels, *The Manifesto of the Communist Party*, p. 61
23. Deroin and Roland in, eds. Bell and Offen, *Women the Family, and Freedom,* p. 289

THE POLITICAL LEGACY OF THE MANIFESTO

Colin Leys and Leo Panitch

I

We are living in interesting times. The tide of reaction is still flowing, but with diminishing confidence and force, while the counter-flow of progressive feeling and ideas gathers strength but has yet to find effective political expression. As the contradictions of unbridled neoliberalism become increasingly plain, fewer and fewer people any longer mistake its real character. 'Stubborn historical facts' are breaking through the illusions fostered by neoliberal rhetoric – and equally through the pseudo-left illusions of 'new times', 'radicalism of the centre' and all similar dreams of a capitalist world miraculously freed from alienation, immiseration and crises.[1]

At the peripheries of the global economy – in most of Africa, in Central America, in South Asia – historical facts have never permitted most people the luxury of such illusions, even if the elites of these countries embrace and foster them. Such recent experiences as the misery and barbarisms provoked by 'structural adjustment' in dozens of countries in Africa, or the rape of the public sector in Mexico, have done nothing to make neoliberalism more beguiling to ordinary people anywhere in the former Third World. Where the propagandists of the 'Washington consensus' did achieve some ideological sway over working people was above all in the 'North'. But there too, after nearly two decades of capitalist restoration, painful reality increasingly prevails over corporate newspeak.

Some 40,000 multinational corporations – fifty of them now receiving more revenue than two-thirds of the world's states – frenetically merge, restructure, 're-engineer', 're-configure' and relocate themselves, in an almost parodic speed-up and trans-nationalisation of Marx's famous Manifesto script. 'Whole populations' – from the

women workers in the free trade zones of southern China and northern
Mexico to the huge new immigrant workforces of Western Europe and
North America – are now 'conjured out of the ground' (in Marx's
unforgettable phrase) in less than a generation; while others – like
older manual workers, and the growing reserve army of young people
– are as rapidly conjured back into it again.[2] Ruthless downward
pressure on real incomes, enforced by the restoration of large-scale
permanent unemployment (thirty-four million people – plus their
families – in the OECD countries alone) through corporate
'downsizing', spectacular failures (Pan Am, British Leyland, Barings,
Yamaichi) and the re-casualisation of work – all of these give new
meaning to the Manifesto's portrait of how 'growing competition',
'commercial crises' and the 'unceasing improvement of machinery'
make people's livelihoods 'more and more precarious'. Nor is it any
longer 'loosely connected provinces' that are being 'lumped together'
by the bourgeoisie, with 'one national class-interest, one frontier and
one customs-tariff'; what the capitalist classes now seek is nothing less
than the abolition of all frontiers and all tariffs, and a Multilateral
Agreement on Investment, a universal treaty giving investors legally –
and if necessary, no doubt militarily – enforceable rights, that would
tie states even more securely to capital's global class-interest.

All this is becoming clear. Journalists can no longer speak, as they
did in the 1980s, of 'the business community', as if it were some
benign college whose interests were more or less identical to those of
the nation as a whole; simply to stay credible they must now talk about
'the corporate agenda' and the threat that capitalism (no longer a taboo
word) poses to the environment, and about the problems of poverty
and homelessness it is creating, the erosion of social security and the
negative impact on standards of health and education.[3]

As Boris Kagarlitsky has recently remarked: 'Reaction is a natural
historical phenomenon, but it becomes exhausted just as revolutions
do. When this exhaustion sets in, a new phase of revolution can
begin.'[4] We are still far from witnessing the exhaustion of the neoliberal
reaction, or restoration, although the symptoms of its fatigue are
accumulating (including the inability of parties too ostentatiously
identified with it to continue to win elections).[5] But as is also normal
with all reactions, this one too is already overreaching itself, partly
because, as Kagarlitsky has also noted, the post-war settlement in the
West was underpinned by fear of the Communist threat and the lifting
of this threat removed a significant constraint on capital's political
ambitions.

Since the collapse of the post-war settlement in the 1970s capitalists had wanted to 'lower expectations', and a clear reaction in the West began to emerge, led by Thatcher and Reagan, aimed at breaking the power of organized labour, expanding the scope for capital accumulation through privatisation, and replacing collective welfare by entrepreneurship and individualism as the legitimating values of liberal democracy. With the collapse of Communism, however, the project could be pursued even more ruthlessly. Unemployment could be raised to mass levels, public services and welfare programmes could be cut more and more drastically, and inequality restored to nineteenth-century levels, without any anxiety about the need to maintain social cohesion in face of the red menace, or to prove to workers in the West that they were as secure as their Soviet bloc counterparts, as well as better paid.[6]

So the social contradictions of capitalist competition returned in force. Even with over 20 million unemployed in Europe, among those still in full-time jobs the weekly hours worked rose, and so did chronic sickness, and so did crime, and the numbers of people in jail.[7] The great economic 'success' story of the mid-1990s, the United States, with an official unemployment rate of only 5% compared to over 11% in the European Union, rests on an unprecedented reduction in American workers' real incomes over the past quarter century. Even during the economic 'recovery' of recent years 'the proportion of people losing jobs is . . . at an all-time high. Between 1992 and 1995, 15 percent of people holding jobs for more than one year lost those jobs; their new jobs, if they found one, paid 14 percent less on average.'[8]

All this could happen without capital any longer feeling even a lingering vestige of concern about the threat of communism. But it could not continue without even the western working class eventually starting to ask themselves again for whose benefit all these sacrifices were being made, and when they would end. By the mid-1990s strikes in France, the USA and Canada once more occupied the front pages alongside reports of strikes in South Korea and 'IMF riots' throughout much of the former Third World from Zimbabwe to Mexico. There was also a sharp rise in class awareness. As even the *Economist* noted, 'Many commentators think that class is dying, but ordinary people are not convinced. In fact class antagonisms may even be worsening – the proportion of voters believing there is a "class struggle" in Britain rose from around 60% in the early 1960s to 81% in the mid-1990s, according to Gallup . . .'[9] And in the United States, a *New York Times*

poll in 1996 found that 55% of Americans now defined themselves as
working class while only 36% defined themselves as middle class, a
major reversal of the traditional American pattern; and no less than
60% of those who had experienced a layoff in their family thought that
'the government should step in to do something' and attributed 'a lot
of the blame for the loss of jobs on the economic system in this
country'.[10]

II

To see the outlines of a new period of class struggle taking shape,
however, is not the same thing as seeing clearly how to engage in it; and
it remains true that the left has been severely disempowered and disor-
ganized by the scope and ruthlessness of the capitalist restoration and
the effects of global deregulation. The independent left, the militant
activists in both the trade unions and the new social movements who
have withstood the pressures to capitulate to market hegemony, are a
potentially far more significant force than the right likes to pretend.
But there is nonetheless an acute sense, within this left, of a political
absence: the lack of a capacity to go beyond 'networking', beyond
pluralism (hard-won and rightly cherished as that is), to find new ways
to give coherence and strategic direction to collective efforts to
mobilise and make effective the developing reaction *against* the
market, *against* capital.

It is this widespread sense of a political absence that makes the
political legacy of the Manifesto especially relevant today. As Rob
Beamish shows in his essay in this volume, the Manifesto, while
drafted by Marx, was 'the product of an extended and intense but open
debate among committed communist-internationalists' who were
trying to fashion political organizations through which the collective
efforts of the working classes to understand and confront the major
problems of their time could cohere and have greater effect. The
eventual result was the mass working-class parties of the late
nineteenth century; and so much did these become part of the political
landscape that it is easy to forget that such autonomous political
organizations of the subordinate classes were an entirely new historical
phenomenon, and that it took the better part of a half-century, after
the defeats of 1848, to make them a reality. By the time of the
Manifesto's centenary in 1948, Social Democratic and Communist
parties were among the leading forces on the world's political stage.
Nevertheless, it was because these parties no longer embodied the

radical legacy of the Manifesto that so many of the '1968 generation', only two decades later, not only rejected these particular parties, but eventually came to doubt the appropriateness of the 'party' as a political form.

Yet most people who are active in political and social struggles today feel the need for something that will perform some essential tasks that used to be performed by parties. This confirms Cynthia Cockburn's premonition in the 1970s that, for all the exciting and energetic pluralism of the new community movements, there was something lacking; that their struggles, if conceived apart from 'an arena of conflict between the dominant and exploited class', would be in danger of failing to cohere despite their proximity to each other

> within the working class and its near neighbours. . . . They shake out as tenants, ratepayers, teenage youth, house owners, swimming enthusiasts and squatters. All are asked to compete and defend their special interests, while the class with real power remains untouched. . . .[11]

The necessity of going 'beyond the fragments', while not replicating the defects of the old parties or their sectarian offshoots, was already being argued brilliantly by Rowbotham, Segal and Wainwright by the end of the 1970s;[12] but the 'articulation' actually achieved between social movements and progressive trade unions – in forms that range from the Rainbow Coalition in the USA and the Action Canada Network in Canada to the Anti-GATT/WTO Movement in India and the Opposition to the Devastation Caused by the World Bank/IMF in Sri Lanka – have consisted mainly of 'popular front'- style strategic networking between the top leaderships of the various organizations. What has always been missing – and this is now strongly felt by many social movement leaders themselves – is something that would be more than the sum of the parts, something which the Social Democratic and Communist parties did partly provide in their heyday.

This is, at one level, simply a matter of offering electoral alternatives. The century-long frustration that American political activists have experienced through being unable to translate political agitation and mobilization into meaningful electoral choices is now increasingly felt elsewhere; the accommodation of the old Communist and Social Democratic parties in Europe to the neo-liberal agenda – epitomised now by 'New' Labour in Britain – is giving activists there a taste of what the absence of a mass working class party in the USA has meant throughout this century (and which the American left is now trying again to rectify with the New Party and Labour Party initiatives).[13]

But it is much more than a matter of what to do on election day. It is about all the things Marx had in mind when he wrote that the 'immediate aim' of all proletarian parties was the 'formation of the proletariat into a class'. These included providing activists with a strategic, ideological and educational vehicle; a political home which is open to individuals to enter (rather than restricted, as today's social movement networking often is, to representatives of groups); a political community which explicitly seeks to transcend particularistic identities while supporting and building on the struggles they generate; and through all of these things, serving as the incubator of a new social force, providing a structure but also an agency which expresses the pre-existing range of identities while also expanding them – 'helping to organize what it claims to represent', as Margaret Keck aptly put it in relation to the Workers' Party of Brazil –[14] and which in doing so achieves the capacity to 'make history'. This, at any rate, is what Marx meant by 'revolutionising praxis', by 'the alteration of men on a mass scale' – and what a party today must be able to do.

The 'formation of the proletariat into a class' is, moreover, not something that once attempted and even partially accomplished, is then finished; the working class, once 'made', is not 'fixed and frozen', as imagined by traditionalists who cling to every cultural as well as socio-economic encrustation – nor by (post?) modernizers who abandon the working class as hopelessly outdated and unchangeable, and go in search of more fashionable agencies. New parties have already arisen and more will arise, profoundly conscious of how much they need to be different from the old Social Democratic and Communist parties if they are to form today's proletariat into a new class, a class once again capable of making history. But 'making history' in what sense? A discriminating view of the Manifesto and its legacy is needed in this respect.

III

We need to ask, first of all, what was the nature of the revolutionary message of the Manifesto, as opposed to the way it has been understood, especially by its critics. It was certainly above all a revolutionary document, and it has always been taken as calling for a political revolution as a prelude to a social and economic one; the October revolution has been seen as a response to its call, and Stalinism as a logical consequence. But it is worth reminding ourselves that this is not true.

The revolution Marx called for (and thought inevitable) was a revolution in social relations. As Bernard Moss points out elsewhere in this volume, Marx, like all his contemporaries, had the example of the French Revolution sixty years earlier very much in mind, and thought a new political revolution – 'the forcible overthrow of existing conditions' – would be necessary in order to achieve the social revolution in most countries, given the predictable resistance that would be offered by the bourgeoisie and its allies to any fundamental change in relations of production. Only in 1872 – twenty-four years after writing the Manifesto – did he cautiously allow that in countries with long traditions of democracy (like the USA, Britain, and perhaps the Netherlands) the workers might 'attain their goal by peaceful means'.[15] In later writings Marx was also apt to put more stress on the possibility of revolution spreading to the capitalist heartlands from the system's unstable 'extremities'; and, as Shanin and others have pointed out, since he was always impatient for action, he backed the revolutionary wing of the Russian populists against their proto-Menshevik opponents, even though this was not fully consistent with his analysis in the main body of his work, whether the *Manifesto* of 1848, or the *Grundrisse* written in the late 1850s, or *Capital* completed in the mid-1860s. What this did show, however, was that he did not believe that all peoples were fated to tread an identical path to socialism.[16]

Revolutions in the 'periphery' would, evidently, also be more or less violent. Marx's attitude to this was practical. The right of revolution – 'the only really historical right', as Engels put it just before his death in 1895, 'the only right on which all modern states rest' – was a democratic right, the right of the majority to make their own history; it would be exercised peaceably if possible, forcibly if not.[17] Marx's profoundest political commitment was to this democratic right, as his subsequent idealisation of the Paris Commune of 1870 as exemplifying an unprecedentedly radical kind of democracy also makes clear; it was from the opponents of socialism that he anticipated violence, and not without cause.

Having said this, it remains true that there was also an unresolved tension in Marx's attitude, reflected in the concept of 'proletarian dictatorship'. On the one hand it meant, for him, 'democracy carried to its fullest' (with the Commune as its example), in the sense of the majority class becoming the ruling class for the first time in history; on the other hand, it meant a period of centralised and repressive rule entailing strict measures to defeat the old ruling classes and prevent counter-revolution. The risk that coercion might become institutionalized and overwhelm the democratic dimension of the revolution, Marx spent little time thinking about. Yet this was to become a tragically familiar pattern in the twentieth century. As Isaac Deutscher, reflecting on the October Revolution, put it:

> Every revolutionary party at first imagines that its task is simple: it has to suppress a 'handful' of tyrants or exploiters. It is true that usually the tyrants and exploiters form an insignificant minority. But the old ruling class has not lived in isolation from the rest of society. In the course of its long domination it has surrounded itself by a network of institutions embracing groups and individuals in many classes; and it has brought to life many attachments and loyalties which even a revolution does not destroy altogether. . . . The revolution therefore treats its enemy's immediate neighbour as its enemy. When it hits this secondary enemy, the latter's neighbour, too, is aroused and drawn into the struggle. The process goes on like a chain reaction until the party of the revolution arouses against itself and suppresses all the parties which until recently crowded the political scene.[18]

Evidently, the subsequent history of the twentieth century has produced no easy answers to this conundrum. But it is no answer at all to take the obduracy of capitalists and their allies as a sufficient reason for the majority to abandon their only 'really historical right'.

Even in the conditions of a capitalist democracy the question of how the state's capacity for repression can be overcome by a mobilised majority bent on exercising its historical right, remains as difficult to answer today as it was a hundred years ago when Engels, just before he died, grappled with it in the text already quoted. Anticipating Gramsci, Engels argued that in Europe the insurrectionary strategies of 1848 had become obsolete by the 19th century's end. The conditions of struggle had essentially changed, he noted, partly due to technical reasons: the modern city with its broad boulevards, the modern army with its firepower. But more fundamentally, the conditions of struggle had changed because the conditions of hegemony had changed. 'Even in the classic time of street fighting . . . the barricade produced more of a moral than a material effect. It was a means for shaking the steadfastness of the military.' By 1849, however, when the bourgeoisie had everywhere 'thrown in its lot with the governments . . . the spell of the barricade was broken; the soldiers no longer saw behind it 'the people' but rebels, agitators, plunderers, levellers, the scum of society. . . .'[19] Now, almost fifty years later, Engels was convinced that 'an insurrection with which all sections of the people sympathize will hardly recur; in the class struggle all the middle strata will probably never group themselves round the proletariat so exclusively that in comparison the party of reaction gathered round the bourgeoisie will well-nigh disappear.' But he did believe that the growth of the mass working class party in Germany by 1895 was such that, operating legally, it had a chance of winning over the middle strata; and, in any case, 'to shoot a party which numbers millions out of existence is too much even for all the magazine rifles of Europe and America.'

> The time of surprise attacks, of revolutions carried through by small conscious minorities at the head of unconscious masses, is past. Where it is a question of a complete transformation of the social organisation, the masses themselves must also be in it, must themselves already have grasped what is at stake, what it is they are going for, body and soul. The history of the last 50 years has taught us that. But in order that the masses may understand what is to be done, long persistent work is required. . . .[20]

Unfortunately Engels immediately went on to treat electoral successes as evidence of this mass mobilisation, as if the entry of Social Democrats into national governments, or even the election of municipal councillors, meant that the masses were really 'in it.'[21] A century of experience of the 'parliamentary road to socialism' has taught us better.

A further problem with the Manifesto's legacy is that it says very little about politics after the revolution, and this is also true of Marx's later writings. His attitude was summed up in the position he ascribed to the working class Communards who, he said, had 'no ready-made utopias', but knew they must pass 'through long struggles, through a series of historic processes, transforming circumstances and men.'[22] In this he was surely right. But his resistance to blueprints kept Marx from addressing the question of what kind of institutional structures socialist democracy would require, and left him open to the charge, advanced by a long line of critics from Bakunin onwards, that simply to declare 'when class distinctions have disappeared' political conflict would disappear too ('the public power will lose its political character', as the Manifesto puts it) was a perfect rationalisation for the permanent dictatorship of an elite ruling in the name of the workers.

This criticism plainly fails to appreciate the whole thrust of Marx's approach; but it is true that for Marx simply to imagine a harmonious collaboration among all 'the associated producers' was indeed to beg fundamental questions about the kind of democratic politics that would be possible and necessary in a world from which the private ownership of the means of production would have been abolished, but in which manifold other differences among people would remain. And it is also true that Marx seriously overestimated, in the Manifesto and later, the extent to which the class structure would be simplified, the 'middle classes' squeezed out and marginalised and the global working class itself homogenized. Things were not going to be simplified in the way he imagined.

But we have to keep a sense of historical proportion. The complex problems that were faced by the new mass working-class parties – including major divisions of interest within the working classes themselves, the rise of the professional middle class, and much else – could hardly be worked through in advance by Marx. In tackling these problems, however, the mass parties – the Communist and Social Democratic parties which have really influenced the history of this century – failed to sustain Marx and Engels' distinctive political practice: the combination of social-scientific analysis, based on their materialist interpretation of history, with engaged political writing and speaking – pamphlets, lectures, articles, addresses, reports, letters – in which they tried to make current history intelligible to activists in such a way that they themselves could draw from the experience of their struggles the lessons they contained, and be better able to try to 'make their own history'. Instead, Social Democrats and Communists increasingly resorted to treating Marx's ideas as a text, a body of findings, either to be followed as dogma (subject to constant quasi-theological reinterpretation) in the case of the Communists, or to be rejected (after repeated revisions) in the case of the Social Democrats. And this was even more true of the numerous small revolutionary groups whose political impact has been marginal (even if their role in developing remarkable activists and intellectuals should not be underestimated).

It was to avoid this that both Marx and Engels often declared their opposition to all attempts to elevate their ideas into a 'system', and insisted that their conception of history was 'above all a guide to study' and that 'all history must be studied afresh'; but very few people in either the Communist or the Social Democratic parties have done this in the way Marx and Engels did it themselves. As vehicles for socialism, however, these parties have in any case run their course; the true political legacy of the Manifesto – to develop a politics concerned above all with ensuring that the masses really are 'in it' – remains to be taken up again by others.

IV

To say this is to go against the current of much so-called left thought and practice over the past two decades. After what can now be seen as a very brief spell of attempting to renew Marxism in the wake of 1968 we have gone through a period since the early 1980s when not only was the idea that 'Marxism is over' quite widespread among people who still defined themselves as being on the left,[23] but the very idea of socialism as a systemic alternative to capitalism was dubbed an 'anachronistic irrelevance'.[24] The resulting vacuum has been filled by social democratic 'modernisers' whose egalitarian commitments are even weaker than those of post-war social democracy in the West.

It is of the utmost importance to assess the reasons for this, as three major recent historical surveys of the century have sought to do. Eric Hobsbawm's *Age of Extremes* portrays the trajectory of socialism in this century as largely determined by the necessary forced march to industrialization in that part of the underdeveloped world where Communist revolutions occurred. Capitalism's powerful tendencies to globalization eroded the determination and capacity of the authoritarian elites in control of those systems to avoid integration into the capitalist order; while the same forces of globalisation also undermined the policies as well as the party and trade union organizations through which Social Democracy in the West had presided over the 'golden age' of the mixed economy in the post-war era. Hobsbawm cannot see any alternative to the path followed either by the Communist or Social Democratic parties. The tragedy of the October revolution was that it could only produce a ruthless, brutal command socialism. The tragedy of Social Democracy was that the Keynesian welfare state could not withstand the corrosive forces of capitalist globalisation.

For all its brilliance, Hobsbawm's argument is also remarkably contradictory. He insists that the failure of Soviet socialism does not reflect on the possibilities of other kinds of socialism; yet he also contends 'that it may well be that the debate which confronted capitalism and socialism as mutually exclusive and polar opposites will be seen by future generations as a relic of the twentieth-century Cold Wars of Religion.' In so far as this is the case, one might expect him not only to proclaim the virtues of the Social Democratic project, but also to provide some grounds for its revival. But far from doing this, he declares he has no solutions to offer, no way out of the process of the erosion of the nation state and democratic politics by capitalist globalisation, no way of halting the process whereby 'human collective institutions had lost control over the collective consequences of human action.'[25]

It is noteworthy that the actual policies and programmes of the parties and labour movements of the left figure hardly at all in

Hobsbawm's text. The rise and fall of the golden age seem determined almost entirely by the dynamics and cycles of capital accumulation. This gap has been filled, however, by the publication of Donald Sassoon's *One Hundred Years of Socialism*, a work of almost 1,000 pages, warmly praised by Hobsbawm, which focusses on the Western European Left in the second half of the century. Sassoon writes very much from the perspective of the accommodation to capitalist global-isation represented by the Blairite 'modernisers' in Britain, the 'renavadores' in Spain, the 'riformisti' in Italy, the 'nouveaux realistes' in Belgium. He sees them as building on and completing the revisionist tradition, from Eduard Bernstein's *Evolutionary Socialism* at the end of the last century to Anthony Crosland's *The Future of Socialism* and the Bad Godesburg programme of the German SPD at the mid-point of the present one. Summarizing his views in the *Guardian*, Sassoon writes that the abandonment of the old class politics and public ownership goals by today's modernisers finally delivers

> socialists of a utopian albatross. Capitalism is not a particular transitory historical phase in historical development but a mode of production. The task of socialists lies in devising a political framework which enables the advancement of certain values, such as justice and equality, while ensuring that the regulatory system does not seriously impair the viability of capitalism.[26]

Sassoon is right to connect Blair to Bernstein, but there was never-theless something very different about the old revisionists. They thought that capitalism was tending towards state collectivism and managerialism, and that this undermined the anarchic and inegali-tarian tendencies of capitalist markets and confirmed and reinforced the reformist strategies of Social Democracy. But in recent decades capitalism has moved in the opposite direction to the one they expected and predicted. It is the arguments of the Marxist critics of revisionism, from Rosa Luxemburg to the founders of the *Socialist Register*, who insisted that capitalism would eventually revert to a competitive and inegalitarian market logic, that are being confirmed today. All that is left linking today's modernizers with their revisionist predecessors is their accommodation to the dynamics of capitalism. Whereas Bernstein and Crosland had believed that this accommo-dation could yield a more planned and egalitarian social order, today's modernizers know (and they mince no words in saying so) that this means accommodating to an ever more competitive and market-driven one.

In light of the modernizers claim to be free of all old illusions, it is worth recalling that much social democratic opinion in the 1950s was inspired by the same idea – the idea that it had become irrelevant to pose alternatives in terms of 'socialism versus capitalism'. The difference lay in the optimistic register in which the theme of reconciliation between capitalist markets and socialist values was expressed then. Anthony Crosland's *The Future of Socialism*, first published in 1956, famously encapsulated the thinking of a whole generation of social democratic leaders and intellectuals in western capitalist countries. It opened with the argument that the post-war 'transformation of capitalism' had, once and for all, proved the Marxist analysis of capitalism wrong. According to Crosland the post-war world had witnessed three 'fundamental changes in the social framework' which no Act of Parliament could undo: (1) in the political sphere, a 'peaceful revolution' had transformed the state, so that 'the capitalist class has lost [its] commanding position' vis a vis governments; (2) in social relations and social attitudes there had been a 'decisive shift' of class power towards the working class at the expense of business; and (3) in the economy, there was a fundamental change in the nature of the business class whereby 'the economic power of the capital market and the finance houses, and hence *capitalist* financial control over industry (in the strict sense of the word) are . . . much weaker. This change alone makes it rather absurd to speak now of a capitalist ruling class.'[27]

In making this case, Crosland refused to adopt what he called 'the current fashion' of sneering at Marx. Marx, in his view, was 'a towering giant among socialist thinkers' whose work made the classical economists 'look flat, pedestrian and circumscribed by comparison . . . only moral dwarfs, or people devoid of imagination, sneer at men like that.' That said, he was convinced that Marx's writings had 'little or nothing to offer the contemporary socialist' because they related to 'conditions that had long since passed.' Yet it is obvious today that what Crosland took as fundamental conditions were in fact temporary – conditions that have long since disappeared. In almost every respect, the analysis of the Manifesto is today more relevant and less anachronistic than Crosland's text, written over a century later.

Yet despite the passing of the conditions on which Crosland built his case, today's modernizers are not only apt to sneer at Marx, but to denigrate anyone with the temerity to suggest the need for an anti-capitalist strategy. The vacuum that 'modernisation' as a political project represents was revealed by Sassoon amidst a detailed discussion of the French Socialist Party's retreat in the 1980s:

> To give up the ambition of abolishing capitalism . . . is not much of a strategy. Modernization as a slogan sounds appealing, but it has done so for over a hundred years. No party of the Left in post-war Europe (and hardly any party of the Right) has ever been against modernization. One suspects the watchword, devoid as it is of any practical content, is used purely symbolically: to be for modernization means to be for progress without abolishing capitalism.[28]

Yet this is precisely where Sassoon ends up. Like the modernizers, Sassoon directs his strongest criticisms at those who do not appear to be sufficiently 'aware' of the limits global markets impose on an anti-capitalist strategy. To be sure, he does not want to join in 'the supine endorsement of the neo-liberal glorification of the market' and he approvingly quotes Keynes as saying that 'capitalism is a beast to be tamed', but he offers no means of doing this, merely endorsing the modernisers strategies.

In sharp contrast, Gabriel Kolko's no less remarkable *Century of War* stresses the mistaken *choices* Communist and Social Democratic parties made, rather than treating their choices as inevitable, as Hobsbawm and Sassoon tend to do. Kolko attributes the mistakes to weaknesses of analysis as well as of organization and leadership:

> Their consistent failure to redeem and significantly (as well as permanently) transform societies when in a position to do so is testimony to their analytic inadequacies and the grave, persistent weaknesses of their leadership and organizations. It is this reality that has marginalized both social democracy and communism in innumerable nations since 1914, providing respites through the century to capitalist classes and their allies that otherwise would never have survived socialist regimes that implemented even a small fraction of the reforms outlined in their program.[29]

While this may bend the stick too far the other way, it is, indeed, only by coming to terms with these mistakes of analysis and strategy that we can begin to delineate an alternative to global capitalism. Social Democrats, no less than Communists, need to face up to their failed analyses and strategies and models, to come to terms with the fact that they were wrong in following Crosland in identifying the 'golden age of capitalism' with 'the future of socialism'.

But the fact that Crosland was so obviously wrong does not make Marx right. To be sure, one increasingly finds today alert columnists once more affirming that Marx was right about the nature of capitalism, and the sneering dismissals of Marxist analysis that became so common in the 1980s are less often heard in the media now.[30] This kind of superficial 'rediscovery' of Marx must not divert us, however, from addressing the real conundrums of socialism in this century; and we must also guard against any tendency to revert to that idiom of the revolutionary left in which fundamental questions were systematically evaded, on the assumption that if the Manifesto, or Marx's other writings, didn't pose these questions, let alone solve them, they could be disregarded. Drawing on the legacy of the Manifesto today means treating it not as a sacred text, but first and foremost as an inspiration to construct a political agenda for our own time.

V

An agenda: hardly the term that comes most readily to mind to describe the Manifesto, certainly not its brilliant Part I, written in the style of an epic prose poem on the rise and impending fall of the capitalist world. Yet this was exactly the point: 'more or less history has got to be related in it', as Engels prosaically noted (perhaps not yet aware of the full extent of his friend's literary powers), shortly before Marx was to begin writing.[31] In other words, the most fundamental political legacy of the Manifesto is that any serious agenda must first include a materialist analysis of contemporary history.

What this means for us now is, first of all, coming to a clear understanding of the twentieth century's passages through uneven development to 'globalization'. The Manifesto foreshadowed, with an accuracy that still astonishes, the 'universal inter-dependence of nations' which it has been the business of our century to realize:

> All old-established industries have been destroyed or are daily being destroyed . . . dislodged by new industries . . . whose products are consumed . . . in every quarter of the globe. . . . The bourgeoisie . . . compels all nations, on pain of extinction, to adopt the bourgeois mode of production . . . to introduce what it calls civilisation into their midst. . . .

What Marx could not specify, of course, was the precise pattern this complex and violent process would actually take in this century, now blocked, now rushing headlong, through world wars, television, electronic banking and the hamburger.

It has also taken a lot longer than he seems to have imagined; with world population increasing more than fivefold since Marx's time, it was only in the decades *following* the first centenary of the Manifesto (when world population had already reached 2.5 billion) that a majority of the world's people ceased to be peasants and whole populations around the globe were transformed into an urban (semi-) proletariat.[32] This goes far towards explaining the spatial pattern of reform and revolution in the twentieth century. In Arrighi's insightful formulation, the 'social power' which labour enjoys because it is indispensable to capitalist production was concentrated in the West and made reformism rewarding, while the immiseration which made for revolution (especially in the former Russian and Chinese empires) was concentrated at the 'periphery'.[33]

This was partly a question of imperialism, as Engels, Lenin and many later theorists argued; cheap food and raw materials and other forms of surplus transfer from the periphery contributed significantly to the living standards of western workers, and imperialist ideology and racism reinforced bourgeois hegemony. Other factors were also involved, however. Down to the 1960s it remained possible for the organised western working class to make major gains through wage bargaining with employers who had limited opportunities to relocate, and to extract reforms from the governments of industrialised economies. It was not till after 1945 that the transnational corporation, developed in the inter-war years, became generalised, and not until the 1980s that, with the aid of computerisation, the TNC's realized their full potential for world-wide control of production and finance. Social changes at the periphery created more and more centres with the requisite externalities for advanced production (security, transport, communications, an elite of high-tech workers and a supply of disciplined semi-skilled wage-labour); changes in the labour process reduced dependence on established labour forces, while a decline in the material element in manufactured goods and falling transport costs increasingly eroded older forms of 'natural protection'; the end of the formal empires in the 1960s, followed by the end of the Soviet system, opened up the whole planet to capitalist penetration. The result of all these changes was that the extraction and realization of *relative* surplus value finally became possible for capital on a global scale – if not exactly everywhere at least somewhere in many parts of every continent and subcontinent – in a way that earlier forms of imperialism had not established.

The longer-run political implications of this, however, are very hard to read. What are the implications, for instance, of the fact that nearly *one billion* people around the world, according to the ILO, were unemployed or underemployed in 1996?[34] Or of the fact that Chinese government reports are now projecting *hundreds of millions* of 'surplus' workers in rural areas by the year 2000?[35] Or of the fact that East Asia, the region of the world that has been the preeminent magnet for the

West's surplus capital, is now plunged in crisis?[36] Or of the fact that whereas the IMF credit the British Government needed to prevent an economic collapse in 1976 was $4 billion (at the time the largest ever requested), the sum needed to do the same job for Mexico in 1994 was $48 billion, while for South Korea in 1997 even $60 billion was not enough. 'Experts' cannot predict when or where the next financial crisis will strike, or the next 'natural' disaster. When we contemplate all this we need to remember that it does not represent the planned outcome of a 'corporate agenda': there is a political project for capital, and it does involve driving down living standards in what used to be called the 'Second' and 'Third' worlds as well as the 'First'. But in the North as well as the South, capital is, as always, driven as much as it is driving. It is being driven by the unrelenting competition between capitals in each sector as well as by the global financial markets which not only impel capital to downsize, merge, reconfigure, restructure and relocate, but also furnish the means of doing so: the increasingly dramatic and unpredictable results are anything but planned.

It was not only social democrats like Crosland who could not have been more wrong on the decline of the financial element in the capitalist class, but also all those, including Galbraith, who thought they saw a new technocratic industrial elite coming to manage the economies of the world. Instead, the Manifesto's image of the capitalist as 'the sorcerer, who is no longer able to control the powers of the nether world whom he has called up by his spells' captures all too well the concerns increasingly expressed by significant elements of the international establishment – from advocates of the Tobin tax to George Soros – that some means must be found of regulating the chaos of contemporary capitalism. This is why the first item on the left's agenda today has to be that of relating every national experience to the widest possible analysis of the accelerating and increasingly uncontrolled contradictions of the global accumulation process. What certainly will become clear, from such analyses, is that through the processes of globalisation, the 'social power' of western labour has declined and impoverishment – or the threat of it – has returned. The 'Chinese walls' that are now being 'battered down' by cheap goods are no longer only the pre-capitalist social structures at the periphery, but also those protecting high wages and welfare-state benefits of all workers – including those in the West – with no more than average global skills.[37] The world taken as a whole has indeed now begun to resemble the pattern Marx's logic led him to foresee, and the conditions that used to sustain western workers' reformism are being undermined.

What might replace that reformism is very hard even to imagine. Throughout the post-war era everyone assumed that a return to mass unemployment would lead to a loss of legitimacy for capitalism; even the western bourgeoisie delayed turning to unemployment as a means of stemming inflation and driving down the price of labour and, even when it did, it watched with apprehension to see how high unemployment had to go before the back of wage militancy was broken. But the legitimacy of capitalism was not brought into question. Many workers saw that they were dependent on 'the goose that laid the golden egg'[38] and accepted the case the goose's owners made for making it well again. They were unfortunately encouraged in this by 'post-Fordist' intellectuals who saw in 'flexible specialization' the path to a new regime of accumulation. Most leaders and activists were less prepared to accept the capitalists' arguments and insisted on the continued viability of the old Keynesian and corporatist arrangements; in effect, they struggled to defend the old managed capitalism. This should not have been surprising: workers have often confronted new insecurities by appealing to idealised memories of earlier times, recalling 'the shadowy image of a benevolent corporate state';[39] and in this they too were encouraged by some social democratic intellectuals who fostered the illusion that stability could be had by clinging to (or imitating) Swedish or German or Austrian corporatism.

After two decades, however, we are in a new conjuncture. Neither the dream of a 'post-Fordist' future nor that of a safe return to the neo-corporatist past is any longer tenable; it becomes more and more obvious that there will be no magic moment when 'prosperity' is restored, unaccompanied by constant demands for still further rounds of sacrifice. Yet at the same time struggles to bring back the Keynesian welfare state have less and less meaning for young people who never knew it, or even for their parents who have ceased to believe in it. It inevitably took some time for the dynamics of neo-liberalism to become familiar and to be seen as normal phenomena of capitalism in the era of globalisation, but it has happened. On the other hand, to understand neo-liberalism objectively does not necessarily induce fatalism. On the contrary, a good many workers, as we have seen, are recognising that they are willy-nilly trapped in a class struggle and are once again blaming the economic system for their situation.

That said, what is still absent is any concrete notion of an alternative system. People in the former Communist countries are learning first-hand that capitalist streets are not necessarily paved with gold;[40] but they, like many workers in the old Third World, have no other model of well-being than that of the western consumer portrayed by the media. Yet there can still be no other way forward for working people anywhere than once more building movements oriented to ending the rule of private property – beginning with imposing effective controls on capital mobility through cooperation between national governments with a popular mandate to do so, and democratizing control over the major means of production, distribution, communication and exchange.

And here the historic failure of Bolshevism weighs like a nightmare on the brains of the living. The Russian and Chinese revolutions and their aftermaths dominated our century; their brute achievements in face of the bitterest odds, the courage and intelligence they mobilised and consumed, the hopes they raised and ultimately disappointed, the immense human costs – the memory of all this is now an extra barrier that the anti-capitalist struggle has to overcome. Giving our goals their proper name – full democracy – will not prevent them being called communist. But the effect of that association will not forever be negative if we can figure out how to make our commitment to democracy genuine and our goals for it viable.

VI

'To win the battle of democracy': this is what the Manifesto saw as 'the first step in the revolution', the primary condition for establishing 'the political supremacy' of the working class.

In the established liberal democracies opinion polls show that representative party politics have never been more despised, and the connection between genuine democracy and an equitable distribution of social and economic power is becoming clear in a way not seen, perhaps, since the struggles for franchise extension in the last century. This is hardly surprising. Not only have national governments transferred power to determine their citizens' economic fates to 'market forces', but as extreme inequality has been restored and welfare-state protections have been stripped away, they have also done their best to close down avenues for popular forces to oppose the process, let alone reverse it. Presidential decrees of dubious constitutionality override parliamentary majorities; legislation curtailing democratic rights is pushed through, contrary to pre-election promises; the powers of local government are usurped; the powers of the police are extended, the powers of juries curtailed; and political parties – including, now, the Labour, Socialist, Social Democratic and Democratic Left parties – are themselves 'modernised' – i.e. power is taken away from their mass membership and given to small groups of professional politicians ('people who make a business of politics') and their market-survey, media-oriented advisers.[41]

Disillusion has also rapidly overtaken the much-touted globalisation of 'liberal democracy', the so-called 'third wave' democratisation announced by Huntington and other apologists for neoliberalism. As often as not it has turned out to mean 'no more than a military despotism and a police state, bureaucratically carpentered, embellished with parliamentary forms' (as Marx said of 1875 Germany).[42] And in any case international agencies are ready to intervene to ensure that elections do not get in the way of the interests of global capital: within a few short weeks in November-December 1997 the IMF extracted public undertakings from all the leading candidates in the South Korean Presidential elections *before* the poll that they would abide by the liberalising conditions of an IMF loan – without which an economic disaster was categorically promised.[43] Perry Anderson's comment is, if anything, an understatement: 'Democracy is indeed now more widespread than ever. But it is also thinner – as if the more universally available it becomes, the less active meaning it retains.'[44]

A further dimension of the emasculation of democracy everywhere is the importance of the mass media. Here the legacy of the Manifesto is not of much help. Marx recognised that 'the class which has the means of material production at its disposal, has control at the same time over the means of mental production, so that thereby generally speaking, the ideas of those who lack the means of mental production are subject to it.'[45] But he also thought a revolutionary class could create its own means of mental production; and while for a time they did so with their publishing houses and newspapers, he did not foresee the way mass-circulation newspapers would become essentially vehicles for selling advertisements, and would in this way eventually bankrupt progressive newspapers that could not raise equivalent advertising revenue.[46] Nor could he foresee how this would be repeated on an even more spectacular scale with radio and television after other means of communication – and especially the public meeting, which was still the key popular medium of communication in Marx's time – had become so much less effective.

The fact is that in most countries of the world the main 'conversation of society' now takes place through a medium – television – from which issues of public concern are increasingly displaced in favour of entertainment and sport, and from which, when public affairs are discussed, left perspectives are often deliberately excluded.[47] This change – whereby not only has public conversation been commodified, but a medium has been developed that effectively gives a monopoly of public conversation to capital – has to be one of the most politically critical developments of the last century; yet the left has still fully to register its immense significance, and develop a commensurate response. Solutions exist: broad public access to mainstream media is not the stuff of fantasy but a democratic necessity, for which institutional models already exist in various countries in Europe, in particular.[48] It is high time to make it a non-negotiable element in a mass campaign for the restoration of democratic rights.

But this is only a beginning. Contrary to the interested arguments of the 'professional representative' class (as Raymond Williams aptly called it), periodic elections – absolutely fundamental as they are – are anything but the only practicable democratic institution that a complex modern society requires. There is an rich legacy of genuinely democratic theory – and of practical experience, from the Paris Commune through Italian Council Communism to the 'social movement' organisations and experiments (east and west, south and north) of our own times – that has still to be assimilated. The range of possibilities is vast, including various kinds of monitoring, reporting and accountability without which elections alone are ineffective as a means of controlling power; deliberative democratic procedures (as in 'citizens' juries') that pre-empt the distortion of democratic debate by adversarial rhetoric; various forms of democratic management (representative supervisory and executive boards, collective managements, job rotation, selection by lot); segmented, coalitional forms of organisation; 'socialised' information systems and institutions of the kind proposed by Diane Elson; the list could be extended almost indefinitely.[49]

The left must make itself the legitimate champion of this legacy by embodying it in its own practice, and driving its significance home to the widest possible public. We need to expose at the same time the way so much local grass roots popular activity is coming to be structured and appropriated by today's modernizing elites (including the World Bank working through NGOs). The capitalist class will undoubtedly not relinquish the power they have recently re-established behind their pseudo-democratic facade without a bitter fight; but the first necessity is still to articulate a convincing, practicable and consistent conception of genuine democracy to set against it. If the point of drawing on the legacy of the Manifesto is indeed 'to exaggerate the given task in the imagination, rather than to flee from solving it in reality, to recover the spirit of revolution, rather than to set its ghost walking again',[50] then bringing to life these visions of radical popular democracy must also be at the very top of our agenda.

The Social Democratic parties – not to mention the Bolsheviks – failed to do this precisely because the political forms they created, or adapted to, sapped the 'spirit of revolution'. It was because Marx was so sensitive to the danger of bureaucracy sapping the spirit of revolution that he made so much of what the Paris Commune suggested about workers discovering new radical democratic means of avoiding this . Yet the notorious 'statism' of socialism in this century was also perhaps inscribed, it must be said, in the Manifesto's own conception of what the proletariat would need to do, at least in the short run, when it achieved power, above all in the stress it placed on the *centralisation* of control over credit, communications and production in the hands of the state – not only to divest the bourgeoisie of its power, but also in order 'to increase the total of productive forces as rapidly as possible.'

What inspired so many Social Democrats and Communists in the twentieth century was precisely this idea that planning would be more efficient than markets. When, however, neither the Communists nor the Social Democrats found that planning production enabled them to displace capitalism ('bury' it, as Khrushchev said), they came to terms with it: the Communists through 'peaceful co-existence', the Social Democrats through the Keynesian welfare state. The radical democratic vision was sacrificed; and this eventually paved the way for the neo-liberal reaction. It was the neo-liberals, in successfully deploying the rhetoric of revolution to promote market freedom as the 'common sense' of the era, who showed that capital, even at the end of the twentieth century, still retained the spirit of bourgeois revolution and the capacity make the world in its image.[51] But capital's idea of freedom brought to the fore once more the contradiction which had first surfaced during the French Revolution, between private capital and political equality.[52] It is this, together with the destructive social effect of global free markets – epitomized in Mrs. Thatcher's notorious statement 'that there is no such thing as society' – that makes the Manifesto's charge that the bourgeoisie is no longer 'fit to rule' seem so very contemporary: 'society can no longer live under this bourgeoisie, in other words, its existence is no longer compatible with society.'

Is it too much to hope that the left can learn valuable lessons from neo-liberalism's sweeping victories over both neo-corporatist and central- command forms of planning? In his Preface to the 1888 English edition of the Manifesto Engels wrote: 'The very events and vicissitudes of the struggle against capital, the defeats even more than the victories, could not help bringing home to men's minds the insufficiency of their favourite nostrums, and preparing the way for a more complete insight into the true conditions of working-class emancipation.'[53] The original new left's critique of both Bolshevism and Social Democracy pointed in the right direction – that is, towards democracy over planning, and towards social revolution rather than co-existence. But the failure of the new left either to transform the existing Social Democratic and Communist parties or to found viable new ones led a strong current of left-wing opinion to give up on both socialism and the working class, in favour of a more diffuse, 'decentred' conception of 'radical democracy'. This stance swept under the carpet the irreconcilability of democracy with private property that the French Revolution had itself so clearly brought to light – and this was something that could hardly be ignored in the era of globalization and neoliberalism. The 'free development of each' can only be 'the condition for the free development of all' in so far as private property is abolished.

This, in other words, must come clearly back onto the agenda. Once again, as in the Manifesto, it must be made clear that this does *not* mean personal possessions, that socialism 'deprives no [one] of the power to appropriate the product of society; all that it does is to deprive [anyone] of the power to subjugate the labour of others by means of such appropriation.' And to this end we too need to put forward practical policies, as the Manifesto did with its ten-point programme, that can begin to make 'inroads on the rights of property', the kinds of 'measures. . . which appear economically insufficient and untenable, but which in the course of the movement, outstrip themselves, necessitate further inroads upon the social order.'[54]

It is sobering to note how far the measures they put forward are still relevant today. John Bellamy Foster, in his important essay in this volume on the Manifesto and the environment, makes this point regarding the passages that have to do with land policy, especially the one which calls for 'the improvement of the soil generally in accordance with a common plan.' Equally relevant is the Manifesto's proposal for 'a heavy progressive or graduated income tax', given the massive redistribution of income and wealth from the poor to the rich over the past twenty years. And the unprecedented power which capital mobility now places in the hands of the bourgeoisie, not to mention the financial instability that accompanies it, makes the Manifesto's call for credit control no less relevant, and moreover prefigures the proposals for capital controls that are now being put forward even on the liberal and social democratic left, not just by Marxist political economists writing in the *Socialist Register*.[55] Contemporary proposals for the radical redistribution of working time and life-long education, such as those advanced by Greg Albo in last year's *Socialist Register*,[56] are also prefigured in the Manifesto's calls for the 'equal liability of all to labour' and 'combination of education with industrial production'. The legacy of the Manifesto is very much present, in other words, in the most sophisticated socialist economic proposals being advanced today, such as Albo's ten-point programme for achieving 'egalitarian, ecologically-sustainable reproduction' through measures directed at 'expanding the scale of democracy while reducing the scale of production'.[57]

The struggle to implement these measures must be both national and global; and this too is very much part of the Manifesto's legacy. While it called on the workers of the world to unite, it also argued that 'the proletariat of each country must . . . *first* of all settle things with its own bourgeoisie' – because to accomplish anything, the workers 'must *first* acquire political supremacy', which meant winning power in the nation-state. But then as now, too, 'united action, of the leading . . . countries at least, is one of the *first* conditions for the emancipation of the proletariat.'[58] It is inconceivable, for example, that effective capital controls can be put in place without such cooperation; yet this implies a wave of national struggles that will commit the leading states to them.

This multiple set of conditions explains the superabundance of '*firsts*' in the Manifesto. Yet all these first steps and conditions are themselves conditional on yet another, even more primary: the 'formation of the proletariat into a class.' The various other kinds of socialist so mordantly criticised in Part III of the Manifesto had one common fault in Marx's eyes: that of seeing socialism in terms of the introduction of measures 'for the benefit of the working class' by people 'outside the working-class movement . . . looking rather to the 'educated' classes for support'.[59] The priority Marx attached to the 'formation of the proletariat into a class' needs to be understood in terms of his commitment to the *self*-emancipation of the workers. But this did not mean merely the formation of unions and parties that would express the particular interests of workers. 'The basic thought running through the Manifesto', as Engels later put it, was that the class oppression and conflict that has marred all previous human history could only be ended once humanity reached 'a stage where the exploited and oppressed class (the proletariat) can no longer emancipate itself from the class which exploits it (the bourgeoisie), without at the same time for ever freeing the whole of society from exploitation, oppression and class struggles.'[60]

The working classes' lack of credibility as general emancipators in our time not only explains why the feminist and ecology movements, engaged in struggles crucial to human emancipation, have often defined themselves in opposition to the working class; it also explains why, for the first time in a century, and despite the rise of the new social movements, we lack a sense that there is an alternative to capitalism. The separation of the social movements from working class politics, unfortunate but understandable, tragically became crystallized into dogma by a generation of intellectuals. As Edward Thompson noted in the *Socialist Register* as early as 1973: 'There were real reasons for this [dismissal of the working class as an agent of general emanci-pation] but the writing off did damage to intellectual growth itself.' He went on to say, in his famous 'Open Letter To Leszek Kolakowski':

> You appear to share this instant dismissal, writing: . . . 'Let us imagine what the "dictatorship of the proletariat" would mean if the (real, not imaginary) working class took over exclusive political power now in the U.S.' The absurdity of the question appears (in your view) to provide its own answer. But I doubt whether you have given to the question a moment of serious historical imagination: you have simply assumed a white working class, socialized by capitalist institutions as it is now, mystified by the mass media as it is now, structured into competitive organi-zations as it is now, without self-activity or its own forms of political expression: i.e. a working class with all the attributes of subjection within capitalist structures which one then 'imagines' to achieve power without changing either those struc-tures or itself: which is, I fear, a typical example of the fixity of concept which characterizes much capitalist ideology.[61]

Of course, the question of how the alteration of people 'on a mass scale' can come about is a huge one, to which there is no ready-made answer. But, to repeat, classes are never frozen and fixed, they are constantly changing; and there is good reason to look forward to – and to work for -developments through which working classes will increas-ingly acquire a broad emancipatory outlook, a 'spirit of revolution' expressive of the full range of identities they comprise. Their potential power can in any case now only be fully realized if, far from trying to ignore or efface these differences, working class organisations express and gain strength from the plurality of identities that make up the proletariat. The recomposition of the proletariat that has been going on in recent decades 'before our eyes' (to employ, in a particularly relevant context, another of Marx's favourite terms)[62] needs to be soberly examined from this perspective, as the essays in this volume by David Harvey, Sam Gindin, Sheila Cohen and Kim Moody seek to do. What is certainly clear is how little help the parties that once based themselves on the working classes have been in this respect. Nothing speaks more clearly than this to the need for new ones.

For the moment we might seek inspiration from the remarkable communist-internationalists of the 1830s and '40s who were then trying to fashion appropriate organizations through which working people could develop themselves. After the leaders of League of the Just were expelled from France in 1839 they made their way to London, where Schapper, Bauer and Moll founded the German Workers' Educational Society. We could do worse today than emulate their efforts, as advertised on one of the Society's posters:

> The main principle of the Society is that men can only come to liberty and self-consciousness by cultivating their intellectual faculties. Consequently, all the evening meetings are devoted to instruction. One evening English is taught, on another, geography, on a third history, on the fourth, drawing and physics, on a fifth, singing, on a sixth, dancing and on the seventh communist politics.[63]

NOTES

We are grateful to Greg Albo, Fred Bienefeld, Martin Eve, Sam Gindin, Margie Mendell, Ellen Wood and Alan Zuege for their comments and criticisms on an earlier draft of this essay.

1. 'Ultimately, when stubborn historical facts had dispersed all intoxicating effects of self-deception, this form of Socialism ['Petty-Bourgeois Socialism'] ended in a miserable fit of the blues' (Karl Marx 'The Manifesto of the Communist Party', in Karl Marx, The Revolutions of 1848: Political Writings Volume I, D. Fernbach (ed.), Harmondsworth, Penguin, 1974, p. 90. On 'new times' see Stuart Hall and Martin Jacques (eds.), New Times: The Changing Face of Politics in the 1990s, London, Lawrence and Wishart and Marxism Today, 1989, a collection of articles published by Marxism Today in the late 1980s. The book ended by suggesting that Gorbachev's perestroika was an inspiring example of the politics needed for 'new times', and Marxism Today closed soon after Gorbachev's fall. On 'radicalism of the centre' as articulated by the Blair leadership of the Labour Party see Leo Panitch and Colin Leys, The End of Parliamentary Socialism: From New Left to New Labour, London, Verso, 1997, chapter 11.
2. On these 'new populations' at the end of the twentieth century, see Nigel Harris, The New Untouchables: Immigration and the New World Worker, London,

Penguin, 1996.

3. A 'teach-in' in Toronto on 'challenging corporate rule', sponsored by the Council of Canadians in November, 1997 drew over 1,500 people. One press report headed its account 'Not Scared of the C-Word', *The Varsity*, 11 November, 1997,

4. Boris Kagarlitsky, 'The Unfinished Revolution', *Green-Left Weekly*, Sydney, Australia, 5 November, 1997.

5. The most dramatic examples are the 'melt-down' of Canada's Progressive Conservatives, who went from being the governing party to holding only two seats in the Federal Parliament in the election of 1993, and the British Conservatives, who after 18 years in office pursuing neoliberal policies were reduced to less than a quarter of the parliamentary seats (and none at all in Scotland or Wales) in the election of 1997. Even without such dramatic collapses, it was noteworthy that by 1997 social democratic parties were in office in 12 of the 15 states of the EU.

6. Giovanni Arrighi, 'Workers of the World at Century's End', *Review* XIX/3, Summer 1996, pp. 339–40.

7. The UK, which had the longest working hours in the EU, also had the fastest rising index of inequality (second only to New Zealand within the OECD), while the numbers of people unable to work due to chronic illness rose steadily from about 600,000 in 1979 to nearly 1.8 million in 1997 (equal to the total of those officially unemployed). Britain was also second to the OECD in the proportion of the population in jail, while in the USA, which ranked first, the probability in 1997 of any adult being jailed at some time in his or her lifetime was 5.1 per cent (9 per cent for all men, and 28 per cent for all black men). *Business Week* August 11, 1997.

8. Alexander Cockburn, 'The Witch Hunt and the Crash', *The Nation* , November 17, 1997. 'Between 1992 and 1995, 15 percent of people holding jobs for more than one year lost those jobs; their new jobs, if they found one, paid 14 percent less on average. The rate of job loss in the nineties 'boom' is higher than in the recession years of the early eighties or of 1990–91.' Cockburn adds that 'about one-third of the U.S. labor force makes $15,000 or less'. This reflects the fact that, as Kim Moody reports: 'The 80% of the total workforce in the US that hold working-class jobs saw their real average weekly earnings slip by 18% from 1973 through 1995. Real hourly earnings in that period fell by 12%, indicating that the growth of part-time work had reduced the average weekly income of US workers by another 6 percentage points.' Kim Moody, *Workers in a Lean World*, London, Verso, 1997, p. 188.

9. 'Fighting the class war', *The Economist*, 27 September, 1997.

10. 'The Downsizing of America', *The New York Times*, 5 March, 1996.

11. Cynthia Cockburn, *The Local State*, London, Pluto, 1977, p. 118.

12. Sheila Rowbotham, Lynne Segal and Hilary Wainwright, *Beyond the Fragments*, London, Merlin Press, 1979.

13. Writing in the mid-1980s, when he was a close adviser to Jesse Jackson, Vicente Navarro chastised 'post-Marxists' whose proposals for 'a constantly shifting pattern of alliances . . . [were] but a recycling of the old pluralist-interest groups' theories that have been the dominant form of political discourse and practice in the US for many years. The emergence and importance of social movements in the US – the main trademark of US political behaviour and mass mobilization – are a direct consequence of the absence of class-based practices by the dominated

classes. . . This is not to deny the enormous importance for the left to be sensitive to forms of exploitation other than class exploitation, nor to ignore the importance of establishing coalitions with strata outside the working class. . . . The operational meaning of this awareness is not, however, the mere aggregate of the demands of each component of the 'people'. Class practices are not the mere aggregate of 'interest group' politics. . . . This was, incidentally, the main problem with Jesse Jackson's 'rainbow coalition' . . . with [its] heavy emphasis on the rights of blacks without providing enough linkage with other components of the working class.' 'The 1980 and 1984 Elections and the New Deal', *The Socialist Register 1985/6*, pp. 199–200.

14. Margaret Keck's account of the Workers' Party of Brazil in the 1980s, offers a rich portrait of what this entails in our own time: 'The PT's origins were deeply influenced by the perception of widespread mobilization around social demands in the late 1970s; in the early 1980s, as it became clear that local organization around specific equity demands did not automatically translate into a societal movement, the party was placed in the ambiguous position of having to help organize what it was claiming to represent.' *The Workers' Party and Democratization in Brazil*, New Haven, Yale University Press 1992, p. 242.

15. 'We know that heed must be paid to the institutions, customs and traditions of the various countries, and we do not deny that there are countries, such as America and England, and if I was familiar with its institutions, I might include Holland, where the workers may attain their goals by peaceful means. That being the case, we must recognise that in most continental countries the lever of the revolution will have to be force; a resort to force will be necessary one day to set up the rule of labour'; Speech on the Hague Congress, in David Fernbach (ed.), *Marx: The First International and After*, Harmondsworth, Penguin, 1974, p. 322.

16. See Teodor Shanin, *Late Marx and the Russian Road*, London, Routledge, 1983.

17. Frederick Engels, 1895 Preface to Marx's *The Class Struggles in France*, in Marx-Engels *Selected Works*, Vol. I, Moscow, Foreign Languages Publishing House, 1962, p. 135.

18. *The Prophet Armed*, Oxford, OUP, 1954, pp. 338–9.

19. Preface to *The Class Struggles in France*, p. 132.

20. *Ibid.*, p. 134.

21. For an excellent discussion of the unfortunate use made of this in the German SPD, see Gugliemeo Carchedi, *Class Analysis and Social Research*, Oxford, Blackwell, 1987, ch. 1.

22. Karl Marx, *The Civil War in France*, in Karl Marx, *The First International and After: Political Writings Volume III*, D. Fernbach (ed.), Harmondsworth, Penguin, 1974, p. 213.

23. This is the phrase that Ronald Aronson repeats like a mantra throughout his *After Marxism*, New York, Guilford, 1995.

24. John Gray, 'Socialism for the unconverted', *The Times Higher Education Supplement*, October 6, 1995.

25. Eric Hobsbawm, *Age of Extremes: The short Twentieth Century, 1914–1991*, London, Michael Joseph, 1994, pp. 564–5.

26. 'Why the Left lost utopia', the *Guardian*, 24 November, 1996.

27. *The Future of Socialism* (1956), New York 1963, pp. 7–16.

28. Donald Sassoon, *One Hundred Years of Socialism*, London, I.B. Taurus, 1996, pp. 558–9.

29. Gabriel Kolko, *Century of War*, New York, New Press, 1995, p. 457.

30. See, e.g., John Cassidy, 'The Next Thinker: The Return of Karl Marx', *The New Yorker*, October 20, 1997, pp. 248–59.

31. Engels wrote to Marx on 23–24 November 1847, just before the London Congress of the Communist League which commissioned Marx to write the Manifesto: 'As more or less history has got to be related in it . . . I am bringing what I have done here [Paris] with me; it is in simple narrative form, but miserably worded, in fearful haste. I begin: What is Communism? And then straight to the proletariat – history of its origin, difference from former labourers, development of the antithesis between proletariat and bourgeoisie, crises, conclusions.' (Marx-Engels, *Selected Correspondence*, Moscow Foreign Languages Publishing House, n.d., pp. 52–53.)

32. See Hobsbawm, *Age of Extremes*, pp. 289–93; and Michael Kidron and Ronald Segal, *The State of the World Atlas*, London, Penguin, 1995, pp. 28–9.

33. Giovanni Arrighi, 'Marxist Century, American Century: The Making and Remaking of the World Labour Movement', *New Left Review* 179, 1990, pp. 29–63.

34. International Labour Organization, *World Employment 1996/97*, Geneva and Washington, D.C., 1996.

35. A projection of 370 million 'surplus' rural workers by the year 2000 appeared in the *China Daily* on December 2, 1997, citing a report by the State Council issued on June 11, 1997.

36. The Swedish/Swiss engineering transnational corporation, ABB, which between 1990 and 1996 'shed 59,000 jobs in western Europe and North America while creating 56,000 chiefly in Asia and eastern Europe' was as a consequence 'heavily exposed in Asia's tiger economies. Confronted with government decisions to abandon investment projects in the region, [ABB] promptly announced it was laying off 10,000 in western Europe and North America . . .' *Financial Times*, October 24, 1997.

37. As the Manifesto puts it: 'The cheap prices of its commodities are the heavy artillery with which [the bourgeoisie] forces the barbarians' intensely obstinate hatred of foreigners to capitulate.'

38. This is a metaphor Marx himself was wont to use, albeit more aptly in relation to Russian agriculture. See Shanin., p. 115.

39. 'Luddism must be seen as arising at the crisis-point in the abrogation of paternalist legislation, and the imposition of the political economy of *laissez-faire* upon, and against the will and conscience of, the working people . . . True enough, much of this paternalist legislation had been in origin not only restrictive, but, for the working man, punitive. Nevertheless, there was within it the shadowy image of a benevolent corporate state, in which there were legislative as well as moral sanctions against the unscrupulous manufacturer or the unjust employer, and in which the journeymen were a recognized 'estate', however low, in the realm. . . These ideals may never have been much more than ideals; by the end of the eighteenth century they may have been threadbare. But they had a powerful reality, none the less, in the notion of what *ought* to be, to which artisans, journeymen, and many small masters appealed.' E.P. Thompson, *The Making of the English Working Class*, London, Penguin, 1968, p. 594.

40. In September 1997 the Russian State Duma reported that life expectancy had fallen far below the levels of other industrialised countries; per capita

consumption of meat, milk and fish had fallen by about a third between 1990 and 1996, the rate of illness among schoolchildren had increased fivefold and only ten per cent of high-school graduates could be considered healthy, with forty per cent chronically ill. *Toronto Star* September 13, 1997.

41. In North America, Engels wrote, 'each of the two major parties which alternately succeed each other in power is itself in turn controlled by people who make a business of politics, who speculate on seats in the legislative assemblies. . . or who make a living by carrying on agitation for their party and on its victory are rewarded with positions.' Introduction to Marx's *The Civil War in France* in Robert C. Tucker (ed), *The Marx-Engels Reader*, New York, Norton 1972, p. 535.

42. Marx, 'Critique of the Gotha Programme' ('Marginal Notes on the Programme of the German Workers' Party'), in Fernbach (ed.), *The First International and After*, p. 356.

43. Report on Business, *The Globe and Mail*, Toronto, 4 December 1997.

44. Perry Anderson, *A Zone of Engagement*, London, Verso, 1992, p. 356.

45. Marx and Engels, *The German Ideology*, New York, International Publishers, 1947, p. 39.

46. James Curran and Jean Seaton, *Power Without Responsibility: The Press and Broadcasting in Britain*, London, Fontana, 1981.

47. See e.g. Brian McNair, *News and Journalism in the UK*, London, Routledge 1994; Douglas Kellner, *Television and the Crisis of Democracy*, Boulder, Westview 1990.

48. For rich analyses of existing and possible ways of restoring the media to democracy see James Curran, 'Mass Media and Democracy Revisited' in J. Curran and P. Gourevitch, eds., *Mass Media and Society*, London, Arnold, 1996; and Don Hazen and Julie Winokur (eds.), *We the Media: A Citizen's Guide to Fighting For Media Democracy*, New York, The New Press, 1997.

49. On citizens' juries see John Stewart, Elizabeth Kendall and Anna Coote, *Citizens' Juries*, London, IPPR 1994. On the idea of a socialised market see Diane Elson, 'Market Socialism or Socialization of the Market?,' *New Left Review*, 172, 1988. On the GLC and democratic 'deepening' in a Swedish women's education centre, see Hilary Wainwright *Arguments for a New Left*, Oxford, Blackwell, 1994, chapters 5 to 7; On democratic management in the workplace and the state, see respectively, Michael Albert and Robin Hahnel, *Looking Forward: Participatory Economics for the Twenty First Century*, Boston, South End Press, 1991, and Gregory Albo, David Langille, and Leo Panitch, eds., *A Different Kind of State: Popular Power and Democratic Administration*, Toronto, Oxford, 1993.

50. *The Eighteenth Brumaire of Louis Bonaparte*, in Karl Marx, *Surveys from Exile: Political Writings: Volume II*, D. Fernbach (ed), London, Penguin, 1973, p. 148.

51. See Leo Panitch, 'Capitalism, Socialism and Revolution: The Contemporary Meaning of Revolution in the West,' *Socialist Register 1989*, London, Merlin, 1989.

52. In addition to Moss, *infra*, see F.L. Bender's excellent introduction to his edition of *The Communist Manifesto*, New York, Norton, 1988, esp. pp. 3–4.

53. Frederick Engels, Preface to the 1888 English edition of the Manifesto, in Bender, ed. p. 47. His claim that lessons had been learned, coinciding as it did with the rise of industrial unionism and mass working class parties, was quite valid.

54. The measures were advanced as only 'generally applicable': they would be 'different in different countries'. And when Marx and Engels a quarter of a century later wrote their first preface to the Manifesto (for the 1872 German

edition), they insisted that 'no special stress' should be laid on the measures proposed, and that the whole 'passage would, in many respects, be very differently worded today.' See Bender., p. 43.

55. See William Greider, 'Saving the Local Economy', *The Nation*, 15 December 1997 as well as the declaration and memorandum by 25 European economists, *Full Employment, Social Cohesion and Equity for Europe: Alternatives to Competitive Austerity*, May 1997. In the Socialist Register, among others essays, see especially Jim Crotty and Gerald Epstein, 'In Defence of Capital Controls' *Socialist Register 1996*, London, Merlin, 1996.

56. Gregory Albo, 'A World Market of Opportunities? Capitalist Obstacles and Left Economic Policy', *Socialist Register 1997*, esp. pp. 27–39.

57. *Ibid.*, p. 28.

58. The text actually says 'leading civilized countries'. Without wishing to burke the question of how far Marx's use of Hegel's concept of 'world-historical' nations (in which the principle of 'freedom' had been most fully realised, etc.) involved assumptions of a racialist nature, we have omitted the word 'civilized' in the quotation in order to focus on the main point, which remains valid – the need for joint action by the leading or major economic powers.

59. Engels, Preface to the 1888 English edition, in Bender, ed., p. 48.

60. Preface to the 1883 German edition in Bender, ed., pp. 45–6.

61. E.P. Thompson, 'An Open Letter to Leszek Kolakowski', *The Socialist Register 1973*, London, Merlin, 1973, pp. 84 and 99–100 n. 69.

62. Marx's observations on the contemporary study of social and economic history are worth recalling: 'Much research has been carried out to trace the different historical phases that the bourgeoisie has passed through . . . But when it is a question of making a precise study of strikes, combinations and other forms in which the proletarians carry out before our eyes their organisation as a class, some are seized with real fear and others display a *transcendental* disdain.' *The Poverty of Philosophy*, Moscow, Foreign Languages Publishing House, 1956, p. 196.

63. Quoted in Bender's introduction to the Manifesto., p. 10.

THE GEOGRAPHY OF CLASS POWER

David Harvey

It is imperative to reignite the political passions that suffuse the *Manifesto*. It is an extraordinary document full of insights, rich in meanings and bursting with political possibilities. While we have not the right, as Marx and Engels wrote in their 1872 preface to the German edition, to alter what has become a key historical document, we have not only the right but the obligation to interpret it in the light of contemporary conditions and historical-geographical experience. '*The practical application of the principles,*' wrote Marx and Engels in that Preface, '*will depend,* as the Manifesto itself states *everywhere and at all times, on the historical conditions for the time being existing.*' This italicised phrase precisely delineates our present task.

The accumulation of capital has always been a profoundly geographical affair. Without the possibilities inherent in geographical expansion, spatial reorganization and uneven geographical develop-ment, capitalism would long ago have ceased to function as a political-economic system. This perpetual turning to 'a spatial fix' to capitalism's internal contradictions (most notably registered as an overaccumu-lation of capital within a particular geographical area) coupled with the uneven insertion of different territories and social formations into the capitalist world market has created a global historical geography of capital accumulation whose character needs to be well understood. How Marx and Engels conceptualised the problem in *The Communist Manifesto* deserves some commentary for it is here that the communist movement – with representatives from many countries – came together to try to define a revolutionary agenda that would work in the midst of considerable geographical differentiation. This differentiation is just as important today as it ever was and the *Manifesto's* weaknesses as well as its strengths in its approach to this problem need to be confronted and addressed.

49

I The Spatial Fix In Hegel And Marx

In *The Philosophy of Right*, Hegel presented imperialism and colonialism as potential solutions to the internal contradictions of what he considered to be a 'mature' civil society.[1] The increasing accumulation of wealth at one pole and the formation of a 'penurious rabble' trapped in the depths of misery and despair at the other, sets the stage for social instability and class war that cannot be cured by any internal transformation (such as a redistribution of wealth from rich to poor). Civil society is thereby driven by its 'inner dialectic' to 'push beyond its own limits and seek markets, and so its necessary means of subsistence, in other lands that are either deficient in the goods it has overproduced, or else generally backward in industry.' It must also found colonies and thereby permit a part of its population 'a return to life on the family basis in a new land' at the same time as it also 'supplies itself with a new demand and field for its industry.' All of this is fuelled by a 'passion for gain' that inevitably involves risk so that industry, 'instead of remaining rooted to the soil and the limited circle of civil life with its pleasures and desires, . . . embraces the element of flux, danger, and destruction.'

Having, in a few brief startling paragraphs, sketched the possibilities of an imperialist and colonial solution to the ever-intensifying internal contradictions of civil society, Hegel just as suddenly dropped the matter. He leaves us in the dark as to whether capitalism could be stabilized by appeal to some sort of 'spatial fix' in either the short or long run. Instead, he turns his attention to the concept of the state as the actuality of the ethical idea. This could be taken to imply that transcendence of civil society's internal contradictions by the modern state – an inner transformation – is both possible and desirable. Yet Hegel nowhere explains how the problems of poverty and of the increasing polarization in the distribution of wealth are actually to be overcome. Are we supposed to believe, then, that these particular problems can be dealt with by imperialism? The text is ambivalent. This is, as Avineri points out, 'the only time in his system, where Hegel raises a problem – and leaves it open.'[2]

How far Hegel influenced Marx's later concerns can be endlessly debated. Engels certainly believed that Marx was 'the only one who could undertake the work of extracting from Hegelian logic the kernel containing Hegel's real discoveries.' The language Marx uses to describe the general law of capitalist accumulation, for example, bears an erie resemblance to that of Hegel.[3] It is even possible to interpret volume 1 of *Capital* as a tightly orchestrated argument, buttressed by a good deal of historical and material evidence, to prove that the propositions Hegel had so casually advanced, without any logical or evidentiary backing, were indubitably correct.[4] The internal contradictions that Hegel depicted were, in Marx's view, not only inevitable but also incapable of any internal resolution short of proletarian revolution. And this was, of course, the conclusion that Marx wanted to force not only upon the Hegelians but upon everyone else. But in order to make the argument stick he also has to bear in mind the question that Hegel had raised but left open.

In this light one other feature in the structure of argument in *Capital* makes sense. The last chapter of the book deals with the question of colonization. It seems, at first sight, an odd afterthought to a work which, in the preceeding chapter announced expropriation of the expropriators and the death-knell of the bourgeoisie with a rhetoric reminiscent of the *Manifesto*. But in the light of Hegel's argument the chapter acquires a particular significance.

Marx first seeks to show how the bourgeoisie contradicted its own myths as to the origin and nature of capital by the policies it advocated in the colonies. In bourgeois accounts (the paradigmatic case being that of Locke), capital (a thing) originated in the fruitful exercise of the producer's own capacity to labour, while labour power as a commodity arose through a social contract, freely entered into, between those who produced surplus capital through frugality and diligence, and those who chose not to do so. 'This pretty fancy', Marx thunders, is 'torn asunder' in the colonies. As long as the labourer can 'accumulate for himself – and this he can do as long as he remains possessor of his means of production – capitalist accumulation and the capitalist mode of production are impossible.' Capital is not a physical thing but a social relation. It rests on the 'annihilation of self-earned private property, in other words, the expropriation of the labourer.' Historically, this expropriation was 'written in the annals of mankind in letters of blood and fire' – and Marx cites chapter, verse and the Duchess of Sutherland to prove his point. The same truth, however, is expressed in colonial land policies, such as those of Wakefield in Australia, in which the powers of private property and the state were to be used to exclude labourers from easy access to free land in order to preserve a pool of wage labourers for capitalist exploitation. Thus was the bourgeoisie forced to acknowledge in its programme of colonization what it sought to conceal at home – that wage labour and capital are both based on the forcible separation of the labourer from control over the means of production.[5] This is the secret of 'primitive' or 'original' capital accumulation.

The relation of all this to the question Hegel left open needs explication. If labourers can return to a genuinely unalienated existence through migration overseas or to some frontier region, then capitalist control over labour supply is undermined. Such a form of expansion may be advantageous to labour but it could provide no solution to the inner contradictions of capitalism. The new markets and new fields for industry which Hegel saw as vital could be achieved only through the re-creation of capitalist relations of private property and the associated power to appropriate the labour of others. The fundamental conditions which gave rise to the problem in the first place – alienation of labour – are thereby replicated. Marx's chapter on colonization appears to close off the possibility of any external 'spatial fix' to the internal contradictions of capitalism. Marx evidently felt obliged in *Capital* to close the door that Hegel had left partially ajar and consolidate his call for total revolution by denying that colonization could, in the long run, be a viable solution to the inner contradictions of capital.

But the door will not stay shut. Hegel's 'inner dialectic' undergoes successive representations in Marx's work and at each point the question of the spatial resolution to capitalism's contradictions can legitimately be posed anew. The chapter on colonization may suffice for the first volume of *Capital* where Marx concentrates solely on questions of production. But what of the third volume where Marx shows that the requirements of production conflict with those of circulation to produce crises of overaccumulation? Polarization then takes the form of 'unemployed capital at one pole and unemployed worker population at the other' and the consequent devaluation of both. Can the formation of such crises be contained through geographical expansions and restructurings? Marx does not rule out the possibility that foreign trade and growth of external markets, the export of capital for production, and the expansion of the proletariat through primitive accumulation in other lands, can counteract the falling rate of profit in the short run. But how long is the short-run? And if it extends over many generations (as Rosa Luxemburg in her theory of imperialism implied), then what does this do to Marx's theory and its associated political practice of seeking for revolutionary transformations in the heart of civil society in the here and now?

II The Spatial Dimension to the Communist Manifesto

Many of these problems arise in the *Communist Manifesto*.[6] The manner of approach that Marx and Engels took to the problem of uneven geographical development and the spatial fix is in some respects deeply ambivalent. On the one hand, questions of urbanization, geographical transformation and 'globalization' are given a prominent place in the argument, but on the other hand the potential ramifications of geographical restructurings tend to get lost in a rhetorical mode that in the last instance privileges time and history over space and geography.

The opening sentence of the *Manifesto* situates the argument in Europe and it is to that transnational entity and its working classes that its theses are addressed. This reflects the fact that 'Communists of various nationalities' (French, German, Italian, Flemish and Danish as well as English are the languages envisaged for publication of the document) were assembled in London to formulate a working class programme. The document is, therefore, Eurocentric rather than international. But the importance of the global setting is not ignored. The revolutionary changes that brought the bourgeoisie to power were connected to 'the discovery of America, the rounding of the Cape' and the opening up of trade with the colonies and with the East Indian and Chinese markets. The rise of the bourgeoisie is, from the very outset of the argument, intimately connected to its geographical activities and strategies:

> 'Modern industry has established the world market, for which the disovery of America paved the way. This market has given an immense development to commerce, to navigation, to communication by land. This development has in turn, reacted on the extension of industry; in proportion as industry, commerce, navigation, railways extended, in the same proportion the bourgeoisie developed, increased its capital, and pushed into the background every class handed down from the Middle Ages.'

By these geographical means the bourgeoisie by-passed and suppressed place-bound feudal powers. By these means also the bourgeoisie converted the state (with its military, organizational and fiscal powers) into the executive of its own ambitions. And, once in power, the bourgeoisie continued to pursue its revolutionary mission in part via geographical transformations which are both internal and external. Internally, the creation of great cities and rapid urbanization bring the towns to rule over the country (simultaneously rescuing the latter from the 'idiocy' of rural life and reducing the peasantry to a subaltern class).

Urbanization concentrates productive forces as well as labour power in space, transforming scattered populations and decentralised systems of property rights into massive concentrations of political and economic power. 'Nature's forces' are subjected to human control – 'machinery, application of chemistry to industry and agriculture, steam navigation, railways, electric telegraphs, clearing of whole continents for cultivation, canalisation of rivers, whole populations conjured out of the ground. . . .'

But this concentration of the proletariat in factories and towns makes them aware of their common interests. On this basis they begin to build institutions, such as unions, to articulate their claims. Furthermore, the modern systems of communications put 'the workers of different localities in contact with each other' thus allowing 'the numerous local struggles, all of the same character' to be centralised into 'one national struggle between the classes.' This process, as it spreads across frontiers, strips the workers of 'every trace of national character,' for each and everyone one of them is subject to the unified rule of capital. The organization of working class struggle concentrates and diffuses across space in a way that mirrors the actions of capital.

Marx expands on this idea in a passage that is so famous that we are apt to skim over it rather than read and reflect upon it with the care it deserves:

'The need for a constantly expanding market chases the bourgeoisie over the whole surface of the globe. It must settle everywhere, establish connexions everywhere. . . . The bourgeoisie has through its exploitation of the world market given a cosmopolitan character to production and consumption in every country. . . . All old established national industries have been destroyed or are daily being destroyed. They are dislodged by new industries, whose introduction becomes a life and death question for all civilized nations, by industries that no longer work up indigenous raw material, but raw material drawn from the remotest zones; industries whose products are consumed, not only at home, but in every quarter of the globe. In place of the old wants, satisfied by the production of the country, we find new wants, requiring for their satisfaction the products of distant lands and climes. In place of the old local and national seclusion and self-sufficiency, we have intercourse in every direction, universal interdependence of nations. And as in material, so also in intellectual production. The intellectual creations of individual nations become common property. National one-sidedness and narrow-mindedness become more and more impossible, and from the numerous national and local literatures, there arises a world literature . . .'

If this is not a compelling description of 'globalization' as we now know it then it is hard to imagine what would be. The traces of Hegel's 'spatial fix' argument are everywhere apparent. But Marx and Engels add something:

> 'The bourgeoisie ... draws all, even the most barbarian nations into civilization. the cheap prices of its commodities are the heavy artillery with which it batters down all Chinese walls, with which it forces the barbarians' intensely obstinate hatred of foreigners to capitulate. It compels all nations on pain of extinction, to adopt the bourgeois mode of production; it compels them to introduce what it calls civilization into their midst, i.e. to become bourgeois themselves. In one word, it creates a world after its own image.'

The theme of the 'civilizing mission' of the bourgeoisie is here enunciated (albeit with a touch of irony). But a certain limit to the power of the spatial fix to work indefinitely and in perpetuity is implied. If the geographical mission of the bourgeoisie is the reproduction of class and productive relations on a progressively expanding geographical scale, then the bases for both the internal contradictions of capitalist and for socialist revolution likewise expand geographically. The conquest of new markets paves the way 'for more extensive and more destructive crises,' while 'diminishing the means whereby crises are prevented'. Class struggle becomes global. Marx and Engels therefore enunciate the imperative 'working men of all countries unite' as a necessary condition for an anti-capitalist and pro-socialist revolution.

III Problematizing the Manifesto's Geography

The geographical element in the *Manifesto* has to large degree been ignored in subsequent commentaries. When it has been the focus of attention it has often been treated as unproblematic in relation to political action. This suggests a two-fold response as we look back upon the argument. First, it is vital to recognize (as the *Manifesto* so clearly does) the ways in which geographical reorderings and restructurings, spatial strategies and geopolitical elements, uneven geographical developments, and the like, are vital aspects to the accumulation of capital, both historically and today. It is likewise vital to recognize (in ways the *Manifesto* tends to underplay) that class struggle unfolds differentially across this highly variegated terrain and that the drive for socialism must take these geographical realities into account. But, secondly, it is equally important to problematize the actual account ('sketch' might be a more appropriate word) given in the *Manifesto* in order to develop a more sophisticated, accurate and politically useful understanding as to how the geographical dimensions to capital accumulation and class struggle play such a fundamental role in the perpetuation of bourgeois power and the suppression of worker rights and aspirations not only in particular places but also globally.

In what follows, I shall largely take the first response as a 'given' even though I am only too aware that it needs again and again to be reasserted within a movement that has not by any means taken on board some let alone all of its very basic implications. While Lefebvre perhaps exaggerates a touch, I think it worth recalling his remark that capitalism has survived in the twentieth century by one and only one means – 'by occupying space, by producing space.'[7] How ironic if the same were to be said at the end of the twenty-first century!

My main concern here, then, is to problematize the account given in the *Manifesto*. This requires – tacitly or explicitly – a non-Hegelian counter-theory of the spatio-temporal development of capital accumulation and class struggle.[8] From such a perspective I shall isolate six aspects of the *Manifesto* for critical commentary.

1. The division of the world into 'civilized' and 'barbarian' nations is, to say the least, anachronistic if not downright objectionable even if it can be excused as typical of the times. Furthermore, the centre-periphery model of capital accumulation which accompanies it is at best a gross oversimplification and at worst misleading. It makes it appear as if capital originated in one place (England or Europe) and then diffused outwards to encompass the rest of the world. Adoption of this stance seems to derive from uncritical acceptance of Hegels' teleology – if space is to be considered at all it is as a passive recipient of a teleological process that starts from the centre and flows outwards to fill up the entire globe. Leaving aside the whole problem of where, exactly, capitalism was born and whether it arose in one and only one place or was simultaneously emerging in geographically distinctive environments (an arena of scholarly dispute that shows no sign of coming to a consensus) the subsequent development of a capitalism that had, by the end of the eighteenth century at least, come to concentrate its freest forms of development in Europe in general and Britain in particular, cannot be encompassed by such a diffusionist way of thinking. While there are some instances in which capital diffused outwards from a centre to a periphery (e.g. the export of surplus capital from Europe to Argentina or Australia in the late nineteenth century), such an account is inconsistent with what happened in Japan after the Meiji restoration or what is happening today as first South Korea and then China engages in some form of internalised primitive accumu-

lation and inserts its labour power and its products into global markets.

The geography of capital accumulation deserves a far more principled treatment than the diffusionist sketch provided in the *Manifesto*. The problem does not lie in the sketchiness of the account *per se*, but in the failure to delineate a theory of uneven geographical development (often entailing uneven primitive accumulation) that would be helpful for charting the dynamics of working class formation and class struggle across even the European, let alone the global, space. I would also argue for a more fully theorised understanding of the space/place dialectic in capitalist development.[9] How do places, regions, territories evolve given changing space relations? We have observed how geopolitical games of power, for example, become interconnected with market position in a changing structure of space-relations which, in turn, privileges certain locations and territories for capitalist accumulation. It is also interesting to note how those national bourgeoisies that could not easily use spatial powers to circumvent feudalism ended up with fascism (Germany, Italy, Spain are cases in point). Since these are rather abstract arguments, I shall try to put some flesh and bones on them in what follows.

To begin with, the globe never has been a level playing field upon which capital accumulation could play out its destiny. It was and continues to be an intensely variegated surface, ecologically, politically, socially and culturally differentiated. Flows of capital found some terrains easier to occupy than others in different phases of development. And in the encounter with the capitalist world market, some social formations adapted to aggressively insert themselves into capitalistic forms of market exchange while others did not, for a wide range of reasons and with consummately important effects. Primitive or 'original' accumulation can and has occurred in different places and times, albeit facilitated by contact with the market network that increasingly pins the globe together into an economic unity. But how and where that primitive accumulation occurs depends upon local conditions even if the effects are global. It is now a widely held belief in Japan, for example, that the commercial success of that country after 1960 was in part due to the non-competitive and withdrawn stance of China after the revolution and that the contemporary insertion of Chinese power into the capitalist world market spells doom for Japan as a producer as opposed to a rentier economy. Contingency of this sort rather than teleology has a lot of play within capitalist world history. Furthermore, the globality of capital accumulation poses the problem of a dispersed bourgeois power that can become much harder to handle geopolitically precisely because of its multiple sites. Marx himself later worried about this political possibility. In 1858 he wrote (in a passage that Meszaros rightly makes much of):

> 'For us the difficult question is this: the revolution on the Continent is imminent and its character will be at once socialist; will it not be *necessarily crushed* in this *little corner of the world*, since on a much larger terrain the development of bourgeois society is still *in the ascendant.*'[10]

It is chastening to reflect upon the number of socialist revolutions around the world that have been successfully encircled and crushed by the geopolitical strategies of an ascendant bourgeois power.

2 The *Manifesto* quite correctly highlights the importance of reducing spatial barriers through innovations and investments in transport and communications as critical to the growth and sustenance of bourgeois power. Moreover, the argument indicates that this is an on-going rather than already-accomplished process. In this respect the *Manifesto* is prescient in the extreme. 'The annihilation of space through time' as Marx later dubbed it (adopting an expression that was quite common in the early nineteenth century as people adjusted to the revolutionary implications of the railroad and the telegraph) is deeply embedded in the logic of capital accumulation, entailing as it does the continuous though often jerky transformations in space relations that have characterized the historical-geography of the bourgeois era (from turnpikes to cyberspace). These transformations undercut the absolute qualities of space (often associated with feudalism) and emphasize the relativity of space relations and locational advantages thus making the Ricardian doctrine of comparative advantage in trade a highly dynamic rather than stable affair. Furthermore, spatial tracks of commodity flows have to be mapped in relation to flows of capital, labour power, military advantage, technology transfers, information flows, and the like. In this regard, at least, the *Manifesto* was not wrong as much as underelaborated upon and underappreciated for its prescient statements.

3. Perhaps one of the biggest absences in the *Manifesto* is its lack of attention to the territorial organization of the world in general and of capitalism in particular. If, for example, the state was necessary as an 'executive arm of the bourgeoisie' then the state had to be territorially defined, organised and administered. While the right of sovereign independent states to co-existence was established at the Treaty of Westphalia in 1648 as a (distinctively shaky) European norm, the general extension of that principle across the globe took several

centuries to take shape and is even now arguably not accomplished. The nineteenth century was the great period of territorial definitions (with most of the world's boundaries being established between 1870 and 1925 and most of those being drawn by the British and the French alone – the carve up of Africa in 1885 being the most spectacular example). But state formation and consolidation is quite another step beyond territorial definition and it has proven a long drawn out and often unstable affair (particularly, for example, in Africa). It could well be argued that it was only after 1945 that decolonization pushed state formation world-wide a bit closer to the highly simplified model that the *Manifesto* envisages. Furthermore, the relativism introduced by revolutions in transport and communications coupled with the uneven dynamics of class struggle and uneven resource endowments means that territorial configurations cannot remain stable for long. Flows of commodities, capital, labour and information always render boundaries porous. There is plenty of play for contingency (including phases of territorial reorganization and redefinition) here, thus undermining the rather simplistic teleology that derives from Hegel but which can still be found in some versions of both capitalistic and communist ideas about what the future necessarily holds.

4 The state is, of course, only one of many mediating institutions that influence the dynamics of accumulation and of class struggle world wide. Money and finance must also be given pride of place. In this respect there are some intriguing questions about which the *Manifesto* remains silent in part, I suspect, because its authors had yet to discover their fundamental insights about the dialectical relations between money, production, commodity exchange, distribution and production (as these are conceptualized, for example, in the Introduction to the *Grundrisse*). There are two ways to look at this (and I here take the question of money as both emblematic and fundamental). On the one hand we can interpret world money as some universal representation of value to which territories relate (through their own currencies) and to which capitalist producers conform as they seek some measure of their performance and profitability. This is a very functionalist and undialectical view. It makes it seem as if value hovers as some ethereal abstraction over the activities of individuals as of nations (this is, incidentally, the dominant conception at work in the contemporary neoclassical ideology of globalization). In *Capital*, Marx looks upon world money differently, as a representation of value that arises out of a dialectical relation between the particularity of material activities (concrete labour) undertaken in particular places and times and the universality of values

(abstract labour) achieved as commodity exchange becomes so widespread and generalised as to be a normal social act. But institutions mediate between particularity and universality so as to give some semblance of order and permanence to what is otherwise as shifting sand. Central banks, financial institutions, exchange systems, state-backed local currencies etc. then become powerful mediators between the universality of money on the world market and the particularities of concrete labours conducted here and now around us. Such mediating institutions are also subject to change as, for example, powers shift from yen to deutschmarks to dollars and back again or as new institutions (like the IMF and the World Bank after 1945) spring up to take on new mediating roles. The point here is that there is always a problematic relation between local and particular conditions on the one hand and the universality of values achieved on the world market on the other and that this internal relation is mediated by institutional structures which themselves acquire a certain kind of independent power. These mediating institutions are often territorially based and biassed in important ways. They play a key role in determining what kinds of concrete labours and what kinds of class relations shall arise where and can sometimes even dictate patterns of uneven geographical development through their command over capital assembly and capital flows. Given the importance of European-wide banking and finance in the 1840s (the Rothschild's being prominent players in the events of 1848, for example) and the political-economic theories of the Saint-Simonians with respect to the power of associated capitals to change the world, the absence of any analysis of the mediating institutions of money and finance is surprising. Subsequent formulations (not only by Marx but also by Lenin, Hilferding and many others) may have helped to rectify matters, but the rather episodic and contingent treatment of the role of finance and money capital in organizing the geographical dynamics of capital accumulation may have been one of the *Manifesto's* unwitting legacies (hardly anything was written on the topic between Hilferding and the early 1970s).

5 The argument that the bourgeois revolution subjugated the countryside to the city as it similarly subjugated territories in a lesser state of development to those in a more advanced state, that processes of industrialization and rapid urbanization laid the seedbed for a more united working class politics, is again prescient in the extreme at least in one sense. Reduced to its simplest formulation, it says that the production of spatial organization is not neutral with respect to class struggle. And that is a vital principle no matter how critical we might

be with respect to the sketch of these dynamics as laid out in the *Manifesto*. The account offered runs like this:

'The proletariat goes through various stages of development. With its birth begins its struggle with the bourgeoisie. At first the contest is carried on by individual labourers, then by the workpeople of a factory, then by the operatives of one trade, in one locality, against the individual bourgeois who directly exploits them. At this stage the labourers still form an incoherent mass scattered over the country, and broken up by their mutual competition. If anywhere they unite to form more compact bodies, this is not yet the consequence of their own active union, but of the union of the bourgeoisie . . . But with the development of industry the proletariat not only increases in number; it becomes concentrated in greater masses, its strength grows, and it feels that strength more . . . the collisions between individual workmen and individual bourgeois take more and more the character of collisions between two classes. Thereupon the workers begin to form combinations (Trades' Unions). . . . This union (of the workers) is helped on by the improved means of communication that are created by modern industry and that place the workers of different localities in contact with one another. It was just this contact that was needed to centralise the numerous local struggles, all of the same character, into one national struggle between classes . . .'

For much of the nineteenth century this account captures a common enough path to the development of class struggle. And there are plenty of twentieth century examples where similar trajectories can be discerned (the industrialization of South Korea being paradigmatic). But it is one thing to say that this is a useful descriptive sketch and quite another to argue that these are necessary stages through which class struggle must evolve en route to the construction of socialism. But if it is interpreted, as I have suggested, as a compelling statement of the non-neutrality of spatial organization in the dynamics of class struggle, then it follows that the bourgeoisie may also evolve its own spatial strategies of dispersal, of divide and rule, of geographical disruptions to the rise of class forces that so clearly threaten its existence. To the passages already cited we find added the cautionary statement that: 'this organization of the proletarians into a class, and consequently into a political party, is continually being upset again by the competition between the worker's themselves.' (p.55) And there are plenty of examples of bourgeois strategies to achieve that effect. From the dispersal of manufacturing from centres to suburbs in late nineteenth century US cities to avoid concentrated proletarian power to the current attack on union power by dispersal and fragmentation of production processes across space (much of it, of course, to so-called developing countries where working class organization is weakest) has proven a powerful weapon in the bourgeois struggle to enhance its power. The active stimulation of inter-worker competition across space has likewise worked to capitalist advantage to say nothing of the problem of localism and nationalism within working class movements (the position of the Second International in the First World War being the most spectacular case). In general, I think it fair to say that workers' movements have been better at commanding power in places and territories rather than in controlling spatialities with the result that the capitalist class has used its superior powers of spatial manoeuvre to defeat place-bound proletarian/socialist revolutions (cf. Marx's 1858 worry cited above). The recent geographical and ideological assault on working class forms of power through 'globalization' gives strong support to this thesis. While none of this is inconsistent with the basic underpinning of the argument in the *Manifesto*, it is, of course, quite different from the actual sketch of class struggle dynamics set out as a stage model for the development of socialism in the European context.

6 This leads us to one of the most problematic elements in the Manifesto's legacy. This concerns the homogenization of the 'working man' and of 'labour powers' across a highly variegated geographical terrain as the proper basis for struggles against the powers of capital. While the slogan 'working men of all countries unite' may still stand (suitably modified to rid it of its gendered presupposition) as the only appropriate response to the globalizing strategies of capital accumulation, the manner of arriving at and conceptualising that response deserves critical scrutiny. Central to the argument lies the belief that modern industry and wage labour, imposed by the capitalists ('the same in England as in France, in America as in Germany'), have stripped the workers 'of every trace of national character.' As a result:

'The working men have no country. We cannot take from them what they have not got. Since the proletariat must first of all acquire political supremacy, must rise to be the leading class of the nation, must constitute itself the nation, it is, so far, itself national, though not in the bourgeois sense of the word.

'National differences and antagonisms between peoples are daily more and more vanishing, owing to the development of the bourgeoisie, to freedom of commerce, to the world market, to uniformity in the mode of production and in the conditions of life corresponding thereto.

'The supremacy of the proletariat will cause them to vanish still faster. United action, of the leading civilised countries at least, is one of the first conditions for the emanciaption of the proletariat.

'In proportion as the exploitation of one individual by another is put an end to, the exploitation of one nation by another will also be put an end to. In proportion

as the antagonism between classes within the nation vanishes, the hostility of one
nation to another will come to an end.'

The guiding vision is noble enough but there is unquestionably a lot
of wishful thinking here. At best, the *Manifesto* mildly concedes that
the initial measures to be taken as socialists come to power will 'of
course be different in different countries.' It also notes how problems
arise in the translation of political ideas from one context to another –
the Germans took on French ideas and adapted them to their own
circumstances which were not so well-developed, creating a German
kind of socialism of which Marx was highly critical in Part III of the
Manifesto. In the practical world of politics, then, there is a certain
sensitivity to uneven material conditions and local circumstances. And
in the final section of the *Manifesto* attention is paid to the different
political conditions in France, Switzerland, Poland and Germany.
From this Marx and Engels divine that the task of communists is to
bring unity to these causes, to define the commonalities within the
differences and to make a movement in which workers of the world
can unite. But in so doing the force of capital that uproots and destroys
local place-bound loyalties and bonds is heavily relied upon to prepare
the way.

There are, I think two ways in which we can read this. On the one
hand the *Manifesto* insists, quite correctly in my view, that the only
way to resist capitalism and transform towards socialism is through a
global struggle in which global working class formation, perhaps
achieved in a step-wise fashion from local to national to global
concerns, acquires sufficient power and presence to fulfill its own
historical potentialities.[11] In this case, the task of the communist
movement is to find ways, against all odds, to properly bring together
all the various highly differentiated and often local movements into
some kind of commonality of purpose. The second reading is rather
more mechanistic. It sees the automatic sweeping away of national
differences and differentiations through bourgeois advancement, the
de-localization and de-nationalization of working class populations
and therefore of their political aspirations and movements. The task of
the communist movement is to prepare for and hasten on the end-
point of this bourgeois revolution, to educate the working class as to
the true nature of their situation and to organise, on that basis, their
revolutionary potential to construct an alternative. Such a mechanistic
reading is, in my view, incorrect, even though substantial grounding
for it can be found within the *Manifesto* itself.

The central difficulty lies in the presumption that capitalist industry and commodification will lead to homogenization of the working population. There is, of course, an undeniable sense in which this is true, but what it fails to appreciate is the way in which capitalism simultaneously differentiates, sometimes feeding off ancient cultural distinctions, gender relations, ethnic predilections and religious beliefs. It does this not only through the development of explicit bourgeois strategies of divide and control, but also by converting the principle of market choice into a mechanism for group differentiation. The result is the implantation of all manner of class, gender and other social divisions into the geographical landscape of capitalism. Divisions such as those between cities and suburbs, between regions as well as between nations cannot be understood as residuals from some ancient order. They are not automatically swept away. They are actively produced through the differentiating powers of capital accumulation and market structures. Place-bound loyalties proliferate and in some respects strengthen rather than disintegrate through the mechanisms of class struggle as well as through the agency of both capital and labour working for themselves. Class struggle all too easily dissolves into a whole series of geographically fragmented communitarian interests, easily coopted by bourgeois powers or exploited by the mechanisms of neo-liberal market penetration.

There is a potentially dangerous underestimation within the *Manifesto* of the powers of capital to fragment, divide and differentiate, to absorb, transform and even exacerbate ancient cultural divisions, to produce spatial differentiations, to mobilize geopolitically, within the overall homogenization achieved through wage labour and market exchange. And there is likewise an underestimation of the ways in which labour mobilizes through territorial forms of organization, building place-bound loyalties en route. The dialectic of commonality and difference has not worked out (if it ever could) in the way that the sketch supplied in the *Manifesto* implied, even if its underlying logic and its injunction to unite is correct.

IV 'Working Men of all Countries, Unite!'

The World Bank estimates that the global labour force doubled in size between 1966 and 1995 (it now stands at an estimated 2.5 billion men and women). But :

'the more than a billion individuals living on a dollar or less a day depend . . . on pitifully low returns to hard work. In many countries workers lack representation and work in unhealthy, dangerous, or demeaning conditions. Meanwhile 120 millions or so are unemployed worldwide, and millions more have given up hope of finding work.'[12]

This condition exists at a time of rapid growth in average levels of productivity per worker (reported also to have doubled since 1965 world-wide) and a rapid growth in world trade fuelled in part by reductions in costs of movement but also by a wave of trade liberalization and sharp increases in the international flows of direct investments. The latter helped construct transnationally integrated production systems largely organized through intra-firm trade. As a result:

'the number of workers employed in export- and import-competing industries has grown significantly. In this sense, therefore, it could be said that labour markets across the world are becoming more interlinked. . . . Some observers see in these developments the emergence of a global labour market wherein "the world has become a huge bazaar with nations peddling their workforces in competition against one another, offering the lowest prices for doing business". . . . The core apprehension is that intensifying global competition will generate pressures to lower wages and labour standards across the world.'[13]

This process of ever-stronger interlinkage has been intensified by 'the increasing participation in the world economy of populous developing countries such as China, India and Indonesia.' With respect to China, for example, the United Nations Development Programme reports:

'The share of labour-intensive manufactures in total exports rose from 36% in 1975 to 74% in 1990. . . . Between 1985 and 1993 employment in textiles increased by 20%, in clothing and fibre products by 43%, in plastic products by 51%. China is now a major exporter of labour-intensive products to many industrial countries. . . . For all its dynamic job creation, China still faces a formidable employment challenge. Economic reforms have released a "floating population" of around 80 million most of whom are seeking work. The State Planning Commission estimates that some 20 million workers will be shed from state enterprises over the next five years and that 120 million more will leave rural areas hoping for work in the cities. Labour intensive economic growth will need to continue at a rapid pace if all these people are to find work.'[14]

I quote this instance to illustrate the massive movements into the global labour force that have been and are underway. And China is not alone in this. The export-oriented garment industry of Bangladesh hardly existed twenty years ago, but it now employs more than a million workers (80 per cent of them women and half of them crowded into Dhaka). Cities like Jakarta, Bangkok and Bombay, as Seabrook reports, have become meccas for formation of a transnational working class – heavily dependent upon women – under conditions of poverty, violence, pollution and fierce repression.[15]

It is hardly surprising that the insertion of this proletarianized mass into global trading networks has been associated with wide-ranging social convulsions and upheavals as well as changing structural conditions, such as the spiralling inequalities between regions (that left sub-Saharan Africa far behind as East and Southeast Asia surged ahead) as well as between classes. As regards the latter, 'between 1960 and 1991 the share of the richest 20% rose from 70% of global income to 85% – while that of the poorest declined from 2.3% to 1.4%.' By 1991, 'more than 85% of the world's population received only 15% of its income' and 'the net worth of the 358 richest people, the dollar billionaires, is equal to the combined income of the poorest 45% of the world population – 2.3 billion people.'[16] This polarization is simply astounding, rendering hollow the World Bank's extraordinary claim that international integration coupled with free market liberalism and low levels of government interference (conditions oddly and quite erroneously attributed to repressive political regimes in Taiwan, South Korea and Singapore) is the best way to deliver growth and rising living standards for workers.[17]

It is against this background tthat it become easier to assess the power of the tales assembled by Seabrook:

> 'Indonesia, in the name of the free market system, promotes the grossest violations of human rights, and undermines the right to subsist of those on whose labour its competitive advantage rests. The small and medium-sized units which subcontract to the multinationals are the precise localities where the sound of the hammering, tapping, beating of metal comes from the forges where the chains are made for industrial bondage. . . .
>
> 'Many transnationals are subcontracting here: Levi Strauss, Nike, Reebok. A lot of the subcontractors are Korean-owned. They all tend to low wages and brutal management. Nike and Levis issue a code of conduct as to criteria for investment; but in reality, under the tender system they always go for the lowest cost of production. . . . Some subcontractors move out of Jakarta to smaller towns, where workers are even less capable of combining to improve their conditions.'[18]

Or, at a more personal level there is the account given by a woman worker and her sister:

> 'We are regularly insulted, as a matter of course. When the boss gets angry he calls the women dogs, pigs, sluts, all of which we have to endure patiently without reacting. . . . We work officially from seven in the morning until three (salary less

than $2 per day), but there is often compulsory overtime, sometimes – especially if there is an urgent order to be delivered – until nine. However tired we are, we are not allowed to go home. We may get an extra 200 rupiah (10 US cents) . . . We go on foot to the factory from where we live. Inside it is very hot. The building has a metal roof, and there is not much space for all the workers. It is very cramped. There are over 200 people working there, mostly women, but there is only one toilet for the whole factory . . . when we come home from work, we have no energy left to do anything but eat and sleep.'[19]

Home is a single room, 2 metres by 3, costing $16 a month; it costs nearly 10 cents to get two cans of water and at least a $1.50 a day to eat.

In *Capital* Marx recounts the story of the milliner, Mary Anne Walkely, twenty years of age, who often worked 30 hours without a break (though revived by occasional supplies of sherry, port and coffee) until, after a particularly hard spell necessitated by preparing 'magnificent dresses for the noble ladies invited to the ball in honour of the newly imported Princess of Wales,' died, according to the doctor's testimony, 'from long hours of work in an over-crowded work-room, and a too small and badly ventilated bedroom.'[20] Compare that with a contemporary account of conditions of labour in Nike plants in Vietnam:

'(Mr Nguyen) found that the treatment of workers by the factory managers in Vietnam (usually Korean or Taiwanese nationals) is a 'constant source of humili- ation,' that verbal abuse and sexual harassment occur frequently, and that 'corporal punishment' is often used.' He found that extreme amounts of forced overtime are imposed on Vietnamese workers. 'It is a common occurrence,' Mr Nguyen wrote in his report,' to have several workers faint from exhaustion, heat and poor nutrition during their shifts. We were told that several workers even coughed up blood before fainting. Rather than crack down on the abusive conditions in the factories, Nike has resorted to an elaborate international public relations campaign to give the appearance that it cares about its workers, But no amount of public relations will change the fact that a full-time worker who makes $1.60 a day is likely to spend a fair amount of time hungry if three very simple meals cost $2.10.'[21]

The material conditions that sparked the moral outrage that suffuses the *Manifesto* have not gone away. They are embodied in everything from Nike shoes, Disney products, GAP clothing to Liz Claiborne products. And, as in the nineteenth century, part of the response has been reformist middle class outrage backed by the power of working class movements to regulate 'sweatshop labour' worldwide and develop a code of 'fair labour practices' perhaps certified by a 'fair labour label' on the products we buy.[22]

The setting for the *Manifesto* has not, then, radically changed at its basis. The global proletariat is far larger than ever and the imperative for workers of the world to unite is greater than ever. But the barriers to that unity are far more formidable than they were in the already complicated European context of 1848. The workforce is now far more geographically dispersed, culturally heterogeneous, ethnically and religiously diverse, racially stratified, and linguistically fragmented. The effect is to radically differentiate both the modes of resistance to capitalism and the definitions of alternatives. And while it is true that means of communication and opportunities for translation have greatly improved, this has little meaning for the billion or so workers living on less than a dollar a day possessed of quite different cultural histories, literatures and understandings (compared to international financiers and transnationals who use them all the time). Differentials (both geographical and social) in wages and social provision within the global working class are likewise greater than they have ever been. The political and economic gap between the most affluent workers in, say Germany and the United States, and the poorest wage workers in Indonesia and Mali, is far greater than between the so-called aristocracy of European labour and their unskilled counterparts in the nineteenth century. This means that a certain segment of the working class (mostly but not exclusively in the advanced capitalist countries and often possessing by far the most powerful political voice) has a great deal to lose besides its chains. And while women were always an important component of the workforce in the early years of capitalist development, their participation has become much more general at the same time as it has become concentrated in certain occupational categories (usually dubbed 'unskilled') in ways that pose acute questions of gender in working class politics that have too often been pushed under the rug in the past.

Ecological variations and their associated impacts (resource wars, environmental injustice, differential effects of environmental degradation) have also become far more salient in the quest for an adequate quality of life as well as for rudimentary health care. In this regard, too, there is no level playing field upon which class struggle can be evenly played out because the relation to nature is itself a cultural determination that can have implications for how any alternative to capitalism can be constructed at the same time as it provides a basis for a radical critique of the purely utilitarian and instrumental attitudes embedded in capitalist accumulation and exploitation of the natural world. How to configure the environmental with the economic, the political with the cultural, becomes much harder at the global level, where the presumption of homogeneity of values and aspirations across the earth simply doesn't hold.

Global populations have also been on the move. The flood of migratory movements seems impossible to stop. State boundaries are less porous for people and for labour than they are for capital, but they are still porous enough. Immigration is a very significant issue worldwide (including within the labour movement itself). Organizing labour in the face of the considerable ethnic, racial, religious and cultural diversity generated out of migratory movements poses particular problems that the socialist movement has never found easy to address let alone solve. Europe, for example, now has to face all of those difficulties that have been wrestled with for so many years in the United States.

Urbanization has also accelerated to create a major ecological, political, economic and social revolution in the spatial organization of the world's population. The proportion of an increasing global population living in cities has doubled in thirty years, making for massive spatial concentrations of population on a scale hitherto regarded as inconceivable. It has proven far easier to organize class struggle in, say, the small-scale mining villages of the South Wales Coalfield, or even in relatively homogeneous industrial cities like nineteenth century Manchester (with a population of less than a million, albeit problematically divided between English and Irish labourers), than organizing class struggle (or even developing the institutions of a representative democracy) in contemporary Sao Paulo, Cairo, Lagos, Los Angeles, Shanghai, Bombay, etc with their teeming, sprawling and often disjointed populations reaching close to or over the twenty-million mark.

The socialist movement has to come to terms with these extraordinary geographical transformations and develop tactics to deal with them. This does not dilute the importance of the final rallying cry of the *Manifesto* to unite. The conditions that we now face make that call more imperative than ever. But we cannot make either our history or our geography under historical-geographical conditions of our own choosing. A geographical reading of the *Manifesto* emphasizes the non-neutrality of spatial structures and powers in the intricate spatial dynamics of class struggle. It reveals how the bourgeoisie acquired its powers vis-a-vis all preceeding modes of production by mobilising command over space as a productive force peculiar to itself. It shows how the bourgeoisie has continuously enhanced and protected its power by that same mechanism. It therefore follows that until the working class movement learns how to confront that bourgeois power to command and produce space, it will always play from a position of weakness rather than of strength. Likewise, until that movement comes to terms with the geographical conditions and diversities of its own existence, it will be unable to define, articulate and struggle for a realistic socialist alternative to capitalist domination.

The implications of such an argument are legion and some clues as to strategies are already embedded in the *Manifesto*. Properly embellished, they can take us onto richer terrains of struggle. It is important to accept, for example, that the beginning point of class struggle lies with the particularity of the labouring body, with figures like Mary Anne Walkley and the billions of others whose daily existence is shaped through an often traumatic and conflictual relation to the dynamics of capital accumulation. The labouring body is, therefore, a site of resistance that achieves a political dimension through the political capacity of individuals to act as moral agents. To treat of matters this way is not to revert to some rampant individualism but to insist, as the *Manifesto* does, that the universality of class struggle originates with the particularity of the person and that class politics must translate back to that person in meaningful ways. The alienation of the individual is, therefore, an important beginning point for politics and it is that alienation that must be overcome.

But, and this is of course the crucial message of the *Manifesto*, that alienation cannot be addressed except through collective struggle and that means building a movement that reaches out across space and time in such a way as to confront the universal and transnational qualities of capital accumulation. Ways have to be found to connect the microspace of the body with the macrospace of what is now called 'globalization.' The *Manifesto* suggests this can be done by linking the personal to the local to the regional, the national, and ultimately the international. A hierarchy of spatial scales exists at which class politics must be constructed. But the 'theory of the production of geographical scale,' as Smith observes, 'is grossly underdeveloped' and we have yet to learn, particularly with respect to global working class formation and body politics, how to 'arbitrate and translate' between the different spatial scales.[23] This is an acute problem that must be confronted and resolved if working class politics is to be revived. I give just three examples.

The traditional beginning point for class struggle has been a particular space – the factory – and it is from there that class organization has been built up through union movements, political parties, and the like. But what happens when factories disappear or become so mobile as to make permanent organizing difficult if not impossible? And what happens when much of the workforce becomes temporary or casualised? Under such conditions labour organizing in the traditional manner loses its geographical basis and its power is correspondingly diminished. Alternative models of organizing must then be constructed. In Baltimore, for example, the campaign for a living wage (put together under the aegis of an organization called Baltimoreans United in Leadership Development – BUILD) appeals to an alternative possible strategy that works at the metropolitan scale – the movement is city-wide – and has as its objective directly affecting the base wage-level for the whole metropolitan area – everyone (temporary as well as permanent workers) should receive a living wage of at least $7.70 and hour plus benefits. To accomplish this goal, institutions of community (particularly the churches), activist organizations, student groups, as well as whatever union support can be procured, get combined together with the aim of unionising temporary workers and those on workfare, targetting the immovable institutions in the metropolitan space (government – including sub-contracting -universities, hospitals, and the like). A movement is created in the metropolitan space that operates outside of traditional labour organizing models but in a way that addresses new conditions.[24] The BUILD strategy of inserting a metropolitan scale politics into the equations of class struggle is an interesting example of shifting a sense of spatial scale to counteract the spatial tactics which capital uses.

Consider a second example. Governmentality for contemporary capitalism has entailed the construction of important supra-national authorities such as NAFTA and the European Union. Unquestionably, such constructions – the Maastricht Agreement being the paradigmatic case – are pro-capitalist. How should the left respond? The divisions here are important to analyse (in Europe the debate within the Left is intense), but too frequently the response is an overly-simplistic argument that runs along the following lines: 'because NAFTA and Maastricht are pro-capitalist we fight them by defending the the nation state against supra-national governance.' The argument here outlined suggests an entirely different response. The left must learn to fight capital at *both* spatial scales simultaneously. But, in so doing, it must also learn to coordinate potentially contradictory politics within itself at the different spatial scales for it is often the case in hierarchical spatial systems (and ecological problems frequently pose this dilemma) that what makes good political sense at one scale does not make such good politics at another (the rationalization of, say, automobile production in Europe may mean plant closures in Oxford or Turin). Withdrawing to the nation state as the exclusive strategic site of class organization and struggle is to court failure (as well as to flirt with nationalism and all that that entails). This does not mean the nation state has become irrelevant – indeed it has become more relevant than ever. But the choice of spatial scale is not 'either/or' but 'both/and' even though the latter entails confronting serious contradictions. This means that the union movement in the United States ought to put just as much effort into cross-border organizing (particularly with respect to Mexico) as it puts into fighting NAFTA and that the European union movement must pay as much attention to procuring power and influence in Brussels and Strasburg as each does in its own national capital.

Moving to the international level poses similar dilemmas and problems. It is interesting to note that the internationalism of labour struggle, while it hovers as an obvious and latent necessity over much of the labour movement, faces serious difficulties organizationally. I again in part attribute this to a failure to confront the dilemmas of integrating struggles at different spatial scales. Examples exist of such integrations in other realms. Movements around human rights, the environment and the condition of women illustrate the possible ways in which politics can get constructed (as well as some of the pitfalls to such politics) to bridge the micro-scale of the body and the personal on the one hand and the macro-scale of the global and the political-economic on the other. Nothing analogous to the Rio Conference on the environment or the Beijing Conference on women has occurred to confront global conditions of labour. We have scarcely begun to think of concepts such as 'global working class formation' or even to analyse what that might mean. Much of the defence of human dignity in the face of the degradation and violence of labour world-wide has been articulated through the churches rather than through labour organization directly (the churches' ability to work at different spatial scales provides a number of models for political organization from which the socialist movement could well draw some important lessons). As in the case of BUILD at the local level, alliances between labour organizations and many other institutions in civil society appear now to be crucial to the articulation of socialist politics at the international scale. Many of the campaigns orchestrated in the United States, for example, against global sweatshops in general or particular versions (such as

Disney operations in Haiti and Nike in Southeast Asia) are organised quite effectively through such alliances. The argument here is not that nothing is being done or that institutions do not exist (the revitalization of the ILO might be an interesting place to start). But the reconstruction of some sort of socialist internationalism after 1989 has not been an easy matter even if the collapse of the wall opened up new opportunities to explore that internationalism free of the need to defend the rump-end of the Bolshevik Revolution against the predatory politics of capitalist powers.[25]

How to build a political movement at a variety of spatial scales as an answer to the geographical and geopolitical strategies of capital is a problem that in outline at least the *Manifesto* clearly articulates. How to do it for our times is an imperative issue for us to resolve for our time and place. One thing, however, is clear: we cannot set about that task without recognizing the geographical complexities that confront us. The clarifications that a study of the *Manifesto's* geography offer provide a marvellous opportunity to wrestle with that task in such a way as to reignite the flame of socialism from Jakarta to Los Angeles, from Shanghai to New York City, from Porto Allegre to Liverpool, from Cairo to Warsaw, from Beijing to Turin. There is no magic answer. But there is at least a strategic way of thinking available to us that can illuminate the way. And that is what the *Manifesto* can still provide.

NOTES

1. G. W. Hegel, *Philosophy of Right*, New York 1967, pp. 150–2.
2. S. Avineri, *Hegel's Theory of the Modern State*, London 1972, p. 132.
3. Compare, for example, Hegel's argument in *The Philosophy of Right* that: 'When the standard of living of a large mass of people falls below a certain subsistence level – a level regulated automatically as the one necessary for a member of the society . . . the result is the creation of a rabble of paupers. At the same time this brings with it, at the other end of the social scale, conditions which greatly facilitate the concentration of disproportionate wealth in a few hands,' and Marx's conclusion in *Capital, Volume 1*, that: 'as capital accumulates, the situation of the worker, be his payment high or low, must grow worse . . . It makes an accumulation of misery a necessary condition, corresponding to the accumulation of wealth. Accumulation of wealth at one pole is, therefore, at the same time accumulation of misery, the torment of labour, slavery, ignorance, brutalization and moral degradation at the opposite pole, i.e. on the side of the class that produces its own product as capital.' The parallel between the two texts is striking.
4. See D. Harvey, *The Limits to Capital*, Oxford 1982, chapter 13 and D. Harvey, 'The Spatial Fix: Hegel, Von Thunen, and Marx, *Antipode*, 13, No. 2, 1981, for further details of this argument.

5. K. Marx, *Capital* volume 1, New York 1976.
6. All citations are from K. Marx and F. Engels, *Manifesto of the Communist party* Progress Publishers edition, Moscow 1952.
7. H. Lefebvre, *The Survival of Capitalism*, New York 1976.
8. I. Meszaros, *Beyond Capital*, London and New York, 1995; D. Harvey, *Justice, Nature and the Geography of Difference*, Oxford, 1996.
9. D. Harvey, op cit., 1996.
10. Cited in I. Meszaros, op cit., 1995, p. xii.
11. I have elewhere tried to adapt Raymond Williams concept of 'militant particularism' to capture this process and its inevitable contradictions – see Harvey, op cit., 1996, chapter 1.
12. World Bank, *World development report: Workers in an integrating world* New York 1995, p. 9.
13. International Labour Office, *World employment 1996/97: National policies in a global context* International Labour Office 1996, p. 2.
14. United Nations Development Program, *Human development report, 1996*, New York 1996, p. 94.
15. J. Seabrook, J. *In the cities of the South: Scenes from a developing world*, London 1996, chapter 6.
16. United Nations Development Program, op cit, 1996, p. 13.
17. World Bank, op cit. 1996, p. 3.
18. J. Seabrook, op cit. 1996, pp. 103–5.
19. loc cit.
20. K. Marx, op cit. 1976, p. 364–5.
21. B. Herbert, 'Brutality in Vietnam,' *New York Times*, March 28th, 1997, A29.
22. Goodman, E., 'Why not a labor label?' *Baltimore Sun*, July 19, 1996, 25A; Greenhouse, S., 1997a, 'Voluntary rules on apparel labor proving elusive,' *New York Times*, February 1, 1997, 1; Greenhouse, S. 1997b, 'Accord to combat sweatshop labor faces obstacles,' *New York Times*, April 13, 1997, 1.
23. N. Smith, 'Geography, difference and the politics of scale,' in Doherty, J., Graham, E., and Malek, M., (eds) *Postmodernism and the social sciences*, London, 1992
24. For accounts of the work of BUILD see M. Cooper, 'When push comes to shove: Who is welfare reform really helping?' *The Nation*, June 2, 1997, 11–15, and D. Harvey, 'The body as an accumulation strategy,' *Society and Space* (forthcoming).
25. *The Socialist Register* for 1994 examines many of these problems at length and the different contributions collectively reflect much of the complexity – both theoretical and practical – of constructing a new internationalist politics.

SOCIALISM 'WITH SOBER SENSES': DEVELOPING WORKERS' CAPACITIES

Sam Gindin

All that is solid melts into air, all that is holy is profaned, and man is at last compelled to face with sober senses, his real conditions of life, and his relations with his kind.[1]

One hundred and fifty years ago, *The Communist Manifesto* announced the arrival of modern socialism. The *Manifesto*'s words rang out with a self-confidence that socialists of today can only dream about: 'A spectre is haunting Europe, the spectre of Communism!'. If the question then – and for much of the next hundred years – was '*how and when*', the question today is a subdued '*if*'. At one time the *Manifesto* was widely read by workers as well as intellectuals. Today, there is a spectre haunting socialists, the spectre of our marginalization.

With the right glorying in its ascendancy, capital has virtually stated – privately in strategy meetings, publicly through its actions – that sensitivity to peoples' needs is incompatible with its own more pressing need for profit. But rather than such a blunt confession detonating, as we once imagined it would, a crisis of legitimacy for capitalism, it is the weakness of the left that has been exposed. It is the left, and not the right, that is mired in a crisis of legitimacy. At a moment when the socialist idea should be more relevant than at any time since the Great Depression, it seems that for all practical purposes socialism simply doesn't *matter*. This historic absence, rather than the ascendancy of the right, is the political story of our times. And the generalized scale of our failures – across a wide expanse of time, experience, and borders – suggests there is more involved here than any list of specific strategic shortcomings.

In spite of a rich legacy of theoretical development and practical experience, we are weighed down by the demoralizing baggage of past failures. Proclaiming 'socialism' – in the abstract – as the answer elicits

75

a collective shrug. Developing lists of policy alternatives is uninspiring: those which are saleable won't work, those that might work have no constituency. Calling for a new political party begs more questions than it answers, and debating how to 'take state power' raises something too distant to take seriously. In the context of a socialist movement all of the above would of course come alive. As things stand, however, we are essentially starting over.

Recent waves of protests, encompassing a broad range of countries and led by the working class, seem to suggest that there is a new basis for socialist renewal. And yet to see in these developments the seeds of a socialist reawakening is to express a hope, not an argument. Socialists have played a role in this revival of militancy, but that role has been based on their credibility as *individual militants* rather than as socialists (even if, over the years, it was their socialism that inspired and sustained that militancy). As exciting and crucial as the new level of resistance is, there is still nothing in its scope which convincingly suggests that the working class *will* go beyond resistance to transform capitalism. The best we can argue is that the resistance which capitalism engenders leaves the door ajar to the *possibility* of socialism.

THE CHASM: SELLING LABOUR, SELLING CAPACITIES

On the face of it, there is something preposterous in the burden Marxists have placed on the modern working class. This *'first class not to own tools'*[2] will somehow create and develop the revolutionary 'tools' to build a new world. No other class in history, ascendant or subordinate, has ever consciously organized itself for something so bold and ambitious as setting out to build an entirely new society. As tattered as the socialist coat looks 150 years after the *Manifesto*, and in full recognition of the fact that only a small minority of workers were actually ever committed to this project, many of us still can't help but be moved by the stunning *chutzpah* and staying power of that most ambitious of dreams.

The fact, however, is that this dream has failed to materialize. More so than at any time since the *Manifesto*, 'liberation from capital is nowhere on the agenda of politics'.[3] Is socialism an impossible dream? Are there reasons for its failure to arrive that go beyond any specific example or temporary circumstance? Is there something at the heart of the socialist project that is inherently contradictory – in particular, the chasm between the essence of socialism and the essence of the proposed agent of socialism, the worker in a capitalist society?

Maxim Gorky, wearily reaching for a grain of hope, once declared:

'. . . life will always be bad enough for the desire for something better not to be extinguished in man'.[4] The history of the working class confirms Gorky's faith. Taking advantage of their strategic role in production or simply rebelling against oppression, working people have resisted and rioted, fought the bosses, confronted the police and private armies, expanded their activity beyond the workplace and immediate self interest, struggled to preserve a sense of dignity and community, taken tactical and creative initiatives, built unions, developed political programmes, formed political parties.

Yet all of this, however heroic and impressive, falls short of demonstrating the collective confidence, sense of mission, and range of capacities necessary to replace capitalism with an alternative social system. Socialism is the society that has never existed, the social order to be invented in the process of revolution, and therefore a world characterized by its 'indeterminate immensity'.[5] Becoming a socialist involves a leap of faith beyond analysis and into the world of possibilities. Is it conceivable that working classes whose visions and potentials have been arrested, if not crippled, by the nature of capitalism, can make – or are even willing to try – that enormous leap?

For workers, capitalism starts with the need to sell their labour power. In exchange, they receive a different kind of power, the ability to consume. What makes the capitalist-worker exchange unequal is not just that workers retain only a fraction of what they produce, but the difference between *access to consumption* and *control over doing*. This distinction doesn't revolve around a snobbish bias against consumption per se, but around an emphasis on what workers have lost in the process. In North America the industrial relations term for what workers receive in this exchange is 'compensation' – money for alienating your labour is treated like insurance payments for losing a limb.

As compensation for a loss, the form consumption consequently takes is, not surprisingly, distorted. Consumption in this context isn't simply about independent needs and enjoyment, but includes an element of the workers *themselves* trying to 'compensate' for the exchange they have been forced to make. Consumption becomes part of a process that includes offsetting the loss of dignity, the frustrations, and the drain in personal energy inherent in alienated labour. Moreover, consumption-as-compensation redirects and fragments the potential unity of workers. Even when workers develop organizations and sufficient unity to challenge their employers, the collective action that emerges is channelled into increasing the price of their labour, increasing their power to consume.

Workers do of course struggle over the conditions of labour and resist their own commodification and subservience – bringing unionization into a workplace is more often about arbitrariness and lack of respect in the workplace than it is about pay. But as the capital-labour relationship is institutionalized, the system's relative openness to gains in wages (because capital has the dynamic capacity to make this concession) stands in contrast to its resistance to any erosion of management rights (the employer's freedom to use, once bought, 'his' labour power).

Since access to consumption is the incentive for *individuals* to offer their labour power, there is a bias to *individual* forms of consumption, reinforced by pressures beyond the direct wage-labour relationship, such as the competitive pressure on companies to develop new markets and hence new individual needs.[6] Between the capitalist's control over the surplus and how it is invested, and the particular biases to individual consumption, communities are structured and restructured in ways that undermine the cultural base for a broader unity – consider, for example, the impact of individual consumption on transportation, housing, recreation, neighbourhoods, cities, the environment.

Let's return to what workers trade off in exchange for the power to consume. What workers are surrendering is their capacity to *do*, the capacity for the creative planning and execution of goals. Equally if not more importantly, they are also handing to someone else control over how that capacity to do is *developed* over time. The new owner of their labour power determines, through the organization of work and the division of labour, which skills are used and which are ignored or allowed to atrophy. The capitalist monopolizes the planning and execution of production, and limits workers to carrying out goals and tasks determined by others.

The owner is the catalyst and stand-in for the 'collective labourer'. He is the actual organizer of what is otherwise an isolated and unproductive mass of workers, and the initiator and hence ostensible embodiment of all useful technical knowledge, past and present. The owner therefore appears as, and in the given context *is*, indispensable. The consequent hierarchical-authoritarian management systems exclude any hint of institutional forms for the running of workplaces in ways that combine efficiency *and* democracy. It is, for example, possible to imagine workers taking over existing technology and modifying it, but much harder to imagine, on any large-scale basis, what entirely different forms of collective democratic co-ordination and 'management' might look like. The *democratic* collective labourer is a 'productive force' yet to be invented.

The lived result is that those very individual (self-development) and collective (institutional-democratic) capacities that need to be nurtured and developed in order to control production, are distorted, undermined, or simply absent. *What workers give up in selling their labour are precisely the kind of capacities and potentials which are absolutely fundamental to one day building a different kind of society: the capacities for doing, creating, planning, executing.* The nature and structure of capitalism guarantees that workers lag behind the productive forces – i.e. are dependent on others and don't have the capacity to control, co-ordinate, or develop the productive forces that already exist. This is not only a future 'technical' problem but an immediate political problem. Our assessment of how we can potentially organize ourselves for production affects how we view the possible, and this directly affects the mobilization for socialism.

The workers' dependency on capital is magnified when addressed at the level of society as a whole. Workers wrestling with alternatives today do so in the absence of planning mechanisms for dealing with the incredible complexity of allocating goods and capital. They face the intimidating power and authority of faceless 'external' forces such as global finance. They have to contend with the ideological impact of Eastern Europe's ubiquitous clamour to join capitalism. They confront the limits of 'politics' (i.e. a politics that takes the basics of economic power as a given). They have to deal with the competition amongst workers induced by their employers' competition. And when militancy does explode, there is the problem of overcoming its localized and fragmented expression, what David Harvey refers to as 'militant particularism'.[7]

Some socialists have always looked to the decline of capitalism's dynamism as the 'answer' to such dilemmas, seeing that decline as both imminent and the base for popular radicalization. But images of a stagnant capitalism unable to address the needs of a majority are either empirically wrong (today's capitalism isn't stagnant) or beside the point. When Marx was writing his polemic the world outside his windows was full of pain and cruelty, yet he still marvelled at capitalism's unprecedented dynamism, its '[c]onstant revolutionizing of production, uninterrupted disturbance of all social conditions, everlasting uncertainty and agitation.'[8]

That dynamism hasn't gone away. Our era is more and more defined by the pervasiveness of capital, its dominance of social and private spaces as well as its international scope, its *everywhere-ness*. As Raymond Williams wrote in the early eighties, 'What is most totalitarian about the now dominant orientation is its extension beyond the basic system of extraction of labour to a practical invasion of the whole human personality.'[9] Through the market and through the state, capitalism continues to revolutionize production, 'sensitize' workers to market disciplines, fragment workers as income is polarized *within* the working class (thereby expanding the effective 'reserve army' to also include the marginally and low-paid *employed*), and to generally restructure life to fit the needs of capital. It penetrates every corner of our communities, crawls into every pore of our personal lives, manoeuvers to imperialize every value and idea.

Especially damaging is the impact of accelerated restructuring on the development of cohesive communities of opposition. The significance of increased capital mobility extends beyond global access to raw materials, markets, and weaker labour. Capitalist restructuring is '... an exercise of capital hegemonic capacity that disrupts the processes by which working class collectivity (its intrinsic capacity) is formed'.[10] When plants close and workers 'relocate', it is not only individual workers that are uprooted. The relationships and common workplace-neighbourhood histories out of which class consciousness emerges are fractured and dispersed.

The comparison with capital is telling. Owners can move plants and expand internationally, yet remain physically in their home base and retain the local and national networks and ties on which their class cohesion depends. In the abstract, the dispersion of workers and their culture may of course also imply the dissemination of radical ideas. But given that such ideas are – even in our strongest communities – still in embryo, the effect of restructuring is to frustrate their emergence.

Through all of this, the *past* dynamism of capitalism exists in the real material gains made by many or most workers. Without a movement and a context, today's concessionary demands that capitalists make on workers produce not just anger over inequities and false promises, but also fear over how much of these past gains might be lost, and therefore a defensive concern to limit concessions rather than risk 'everything'. In this context, the alternative to the mean capitalism of today isn't socialism, but the (nicer) capitalism of yesterday.

Even when workers look to collective solutions at the *political* level, their own lack of developed capacities is compounded by the state's failure to democratize life. A capitalist state has no historical reason for developing structures and supports for direct popular intervention in daily production, or for democratizing the application of surpluses within our communities. Within the state's own sphere, it increasingly emulates the private sector in the way it provides goods or services and 'manages' its own activities. State activity may, because of the absence of direct market discipline in buying and selling, seem to have some space to be 'different'. But this has so far rarely led to innovative democratic structures, and even where it does, there is still the indirect discipline on those structures of class pressure exercised through capital and financial markets sounding the alarm over government deficits and debts.

As the focus of politics and therefore democracy, the capitalist state plays a special role in limiting the democratic imagination. The historical transfer of economic power from the state to a specialized and relatively autonomous sphere was the basis for the evolution of a new kind of state. With the privatization of economic power, a ruling class facing democratic pressures could, even if reluctantly, indulge the broadening of participation in the state. As Ellen Wood puts it: 'Only in capitalism has it become possible to leave the property relations between capital and labour fundamentally intact while permitting the democratization of civic and political rights.'[11] Perry Anderson focused directly on the resultant form of the state, asserting that 'bourgeois democracy . . . is itself the ideological lynchpin of Western capitalism'.[12] For the first time in history, the state that emerged (with working class struggles playing a prominent role) included a legislative authority – parliament – chosen by universal suffrage, and tolerated the formation of non-state organizations of the subordinate classes such as unions and working-class parties.

Anderson overstated the case, but the legitimating role of this particular kind of state remains crucial. We cannot successfully demystify the capitalist state by limiting ourselves to its coercive role. Even as the state limits basic democratic rights (e.g. those of trade unions) in order to increase freedom for capital (e.g. free trade), it seems to retain its authority and, more importantly, cramps how we think about democracy. After all, how bad can this state be if it has been the site of past gains and even the institutional guarantor of those gains? And the always-open ostensible invitation to seek change through electoral participation transfers failure to the participants. If we don't try, who can blame the state? If we tried and failed, we must have been trying the impossible.

There is a particular genius in the way capitalist structures obscure the 'real conditions of life' and prevent an understanding of 'man['s] relations with his kind".[13] *The fact that capitalism is so present and socialism so absent, combines with capitalism's remarkable economic dynamism and its 'open' state to channel resistance into reform.* As Mike Lebowitz puts it in a brilliant and insufficiently known work, '[T]he inability to satisfy their needs..leads workers not beyond capital but to class struggle within capitalism'.[14] Workers make their choices in the context of 'options under pressure',[15] and the target of their militancy is change within the system. When workers strike, the point is to get a settlement. The unemployed want jobs, not a revolution – even if their labour is 'exploited'. Unions want to protect what a dynamic capitalism previously provided, rather than gamble with radical change. Political parties with a working class base are both awed and seduced by the power of capitalist restructuring, and define their role as 'influencing' that restructuring in a positive way rather than challenging it.

The point is that if we wait for capitalism to go into terminal crisis because its social relations have become a fetter on the productive forces, we are likely to wait forever. Threats to the continued expansion of the productive forces (i.e. threats to capital accumulation and capitalist economic growth) are, as we've learned since the mid-seventies, at least as likely to lead to a *consolidation* of capitalist social relations as to any fundamental questioning of their inevitability. Moreover, the truly serious threats to the continued expansion of the productive forces will come not from capitalist social relations, but from the implications of a radical move to transform those relations. Any transition to socialism is bound to dramatically disrupt the expansion of the productive forces – and not just in the short term. The contradiction to address is therefore not that between the social relations of capitalism and the expansion of the productive forces, but between those social relations and the *expansion of human needs and potential capacities.*

For the ruling class, the idea of ruling is 'in their bones', assumed by osmosis from everything around them – from the nervous care of a series of nannies, to the games they play as children, the walls that surround their homes and gardens, the trees that shade their houses, their generational expectations, and, of course, their privileged access to resources of every kind. The ruling class literally breathes power.

But for workers, the idea of 'ruling' is an absence. It is not even a distant goal facing possibly insurmountable problems; it hasn't, generally, yet manifested itself as an *idea* to be confronted. For reasons rooted in the working class family and the workplace, and well culti-vated beyond, the tendency of capitalism is to reduce a working class with the potential capacities to do, enjoy, and act politically, to a collection of 'just workers'; 'just consumers'; and 'just voters'. In contrast to the ruling class, workers know their place even as they resent it and must go through a process of *unlearning* before the idea of collectively running their lives, and not just occasionally influencing them, can be born.

SOCIALIST IDEOLOGY: DEMOCRATIZING THEORY

Socialist renewal is today fundamentally about ideology – developing, deepening, and disseminating a particular system of ideas. That set of ideas expresses, through its values and vision, an opposition to capitalism as a social system; theorizes the dynamics of change within capitalism; and locates itself within a movement to replace capitalism. Socialism may be a product of history, but it is also a *break* with history. However encouraged or limited by objective conditions, the socialist project is in the end a creative act of collective will. Articulating that 'will' is the purpose of socialist ideology.

It is not struggles per se that define us as socialists, but those struggles that lead us to leap beyond resistance to a self-conscious identification, by way of a socialist ideology, with the socialist project. Socialist ideology-as-vision connects and sustains us in a struggle that will necessarily be long, painful, uneven and uncertain. In the form of ideology-as-common-sense, it equips us to challenge the everyday (il)logic of capitalism. As a coherent set of goals, assumptions, and insights into society, that ideology must be rich enough to suggest concrete policies and strategic directions for our struggles.

In saying this, I don't mean to make any artificial distinctions between ideology and other dimensions of building for socialism. Ideology doesn't exist apart from on-going struggles and organizational issues. What I *am* arguing is that at this particular historical moment when our socialist presence is so weak, consideration of any struggle, policy, or organizational direction must give special weight to its impact on how our counter-ideology – our declaration of the socialist project – is developed and given practical life.

Every ideology is unique in ways related to its particular project. The uniqueness of socialist ideology stems from the radical and remarkable thing it is trying to do: create a new world and do it through a truly popular mobilization in which 'the masses' are more than foot soldiers for someone else's revolution, but are organizing themselves, for themselves. What does this imply?

Socialists must obviously have something substantive to say about the future society. And creative ideas about resolving expected problems under a socialist future can of course contribute constructively to the socialist project. But any attempt at a concrete outline of socialism (as opposed to 'direction') inevitably raises further problematic questions that, from the perspective of the present, are unconvincing to non-believers. And that scepticism is justified – the truth is we don't and can't know what socialism will, in any detail, look like. We don't know because socialism is not a state of affairs, but a *process*.

Central to that process is a preoccupation with human capacities. This emphasis was at the centre of the links between Marx's critique of capitalism (class control of the capacities of others) and his vision as a revolutionary (the potential political capacities of the working class as the agency morally and strategically placed to challenge capital). Underlying this focus on capacities was a particular philosophy of 'man'. Marx argued that humans were that *part* of nature characterized by self-consciousness (hence *human* nature). Unlike animals, the human species acted beyond immediate material needs and instincts. It had the capacity to *imagine* what did not yet exist and to plan and execute those imaginings. Its this capacity for conscious and purposive activity that 'distinguishes the worst architect from the best of bees'.[16]

Human activity occurs in place and time. It is social and historical. As we interact with nature and each other to address our needs, we affect the world in which we live. In the process, we develop and extend our individual and collective capacities; we change ourselves. In contrast to his contemporaries, the socialism Marx addressed wasn't something to be *invented* by a minority, but something to be *created* by people in struggle.[17] Socialism could not emerge from top-down plans, however well-meaning, nor draftsmen's blueprints, however elaborate. It wasn't something to be given and received. The socialist utopia wouldn't come from ideal communities established on the margins of capitalist society, but through engagement with and *within* capitalist society (i.e. political struggle). By way of that engagement, people could (which doesn't necessarily imply *would*) change themselves and develop the collective capacities to change society.

This stress on humans as *doers,* with the capacity to create our material and social environment and thereby make history and ourselves, transforms 'human nature' from being a limit on the possible, to a contingency dependent on lived history, on what human beings actually *do*. Gramsci concisely summarized this: 'by putting the question "What is man?" we really mean: "What can man become?".'[18] The development of capacities is, accordingly, both a goal and the crucial connection to achieving that goal.

What Marx pinpointed as so historically significant in capitalism was its demonstration of the amazing capacity of humans to act socially to produce their material means of existence. Capitalism showed the remarkable degree to which the capacities of the whole, the social collective, could exceed the sum of the parts. Linking individuals and communities through markets, combining workers into factories, accumulating and transforming profits into expanded means of production, subordinating science and other social institutions to the productivist drive, capitalism revealed a potential previously unknown and uncontemplated. '. . . what earlier century had even a presentiment that such productive forces slumbered in the lap of social labour?'[19]

But this overwhelming focus on *production* narrowed the potential richness of human activity to that single dimension. And the socialization of labour came by way of individual alienation and class control. Capitalism, for all its achievements in opening up new possibilities for humanity, inherently limits 'what man can become'. Socialism is the response. The question 'What is socialism?' is transformed from speculation about the future into an encounter with the present: 'Can we transform capitalism?'.

The kind of movement that could develop the confidence, understanding, unity, collective capacities, and innovative organizational structures to one day defeat capitalism, would certainly have established its potential for completing the invention of socialism. Although the specific questions of 'how to run' socialism remain important, C.B. Macpherson was right to insist that

> . . . the main problem is not how to run it but how to reach it. It seems likely that if we can reach it, or any substantial instalment of it, our way along the road to reaching it will have made us capable of running it, or at least less incapable than we are now.[20]

The demand socialism makes on itself – the popular capacity to transform the world – translates into distinct expectations of its members in terms of understanding and participating in change. *Socialist ideology looks to be the bridge, carrying traffic both ways, between the practice of theory and the practice of revolution.* The structural power of capitalism to obscure social relations placed an ideological responsibility on Marxist theorists: reveal what capitalism really is and help us see through it. But socialist ideology can't just popularize theory, making it accessible in content, style and availability. Socialist ideology must also *democratize* theory.

As important as it is to 'educate the masses' by 'sharing' theory, the issue is to engage the potential creators of a new society directly in developing their *own* theoretical capacity to understand and see through capitalism. As an American journalist, Sally Kempton, once said: 'You can't fight an enemy that has outposts in your head'. Without the widespread capacity to think in a way independent of capitalist ideas, building a movement to match the task we have set for ourselves would be inconceivable (all the more so at a time when the capitalist castle, wrapped in its aura of invincibility, sits so smugly on its hill).

This does not meant that our need for some activists who devote the majority of their lives to *full-time* theoretical work would disappear. It is that their monopoly over theory would end. With this comes a change in both their relationship to the rest of the movement and the further development of theory. Activists not engaged in full-time theory would not only demand greater clarity, but pose new theoretical questions based on the interaction of their experience and a maturing theoretical framework. Theory, and its democratization as socialist ideology, would consequently be in perpetual change and development, reflecting the unevenness of how class consciousness develops, how *socialist* class consciousness emerges, and how the struggle proceeds.

'MAKING' SOCIALISTS

That said, the standard questions of socialist mobilization still confront us. Can we reinvent a socialist language for our time with which to address non-socialist workers? How do we participate in working class and popular struggles in a way that both supports them and introduces the 'political exposure'[21] that takes them beyond the local, and beyond resistance? Can we play a role that structures these struggles so that the issues addressed, the articulation of goals, the tactics, and the assessment of victories and defeats have a socialist content – that is, contribute to the introduction of socialist ideas and the 'making' of socialists? How do we ensure that experiences and lessons are cumulative, and avoid repeated memory loss and the separation and isolation of struggles across sectors and time? How do we *build* something that lasts and grows?

The *Manifesto* still sets the stage for such questions. It attempted to integrate ideology and theory through exposing the class inequality underlying free market exchanges and through locating capitalism as a historical, and therefore potentially transitory, social system. Its analysis of the internal dynamics of capitalism was directed at drawing out the political possibilities that came with competition, crises, the concentration of capital, and above all the formation of the modern working class.

The problem from the perspective of the present, however, lies in the fact that we can no longer, 150 years later, think and strategize as if socialism is in any way imminent. What we now need is a theory appropriate to the long march *within* capitalism – a new political economy, a *political economy of transition*.[22] This political economy would live between the reality of capitalism and the socialism to come. It would be unashamedly ideological in the sense that its assumptions, categories, and dynamics strengthen and give concrete direction to our project. This isn't a matter of finding an alternative to Marxism, but of adding a new *layer* to it.

Parallel to this gap in Marxist political economy is our failure to solve the problem of how we organize ourselves as socialists. The answers from the beginning of the century, that tried to go beyond Marx in terms of solving this through the 'party question', are in the end inadequate. The reality of the failures of Leninism and social democracy, and especially the need to redefine how to think about what we face, have pushed them aside as models. The judgement of Marx and Engels in 1872, looking back at the Manifesto and its time, is valid again now:

> the political situation has been entirely changed and the progress of history has swept from the earth the greater proportion of the political parties there enumerated.[23]

The two main historical wings of socialism, social democracy and communism, generally considered victory possible in the relative near term and directed their attention to the *taking of state power*. In setting a different agenda, we are not suggesting that it is possible to ignore the issue of the state – all struggles in capitalist society are related to or reflected in state power at some level, and any socialist movement will always include an on-going debate over the theory and strategy of addressing the state. But the nature of socialist organizations is insepa- rable from the identification of the *stage* of the struggle. Since our immediate goal is the 'less ambitious' one of just getting the *idea* of socialism seriously on the agenda again, we are addressing a different issue from that of social democratic and communist parties.

Social democracy wandered between underestimating capitalism's power, which led to the naive equation of electoral victory with radical change, and a pragmatism that was overwhelmed by the economic power of capital. It consequently slid into reformism.[24] Social democratic parties, based on the electoralist road to a technocratic socialism, had little need for, or interest in (if not active fear of), the development of a militantly class-conscious activist movement and therefore ended up as centralized, in crucial respects, as their communist antagonists. Communist parties, based on the cataclysmic revolutionary event and so strongly influenced by the particularities of the first successful revolution, emphasized unity, discipline, and centralization. In the case of the Soviet Union, defeating capitalism meant the confluence of the strong party with the state. Communist parties in the West, hampered by the way their ties to the Soviet Union limited their theoretical development, made defensive by the Cold War, and suffering from top-down bureaucratized structures, proved incapable of addressing, let alone challenging, the ideological hegemony of capitalism (France and Italy were partial and brief exceptions for a period).

In contrast, socialists at the end of the twentieth century, facing no pressure to immediately 'win' the state or establish a new state, need be less obsessed with organizational strength and less enamoured of centralization. They may focus instead on the widespread development of ideological activity – the democratization of theory. This takes us beyond the question of a *different* kind of party, and opens the question of whether there is any reason today to insist on there being only *one* party (with its single party paper), as opposed to a plurality of socialist parties/movements. In addition to any debate over the relationship between unity and democracy *within* a single socialist structure, we would therefore also face the issue of developing practical working relationships *between* organizationally separate groups. Moreover, the legitimacy of different levels of activity also comes to the fore. In the focus on the state, life is about 'big politics' and the politics of the small – the non-directly economic, the local as opposed to national – is, if not ignored, then certainly underplayed. With the shift to developing capacities, the potential of the politics of the small rises.

More generally, if we acknowledge that capitalism will not simply self-destruct and also reject the Big Bang theory of creating a socialist universe; if we truly recognize the staying power of capitalism and especially the protracted process of developing our capacities to both change and run the world; if the reality of on-going risks of reversal forces us to address how to *sustain* our ideas and direction; if we explicitly agree with Dennis Potter's depiction that we have 'Lots of clues. That's the way things are. Plenty of clues. No solutions.';[25] then it becomes clear that fundamental to all organizational questions is the priority of developing a rich socialist subculture. That is, a subculture blossoming in every backyard, full of confidence in its capacity to interact with and change the broader culture's assumptions, common sense and therefore 'political climate'.

None of this can happen without the greatest amount of improvisation. Duke Ellington had it right: 'It don't mean a thing if it ain't got that swing'.

THE CANADIAN AUTO WORKERS: BETWEEN MILITANCY AND SOCIALISM

In light of the limitations shown by unionism, it is perhaps not surprising that many socialists turned away from workers and unions. Their Marxism apparently proved incapable of shielding them from the temper of the times. But the fact is that unions remain central to the socialist project, even though the relationship between socialists and unions is characterized, at best, by an uncomfortable tension. Socialists are other-worldly, unions too-worldly. Socialists dream, unions bargain. Socialists look ahead to a society in which labour is no longer a commodity, unions live to deal with that commodification.

Today, both socialists and unions confront an impasse that only their interaction can address. For socialists, the predicament might be summarized as follows. Capitalism's crime is that it commodifies labour. As long as capitalism exists, labour power will be a commodity. This can only be overcome after a socialist revolution ushers in a socialist society. That revolution depends on working class leadership. But commodities can't make revolutions. How then do we get to socialism and end labour's commodification? For unions, the predicament is that recent history has revolved around capital's determination to *intensify* the commodification of labour and therefore increasingly limit the possible role and impact of unions. This drive to commodify and regulate workers so comprehensively *through the market* necessarily marginalizes unions unless they go *beyond* the market.

These dilemmas set the stage for a mutually beneficial dynamic. To continue the socialist project, agitation is not enough. Socialists must engage workers in winning the kind of reforms that so change the *context* in which workers sell their labour power that the exchange of a worker's time for income no longer completely dominates the rest of their being, whether in the workplace or outside. That is, concrete changes in the here and now are absolutely crucial to create amongst workers – through the struggles for the changes, and through the results achieved – a sense of their remaining and on-going humanity. Unions, meanwhile, may have a moral language to counter capital (fairness, sharing in progress) but no language for challenging the capitalist *logic* behind what is happening to the workers they represent. There are, consequently, the best of reasons for both socialists and unionists to edge closer together.

In the late seventies, the growing aggressiveness of corporations and hostility of governments led to debates within unions over an appropriate response. Unions that rejected the 'new reality' found that keeping their traditions of militant unionism unchanged now required radical changes in their structures and activities. The Canadian Auto Workers (CAW), for example, not only ended up breaking away from their more compliant parent (the American-based UAW), but found themselves drawn into a world of uncertain strategic demands and pressures for new ideological responses and alternatives.[26] Through the resultant struggles and campaigns, the CAW evolved towards a 'movement unionism'.

> [Movement unionism] means making the union into a vehicle through which its members can not only address their bargaining demands but actively lead the fight for everything that affects working people in their communities and the country. Movement unionism includes the shape of bargaining demands, the scope of union activities, the approach to issues of change, and above all, that sense of commitment to a larger movement that might suffer defeats, but can't be destroyed.[27]

Central to consolidating and sustaining the union's culture of struggle and resistance was a response to the strait-jacket of 'competitiveness'. Competitiveness presents itself as not only the best, but the *only* model of economic development. As such it obscures class relations, structures economic debate and acts as the ultimate ideology of the status quo. Since competitiveness is, however, not just an idea but a reflection of structures already in place, competitiveness represents a constraint we have to deal with. The trick is to prevent that *constraint* from slowly insinuating itself into our *goals*.

Within the CAW a group of staffers working in research and education have been trying to flesh out an alternative direction that addressed this challenge. It is based on moving beyond questions of distribution, and working through the implications of shifting from capitalism's focus on the accumulation of *capital* and control over labour power, to socialists' concern with the accumulation of *capacities* and democratic intervention. Democracy is here thought of in the broadest terms: '. . . we are not only emphasizing popular control over the economy, but also equal access to participation (democracy must be universal) and the development of individual capacities (democracy must aspire to meeting and developing each individual's potential)'.[28] Without the development of our capacities, we could neither progress towards socialism nor – as Marx understood – know what to do with the economy even if it were magically handed to us: '. . . private property can be abolished only on condition of an all-round development of individuals, because . . . only individuals that are developing in an all-round fashion can appropriate them'.[29]

This entry point – the 'democratic development of capacities' – is primarily an ideological counter-weight but it also affects how we approach a number of inter-related issues, particularly the relevant unit of production, the appropriate unit to address needs, the centrality of protecting spaces for experimentation, the relationship between the economic and political, the tactical and strategic urgency of taking on finance capital.

The CAW, in its leadership training programme, carries out the following exercise. Participants identify a series of issues relevant to their lives – unemployment, training, economic restructuring, working conditions, social programs, equality, etc. For a set of issues, some participants are asked to identify the implications of assuming the goal is competitiveness; others are asked to follow through on the logic of pursuing the democratic development of capacities. Reports are given, answers hotly debated and discussed, and the process is repeated with other sets of issues and participants switching their starting perspectives.

For example, the logic of competitiveness incorporates the need for significant unemployment to discipline workers and boost corporate performance. The democratic development of capacities asserts that the underutilization of human potentials contradicts development; if economic structures don't make full employment a priority, it is those structures rather than workers that must be 'adjusted'. Competitiveness sees workplace closures as essential to economic restructuring. Our alternative doesn't deny the need for change but asks whether the closure involves the removal of tools and equipment that might be useful for the community and for the on-going development of skills that would otherwise go unused. If this is the case, then the issue shouldn't be closures, but supportive mechanisms to revitalize those workplaces.

Similarly, competitiveness does express concern with skill development through training. But training driven by competitiveness is generally concentrated on a small part of the workforce, and the training the rest of the workforce gets is generally about fitting people into the requirements of externally-determined technology and work reorganization (Fordism, contrary to popular conceptions, exists comfortably alongside all the new allegedly post-Fordist production paradigms). The 'democratic development of capacities' demands training for everyone – as a need, a democratic right, and a personal-social investment in the future. And the scope of the training extends to developing the skills and confidence to control, rather than be adapted to, technology and the organization of work. Competitiveness would lament this as an 'over-investment' in skills,[30] wasteful and even potentially counter-productive. Our alternative agrees that 'excess knowledge' (re existing work structures and division of labour) might create problems. But that's positive if it implies the kind of conflict over basic issues that could stimulate structural change.

The discussion groups articulating competitiveness note that it is export-oriented and that we are consequently pushed towards strengthening 'our' companies and improving the 'investment climate' so 'our company', and not others, will attract private investment and be successful. In contrast, for those starting with the democratic development of capacities, the unit of production isn't the company (a property relation) but the workplace (the basic unit of social production) and groups of workplaces with common economic ties (clusters or sectors).[31] This opens up an economic-political-ideological perspective in which 'strengthening the economy' doesn't automatically translate into bolstering the private power of companies, but shifts attention to developing the productive capacities of workplaces and sectors. Moreover, without a national space free of the undermining pressures of global markets, there can be no experimentation[32] and without experimentation no new democratic structures could emerge or suggest themselves. In the discussions, we emphasize that international economic relations will not thereby cease; rather, they would be put in a regulatory framework that permits the passage to substantially more inward-oriented development strategies.

What emerges from all of this is a growing clarity about competitiveness as an ideology, and – more slowly – the democratic development of capacities as an alternative ideology with implications for different directions. Seriously broaching any of these ideas also adds to what unions do, and affects all aspects of how they do it. The process of workers moving from primarily seeing themselves as – and living the lives of – inputs into the production process and consumers in an economy, to a self-identification as *producers* and *political actors*, implies a change in not just goals but the everyday culture of their organization: the reallocation of research resources to address jobs; the challenges that come from an awakened membership to improve democratic structures and to create new vehicles for participation; links to the community based on joint mobilization; an expanded scope of bargaining. A reorientation in the role of unions could not, for example, be imagined without unions simultaneously moving beyond defensive challenges to management rights to negotiate – under their new mandate to represent 'producers', and as part of a redefinition of what a 'job' includes – regular time *during* working hours for ergonomic training, access to engineers to improve work stations, updates on production and restructuring trends, and access for workers' to their own 'experts'.

In contrast to the ideological work being done within the union, the implications of all of this in terms of political strategy have as yet not been systematically integrated into our work. What follows outlines some ideas being discussed as a way to move ahead; they have been raised only tentatively in various union educational and strategic settings.

The political economy of transition we are reaching for through the 'democratic development of capacities' approach must explicitly overcome the structural separation between the economic and political by *politicizing the economy*. This involves rethinking the state's direct role in the economy. Over and above the democratization of its existing economic functions, this means thinking about *'a different kind of state'*:[33] inventing state structures to simultaneously develop the productive capacities of the community and develop a popular capacity to participate in, influence, and regulate the direction of production in what will still be a capitalist economy. Consider the following two examples, one community-based and one sector-based.

Suppose each community elected 'job development boards', mandated to provide everyone in the community with either paid work or training (or both). These boards would survey community needs beyond market demands to match them with the community's

potential human, natural, and capital resources. They would have the
defensive right to postpone closures and – backed by supporting institutions – to evaluate corporate finances, provide technical and financial
support, initiate the possibility of workplace conversion or cooperation
across workplaces to achieve economies of scale, and over time develop
the direct capacity to organize production/services through co-ops and
the introduction of municipal ownership. Campaigns for seats on these
boards would debate how to create jobs, but would inevitably also raise
questions about how we define 'needs'. This public involvement would
be institutionally encouraged between elections through forums and
on-going classes on the structure of the local economy and the
technical aspects of addressing its development. These embryonic
councils – an alternative to units of capital as the core administrative
unit for organizing economic activity – would be the base for moving
towards a community-based democratic planning capacity.

This emphasis on the 'community', like that on 'sectors' in what
follows, is part of a more general attempt to rethink and redefine how
we think about economic activity. Our focus here is not on the
consumer (someone with money to spend) but on a tiered range of
social units that include the household (the basic unit that supplies
labour in order to make a livelihood), the community (the social
network and its sense of place within which households live and work),
and the nation (communities bound by a geographical-historical-
administrative nexus). The concern is not consumption but *needs*
(which do not necessarily correlate with market signals). And within
the hierarchy of needs, the development of capacities ranks foremost
because it includes an expansion of future options and possibilities –
ultimately, social change itself. This reorientation highlights particular
questions dealing with the family (e.g. the division of labour within the
family and its impact on women's options to develop their potentials).
And it shapes how we view the role of physical and social infrastructure
in providing the base for developing communities and equalizing
access to economic participation (e.g. the role of transportation,
health, education, training, child care).

At the sectoral level, where economic activity extends across and
beyond specific communities, the thrust would be to develop an
independent working class capacity to intervene in the direction of
that sector. Unions would demand that state agencies put their bureaucracies to work preparing detailed sectoral information specifically for
the *workers* involved. Unions would also insist, on democratic grounds,
that they be given resources to partially offset what companies take for

granted: to hire researchers, carry out surveys of local productive potential, engage their members in creating internal workplace structures for input, and for developing the broader sectoral councils. With a sympathetic policy framework around trade policy, financial levers, and newly-established sectoral 'service centres' (won through political mobilization), unions would be in a position to negotiate/struggle for sectoral directions with companies and the state.

These 'service centres' would overlap with the community structures created under the job development boards, since such centres would be physically located in one community or another. They would address particular sub-sectoral needs and be linked to other public institutions like universities. They could pool resources to address the improvement of working conditions and the quality of goods; look ahead to new materials, technologies, and outputs; consider the potential spin-offs for other sectors. There might, for example, be a tool-and-die centre in Windsor experimenting with new tooling; a stamping research centre in Kitchener to link new developments in steel and plastics; an ergonomics centre in Oshawa to study the engineering of workstations. Unlike the private capacities which come and go with companies (the threat of withdrawal being used against workers and the community), these institutions would represent *social* capacities, rooted in our communities and integrated into domestic sectors.

The local and sectoral initiatives raised above could not occur without a funding base and we try to link this to 'taking on the banks'. Although capitalist restructuring of the economy is carried out by the 'real' sector, the financial sector plays a special role in the accumulation and allocation of society's surplus. As capital in its most mobile form, it is the medium through which capitalist logic and discipline is implemented. In the process it takes on, to a degree, a life of its own. Challenging the financial sector is an immediate priority because this sector lies in waiting to undermine any of our initiatives, and because we can't move on to the complexities of socializing the real economy without some social control over society's overall surplus.

Viewing the financial sector as a public utility for regulating and facilitating the investment that shapes our workplaces, sectors, and communities raises a number of issues about planning capacities. At a minimum, finance-as-a-public-utility means controlling the international outflow of capital and the establishment of a 'social investment fund'. The financial base of that fund might come from a levy on *all* financial institutions (banks, insurance companies, investment houses, pension funds; to limit ourselves to voluntary 'solidarity' funds that leave financial capital's resources untouched would guarantee failure). Those funds would be allocated, through national and regional democratic structures, to national projects (e.g. housing) and to the sectoral and community structures discussed earlier. Together, this control on capital outflows, access to a growing portion of private capital, social allocation of the funds, and union/community involvement in their concrete application, constitute a process of moving towards the politicization and democratization of finance.

Facing both external attacks and preparing for a generational change within the union, the CAW has made an impressive commitment of institutional resources (in addition to political space) for maintaining its culture and developing an ideology independent from capital. The union dramatically increased its educational programmes through the nineties, largely on the basis of negotiating monies from the corporations that were *completely* controlled by the union.[34] Those educationals are heavily oriented to political economy and ideology as fundamental to building the union. New educationals were negotiated to provide forty hours of training for every steward at GM, Ford, and Chrysler on their workplaces, the industry, union history, and movement unionism. Research resources were expanded and shifted to supporting educational work. A department of work organization was established to provide an independent capacity to understand workplace changes and act as a catalyst for our response. An economist was hired to prepare background material for sectoral interventions and to provide ammunition for taking on the banks. Sectoral co-ordinators were appointed in some sectors (aerospace, auto parts) not only to co-ordinate bargaining but act as a catalyst in developing sectoral strategies with elected sectoral councils. Resources and organizational skills were put into communities (e.g. around the educational system) to expand the self-definition of what workers are and what unions do.

What has been the response from workers? At one level, there is nothing surprising. Some workers raise legitimate but narrow concerns like whether the restrictions on investment might affect their pension. Others are intrigued and raise practical questions: Won't the local elite still dominate any boards we set up? How will we control those who run the massive Social Investment Fund? There are those that take the ideas in a populist direction, underestimating the difficulties; and those who remain convinced that neither workers nor state institutions can do what companies now do. Even where workers are engaged in lively discussions about these ideas, we still need to question how deeply these discussions have penetrated the participants' consciousness; and – since it is these workers who are to take the message back to the workplace – how widespread the impact of this exercise ultimately is.

Another set of concerns comes directly from the every-day reality of union survival. In chasing after the restructuring, resources are 'diverted' to bringing new members in, often only to keep the union in the same place in terms of membership numbers. Staff are overworked and activists – precisely because their activism is 'in addition' to what they are *expected* to normally do – are always exhausted. Even with the best of intentions, and in spite of the leadership support, is it possible to take on the kind of challenge we're posing when it remains *secondary* to the main function of organizations already hard-pressed? Without political attitudes being a condition of membership, can there be any broadly-based internal political consensus and a priority focus on political issues?

The answer – in spite of the reservations, problems, and limits – is an exciting yes. The discussion and debates in the classrooms and workshops are at remarkably high levels. Even where workers remain unclear and unsure of specifics, they are affected by the general orientation towards an independent working class perspective, the emphasis on thinking about capacities, the broadening of the theme of democracy and a new self-consciousness of their history. Most go back ready to challenge the union and supplement or rejuvenate the existing cadre. Although it wasn't intended as an explicit goal, the workers trained to deliver the programmes have emerged as a new layer of ideologically-confident activists.

Beyond the *content* of the educationals, and no less significant, were two other factors. Bringing workers together across workplaces, companies, and sectors was crucial. An auto worker hearing a fish plant worker or airline worker talking about lean production brings home lessons about class identity that sociological lectures could otherwise never do. Moreover, this horizontal mixing of diverse workers and activists (as opposed to vertically between specific workplaces and a national office) allows workers opportunities to discuss their problems directly, introducing a level of democracy that unions – through inertia or bureaucratic design – too often block. And bringing workers together in their own educational centre, in an environment – the CAW's education centre at Port Elgin in Ontario – full of the history of past struggles (posters, art, photos) and where they share not just class time, but meals and evenings, not only intensifies the learning experience, but gives it a cultural base. The centre's sheer physical existence seems to say

'We're in this for the long haul and aren't going away'.

Above all, it must be stressed that in the absence of on-going struggles and campaigns, none of this would be relevant. Ideology would be rhetoric, education would be excuses, cynicism would block excitement, alternatives taken back would have no audience and ideas introduced no reason to mature.

Given the heightened struggles and mobilization that in fact have occurred within the CAW, the main limitation we faced and still face is an old one – the absence of significant socialist movements. Without this, openings created at the national union level have not been taken up and developed locally; there has been little attempt to take the material and perspectives into other unions and organizations; and we have only had ad-hoc and sporadic support and criticism from socialists intellectuals to take this work further. As individuals in unions and as part of networks, we have to get on with developing and engaging workers in the ideas that can make the socialist project relevant again. This *will* lead to battles within the labour movement – if not now, then when we show signs of success – because it ultimately threatens the 'normal' life of unions and the pragmatic ambitions of social democratic 'modernizers'. But the potential is there, and the creation of networks of socialists linked to sympathetic union activists to work on this is the minimum we can expect of ourselves today.

Capital's success in getting its way in terms of structural change depended on people accepting that the national interest lies with making capital stronger so 'we' can be competitive. The failure of that victory to deliver the promised goods has left both corporate authority and corporate ideology vulnerable. Capital's own insistence that the times demanded major overhaul rather than tinkering has created a more receptive audience to new ideas. And the failure of collective bargaining and electoral representation to adequately address working class needs has, after a long hiatus, led to more militant and creative responses and a corresponding radicalization of rhetoric. There is now an interest, at least amongst a significant *minority* of workers, in alternative ideas. *This* is the fight socialists must take on.

CONCLUSION

Proletarian revolutions..deride with unmerciful thoroughness the inadequacies, weaknesses and paltriness of their first attempts.
— Karl Marx[35]

Marx brought us the gift of historical optimism, but one hundred and fifty years after the *Manifesto*, doubt threatens to overwhelm us. We are, in spite of the long stretch of history since Marx wrote the above lines, still engaged in our 'first attempts'. From the perspective of the heady sixties, the 'paltriness' of a strategy which begins by postponing the revolution to a distant and indefinite tomorrow would be dismissed with a quick wave of the hand as reformist. Today, the modest goal of simply getting socialism seriously on the agenda is more likely to be labelled *utopian*.

Towards the end of *What is To Be Done?*, Lenin, in the midst of the most hard-headed and unsentimental of polemics, quoted the journalist Pisarev:

> . . . if man were completely deprived of the ability to dream..if he could not from time to time run ahead and mentally conceive . . . the product to which his hands are only just beginning to lend shape, then I cannot at all imagine what stimulus there would be . . . [for] art, science, and political endeavour . . . The rift between reality and dreams causes no harm if only the person dreaming believes seriously in his dream, if he attentively observes life, compares his observations with his castles in the air..and works conscientiously for the achievement of his fantasies. If there is some connection between dreams and life then all is well.[36]

To which Lenin added:

> Of this kind of dreaming there is unfortunately too little in our movement. And the people most responsible for this are those who boast of their sober views, their 'closeness' to the 'concrete' . . .[37]

That connection between 'dreams and life', it turned out, eluded the Russian Revolution and the dream became a nightmare. Social democracy, for its part, completely lost its capacity to dream. Even today, however, some of us choose to carry on. We contemplate our inability to build on the past – a past characterized not so much by the gains of the welfare state, as by the movements that lay behind it. We note, without recrimination but with sadness, the past gains in consciousness and the pockets of socialist confidence that have faded with disuse. We challenge the credibility and authority of those with power. We shake angry fists at those who in the name of a frightened realism give up on socialist ideals. Even when it is out of fashion we still have faith. This faith is connected to the real world, is a secular faith, but no other word honestly explains our hanging on to socialism. We refuse to accept that what is, or has been, is all that can be, and insist on the human species' capacity to *develop* its capacities. We dream with sober senses.

NOTES

1. Karl Marx and Friedrich Engels, *The Communist Manifesto*, London, Penguin, 1967, p. 83.
2. 'If we disregard slaves . . . there has been, in the history of men who work with their hands, no group, stratum, or class which has not owned at least a substantial portion of its tools. Workers in the modern sense of the word are the first class not to own tools.' Jurgen Kuczynski, *The Rise of The Working Class*, New York, World University Press, 1967, p. 10.
3. Ralph Miliband, *Socialism for a Sceptical Age*, London, Verso, 1994, p. 188.
4. Maxim Gorky, quoted by John Berger in *Permanent Red*, London, Writers and Readers Publishing cooperative, 1960, p. 93–4.
5. Karl Marx, *The Eighteenth Brumaire of Napoleon Bonaparte*, New York, International Publishers, 1969, p. 19.
6. It is, as we emphasized earlier, not only that consumption is individualized but that the content of consumption-as-compensation is not necessarily individually enriching.
7. David Harvey, *Justice, Nature, and the Geography of Difference*, Oxford, Blackwell, 1996, p. 44.
8. Marx-Engels, *Manifesto*, p. 83.
9. Raymond Williams, *Towards 2000*, London, Verso, 1983, p. 262.
10. Jerry Lee Lembcke, 'Labor History's "Synthesis Debate": Sociological Interventions', *Science and Society*, Summer 1995, p. 162.
11. Ellen Meiksins Wood, *Democracy Against Capitalism: Renewing Historical Materialism*, Cambridge, Cambridge University Press, 1995, p. 202.
12. Perry Anderson, 'The Antinomies of Antonio Gramsci', *New Left Review*, No. 100, November, 1976, p. 28.
13. Marx-Engels, *Manifesto*, p. 83.
14. Mike Lebowitz, *Beyond Capital*, London, MacMillan, 1992, p. 131.
15. Raymond Williams, 'Notes on British Marxism since the War' in *New Left Review*, No. 100, November, 1976, p. 87.
16. Karl Marx, *Capital, Volume 1*, London, Penguin, 1990, p. 284.
17. A third of the *Manifesto* concentrated on a critique of a-historical and elitist notions of socialism.
18. Antonio Gramsci, *The Modern Prince and other writings*, New York, International Publishers, 1970, p. 76.
19. Marx-Engels, *Manifesto*, p. 85.
20. C.B. Macpherson, *The Life and Times of Liberal Democracy*, London, Oxford University Press, 1977, p. 98.
21. Lenin, *What Is To be Done?*, New York, International Publishers, 1972, p. 70.
22. '[Its] principles should be envisioned as transitional [not socialist] in the sense of 'structural reform' that initiates democratic modes of regulation against market imperatives.' Greg Albo, 'A World Market of Opportunities', in L. Panitch, ed., *The Socialist Register 1997*, London, Merlin, p. 30.
23. Marx-Engels, first preface to the German edition of the *Communist Manifesto*, June 24, 1872 included in *Manifesto*, p. 54.
24. In an eerily contemporary passage in the *Manifesto* Marx notes: 'Ultimately, when stubborn historical facts had dispersed all intoxicating effects of self-deception, this form of Socialism ended in a miserable fit of the blues.', p. 109.

25. Dennis Potter, *The Singing Detective*, New York, Vintage, 1988, p. 140.
26. 'Over the past two decades, our union resisted the pressures to get into line with the so-called new reality. . . . Out of that experience, a 'culture of struggle and resistance' grew within the union. That culture united us, kept us in motion, defined us as a union. How do we now expand and deepen this legacy as we search for new strategies and new responses'. CAW Collective Bargaining and Political Action Convention, 'False Solutions, Growing Protests: Recapturing the Agenda', June, 1996.
27. Sam Gindin, *The Canadian Auto Workers: The Birth and Transformation of a Union*, Toronto, Lorimer, 1995, p. 268.
28. Sam Gindin and Dave Robertson, 'Alternatives to Competitiveness' in Daniel Drache, ed., *Getting on Track*, Montreal and Kingston, McGill-Queen's University Press, 1992, p. 33–34.
29. Karl Marx, *The German Ideology*, New York, International Publishers, 1972, p. 117.
30. Wolfgang Streeck, 'Training and the New Industrial Relations' in Marino Regini, ed, *The Future of Labour Movements*, London, Sage Publishers, p. 262.
31. This reorientation in the unit of analysis from the company (capital) to groups of workplaces (sectors) is returned to a few pages ahead with the example of sectoral strategies.
32. Albo, op. cit., p. 30–2.
33. Leo Panitch, 'A Different Kind of State?' in Greg Albo, David Langille and Leo Panitch, eds., *A Different Kind of State? Popular Power and Democratic Administration*, Toronto, Oxford University Press, 1993, p. 5.
34. Through the 1980s and nineties, a total of over 5000 workers went through the four week residential course at the union's education centre. The course content focuses on political economy, union structures and strategies, labour history, class and social identity, mobilization and politics. Each year, thousands more go through two week, one week, and weekend schools with courses on such topics as work organization and health and safety, and courses for activist women and people of colour.
35. Marx, *Eighteenth Brumaire*, p. 19.
36. Pisarev, quoted by Lenin, op. cit., p. 167.
37. Lenin, ibid., p. 167.

UNIONS, STRIKES AND CLASS CONSCIOUSNESS TODAY

by Sheila Cohen & Kim Moody

One hundred and fifty years after the publication of the *Communist Manifesto*, the 'spectre' of Communism can no longer be said to be haunting Europe – whether in the form of mass parties devoted to revolution or the states that inaccurately claimed that title. But class struggle, the inextinguishable source of everything the authors of the *Manifesto* meant by Communism, is, it seems, as irrepressible as ever. Despite ever-stronger siren calls by social democratic and union leaderships for 'partnership' and 'co-operation' with capital, old-fashioned mass strikes have recently stalked not only Europe but almost every other continent.

By the mid-1990s, this could be seen in the dramatic confrontations between major labour federations and the neoliberal, populist, and even social democratic governments of such seemingly dissimilar capitalisms as France, South Korea, South Africa, Canada, Peru, Brazil, Argentina, Belgium, Italy, and a dozen others. Alongside, sometimes preceding, and often following these political outbursts was a return to militant confrontation with capitalist employers far larger and more powerful than any Marx and Engels could have envisioned in 1848. If no manifestos appeared, no barricades were thrown up, and the red banners typically bore the initials of a trade union federation rather than a revolutionary party, the dynamics dramatically evoked throughout the original *Manifesto* were nonetheless clearly at work and a renewed class consciousness was evident across much of the industrial and semi-industrial world.

Despite all the real and apparent differences between Europe 150 years ago and today's capitalist world, two fundamental issues remain equally unresolved: the lack of fully-fledged and widespread socialist consciousness, and the absence of large-scale organization directed at fostering such consciousness. If Marx and Engels saw in the rise of class

102

conflict the birth of such organisation, the moves cited above towards some resurgence of class struggle may offer the opportunity for its rebirth – providing, of course, the socialist left can overcome its own isolation from the reality of this struggle. In many ways, we are faced with the same problems and limitations within the socialist movement itself as were the authors of the *Manifesto*.

I

In 1848 as now, the socialist movement consisted of a variety of 'socialisms' ranging from the idealist/populist/utopian to the avowedly revolutionary, or at least insurrectionary. The *Manifesto*'s survey of 'Socialist and Communist Literature' identified the three categories of Reactionary Socialism, Conservative or Bourgeois Socialism and Critical-Utopian Socialism or Communism, and the forceful rejection by Marx and Engels of all these forms of 'socialism' had one common theme; their mistaken abnegation of class. 'German or "True" Socialism', for example, prides itself in representing 'not the interests of the proletariat, but the interests of human nature, of man in general, who belongs to no class, has no reality, who exists only in the misty realm of philosophical fantasy'.[1] While more aware of 'the working class, as being the most suffering class', utopian socialists like Fourier and Owen are equally castigated for considering themselves 'far superior to all class antagonisms . . . Hence, they habitually appeal to society at large, without distinction of class . . .'.[2] The sectarians of the era receive no gentler treatment: 'They hold fast by the views of their masters [i.e. Fourier, Owen, et. al.], in opposition to the progressive historical development of the proletariat'.[3]

Even in the apparently revolutionary era when the *Manifesto* was written, then, the class-oriented politics of Marx and Engels placed them at a peculiar distance from many of the other socialists of their time. One of the most central features of this difference revolved around their consistent adherence to what they referred to as 'the real working class movement'; and this was shown most clearly in what was then an almost unique focus on, and endorsement of, trade union organisation.

The general absence of this orientation within the intellectual and political milieu of Marx and Engels – mirrored in an equivalent distaste for 'economistic' struggles in our own era – is recognised by Hal Draper: 'Marx was the first leading figure in the history of socialism to adopt a position of support to trade unions and trade-unionism, on principle'.[4] Most other socialists, as Draper points out, were often not only indifferent but positively hostile to trade unionism; and he shows this was even true of Owen as well as Proudhon, who 'not only condemned trade unions and strikes on principle but vigorously approved gendarmes' shooting down strikers as enemies of society, that is, enemies of small property'.[5] Even the leading Chartist Ernest Jones rejected trade unionism as a 'fallacy', despite the fact that his views were published only a few years after the mass Chartist struggles which centred, at their height, on a general strike and the attempt to found the Grand National Consolidated Trade Union.[6] Marx and Engels were in effect unique, then, among their socialist contemporaries, in consistently following an orientation towards basic trade union organisation and struggle as expressions of what they referred to as the 'real class movement'.

But were they correct? Richard Hyman, in his 1971 pamphlet on 'Marxism and the Sociology of Trade Unionism', comments that despite their lifelong involvement with both theoretical and practical aspects of trade unionism, the attention of Marx and Engels to this question is 'remarkably slight'. Although he acknowledges that they provided a sufficient base in their writings 'to be considered as a coherent theory of trade unionism', Hyman evidently regards this theory as essentially naive. 'One need scarcely document the failure of subsequent experience to validate [the Communist Manifesto's] optimistic prognosis; yet Marx and Engels never produced a comprehensive revision of their earlier analysis'.[7] This view is echoed in John Kelly's comment, in *Trade Unions and Socialist Politics*, that '. . . despite their contact with, and interest in, trade unionism they left behind no systematic or coherent analysis of the limits and possibilities of trade union action'. The 'array of seemingly contradictory insights and arguments' said to be presented by Marx and Engels on the question is contrasted, critically, to the sustained and internally consistent logic of Marx's economic analysis and his 'constant endeavour to penetrate between the 'surface appearances' of capitalism and its *underlying essence*'.[8]

There is, however, no unified 'underlying essence' to the character of trade unionism; it is an essentially *contradictory* phenomenon, and this is what accounts for Marx and Engels' apparently 'contradictory' responses to the class struggle (or lack of it) taking place around them. The contradictory character of trade unionism, and the dialectical nature of the necessary political response, is not sufficiently or explicitly theorised in the writings of Marx and Engels on trade unionism. Yet the distinction between the consistently subversive potential of basic industrial organisation, the grass roots of trade unionism, and 'trade unions' *as organisations* and, incipiently, bureaucracies, was the underlying reason for their apparent vacillations between feverish excitement about union struggles during working-class upsurges and strong disapproval of the general orientation of the trade unions during periods of acquiescence.

This instinctive 'nose' for the class struggle potential of grassroots trade unionism is evident in Engels' delighted response to the eruption of basic class conflict into the New Unionism of the late 1880s; a development which, though sadly too late for Marx, was greeted by Engels like a draught of water in the desert of 19th century craft trade unionism. As he wrote excitedly to Lafargue in 1889: 'These new trades unions of unskilled men and women are totally different from the old organisations of the working class aristocracy and cannot fall into the same conservative ways . . . In them I see the *real* beginning of the movement here'.[9] His estimation that these new unions could not 'fall into the same conservative ways' was before long revised by Engels himself, with a disillusioned re-assessment of leaders like John Burns and Tom Mann as symbolising 'the bourgeois "respectability" which has grown deep into the bones of the workers'.[10] But his instinctual awareness of the always subversive undercurrents of exploitation-based grass-roots class conflict had ensured that the *potential* for undermining the labour 'aristocracy' was, in Engels' mind, always a possibility. This class-centred 'optimism' is more than a simple naivety; it challenges the essentially *static* conception of class consciousness frequently embodied in assessments of the 'the unions' as implicitly monolithic organisations.

Twentieth century analysis of trade unions is, of course, more sophisticated in its understanding of the internally stratified nature of unions as social phenomena. Yet, in most of the renditions of economists and sociologists, 'modern' analysis is far more one-sided than Marx and Engels' instinctive understanding. The internal dynamics and contradictions of trade union life have been buried in a series of static theories, from the Webbs' glorification of union bureaucracy and Michels' declaration of its inevitability in his 'Iron Law of Oligarchy,' through the 'institutional' analyses of the American Wisconsin School and the 1950s 'maturity' theorists. All shared a belief in the inevitability and desirability of bureaucracy and stable labour relations. All imagined the direction of development to be a one-way street toward order and the professionalization of labour relations.[11] Marx and Engels, in contrast, saw something deeper beneath the organizational surface, in the living force of the workers themselves. The focus on the working class as the fundamental force in the struggle against capital; the recognition of the common *interests* of that class which lend it the potential, through struggle, to grow from 'class-in-itself' to 'class-for-itself'; the orientation, through this focus, towards the potential of basic trade union struggles as an aspect of class activity – all these aspects of Marx and Engels' analysis both flowed from, and led to, their consistent awareness of where the class was, rather than where they, and certainly their contemporary fellow-socialists, might have liked it to be.

This crucial orientation towards *existing* class realities is expressed in the *Manifesto* in its presentation of the 'theoretical conclusions of the Communists . . . [which] merely express, in general terms, actual relations springing from an existing class struggle, from a historical movement going on under our very eyes'.[12] As Engels wrote later, discussing the impact of the concept of historical materialism, '. . . communism now no longer meant the concoction, by means of the imagination, of an ideal society as perfect as possible, but insight into the nature, the conditions and the consequent general aims of the struggle waged by the proletariat'.[13]

This orientation on the part of Marx and Engels towards the 'actually existing' consciousness and organisation of the working class, rather than towards some separate, idealist construction of socialism, has been widely dismissed as implying a simplistic conflation of class activity with revolutionary consciousness. Certainly, the blithely determinist logic of the *Manifesto*'s statement that 'What the bourgeoisie . . . produces, above all, are its own grave-diggers. Its fall and the fall of the proletariat are equally inevitable' appears to sum up the crude historicism for which Marxism has been most frequently lampooned.[14] But what intervenes between such 'inevitability' and the reality of reformism is, of course, the issue of class consciousness; the *subjective* arena of which objective social and material realities can at best be regarded as an erratic and unpredictable undercurrent – a 'determinant in the last instance'. The consistent orientation of Marx and Engels towards such objective material conditions as *generators* of working-class struggle and organisation has been well noted; their awareness of the complex balance between such factors and the nature and progress of working-class consciousness and *realpolitik* has perhaps received less attention.

While, as we have pointed out, Marx and Engels failed to develop any explicit theory of the mutually influential relationships between concrete working-class conditions and class interests, activity and consciousness, they were clearly aware of the importance of more than simply the 'economic base' in conditioning such relationships. The essentially *dialectical* nature of the Marxist view of class consciousness, though never fully explicated, was rooted firmly in an awareness of the interrelation between material realities and the uneven, erratic but always materially-based development of such consciousness. In *The Poverty of Philosophy*, written a few years before the *Manifesto*, Marx developed the famous distinction between class-in-itself and class-for-itself, which bases the development of class consciousness not in theoretical abstractions but in the concrete requirements of capitalism and the organisational forms thus generated: 'Economic conditions had first transformed the mass of the people of the country into workers. The combination of capital had created for this mass a common situation, common interests. This mass is thus already a class as against capital, but not yet for itself. In the struggle, *of which we have noted only a few phases*, this mass becomes united, and constitutes itself as a class for itself. The interests it defends become class interests'[15].

The crucial reference here is to some earlier paragraphs in which Marx enunciates a description of the significance of working-class 'combinations' very similar to that put forward in the *Manifesto*: 'In England they have not stopped at partial combinations which have no other objective than a passing strike, and which disappear with it. Permanent combinations have been formed, *trade unions*, which serve as ramparts for the workers in their struggles with the employers'[16].

The significance of this argument is that 'economistic' struggles are not dismissed, as by so many socialists in Marx's time and since, as removed from any connection with political consciousness and socialism; rather, they are identified as the *central element* in the development of more explicit class consciousness and thus, potentially, a wider politicisation. In this sense the conception of 'class for itself' does not have to be confined to those historical moments when the working class consciously recognises its historic mission at the wholly political level of state power; it refers to a *transitional* dynamic, a *pull* through the materially-based necessity of basic struggles for what are *objectively* class interests towards the beginnings of a conscious, *subjective* awareness of class identity.

Of course, this 'pull' does not automatically take the form of an uninterrupted progress towards class unity, as implied by the enthusiastic young authors of the *Manifesto*. But the crucial insight around which Marx and Engels built their political lives was that the roots of *any* meaningful movement towards socialism by the class defined in terms of its potential for social transformation lie in the objective realities of class conflict which push workers, whatever their subjective consciousness, into resistance against capital.

Whatever the optimism of the clarion call rolled out in the *Manifesto*, it is these crucial insights we invoke in calling for a return by the left to 'class consciousness' – for a shift of emphasis away from programmatic rectitude on the one hand, and theoretical fixation on text or 'discourse' on the other, to the perhaps difficult recognition that the key to socialist advance lies in that most despised and least acknowledged expression of 'socialism from below', basic material class struggles.

II

The *zeitgeist* of the 1840s, when meetings of thousands of workers inspired by the 'People's Charter' took place on the Yorkshire moors, and even of the second decade of the 20th century when American workers travelled miles across the Great Plains to attend socialist tent meetings in equal numbers, seem to belong to another world from that of late 20th-century consumerism and individualism. In this 'post-modern' age, consciousness of so 'fundamentalist' a category as class appears to have shrunk to a scarcely discernible pulse, a sluggish bleep on the blank screen of a commodity-based culture pushed relentlessly to the wildest shores of the 'global village'. And yet there remains a countervailing force, all the more significant for swimming *against* this overwhelming ideological stream. The persistence of highly conflictual economic struggles entered into by workers whose subjective consciousness may be profoundly reformist, not to say conservative, continues to confound prophets of 'post-industrial' stability and to demonstrate, as we argue below, a transformative potential in terms of both consciousness and *praxis*.

Recent events in the US such as the change in leadership of the AFL/CIO, the waging of a number of climactic strike struggles and, at the time of writing, a key national victory – in a strike for jobs and greater pay equality – have opened up a new receptiveness to class thinking in that most individualistic of cultures. During roughly the same period, the simmering anger provoked by years of neo-liberalism has been reflected in open political protest on the streets of France, South Africa, South Korea, and many other countries. Such developments can be taken to illustrate the potential for renewed class-based revolt even after years of apparent quiescence.

How and why do apparently 'hegemonised' workers achieve such qualitative leaps into outright conflict with employers and the state? Marxist theoretical development in the wake of the distortions of Stalinism has concentrated almost entirely on the domination of such 'superstructural' factors as ideology, culture, and political process, and their role in structuring consciousness and blanking out dissent. In urging a more thorough exploration of the complexities of working-class consciousness and 'common sense', our own argument sets out to challenge this widespread assumption of the uncontested hegemony of ruling ideas.

We begin by reversing the critique. Just as a crude determinism of economic structures and interests cannot be assumed in the trajectory of class consciousness, nor can an uncontested 'overdetermination' of ruling-class or even reformist ideology be assumed to be a stable property of the capitalist system. Rather than positive endorsement of the ruling ideas of the epoch, a 'dull compulsion' to accept the apparently inevitable may be a more accurate description of at least some strands of working-class response to the prevailing system. And if we substitute fatalistic acceptance for coherent and positive consent, it becomes possible to sight gaps – potential breaks in the apparently seamless canvas of late 20th century 'common sense'.

We start by citing an *absence*: the absence of ideology. What is being proposed here is not that workers do not subscribe to ruling-class ideas wholly or in part, or that they do not accept, in one or other sense, the parameters of reformist ideology; the boundaries of that acceptance, and the pervasiveness of reformist ideology, are realities which if anything deserve much greater recognition in many segments of the left. Yet the impermanence, the instability, in many ways the fragility of this acceptance is also indicated when we probe more deeply into the precise nature of 'actually existing' working-class consciousness. Here we discover, rather than coherent and explicit assent to a consistent set of ideas and 'values', a more complex mix; one charac-terised less by undifferentiated ideological domination than by incon-sistency, contradiction, and lack of information.

The essentially incoherent nature of working-class social and political attitudes was noted in a cluster of studies produced in the 1970s which united in indicating that workers' views on general social issues tend to exhibit a mixture of indifference and inconsistency rather than active 'legitimisation' of the *status quo*.[17] The term 'pragmatic acceptance' was used by Michael Mann to express the essentially fatal-istic, rather than actively participatory, dimension of workers' outlooks.[18] Later, Scott Lash provided strong grounds for a dismissal of workers' perceptions of class and similar political concepts as confused and incoherent.[19] But workers' consciousness is also *contradictory* – a crucial feature allowing a corresponding potential for struggle and subversion of ideology. Edward's and Scullion's 1982 study of workplace organisation shows shop stewards subjectively endorsing the profit-related ethos of their management while objectively under-mining it with their own actions: 'There was, as it were, an uncon-scious form of resistance whereby stewards' everyday actions challenged managerial rights in many ways even though their articu-lated ideology involved commitment to the same aims . . .'.[20]

More recent research is less directly concerned with 'consciousness' but touches nevertheless on workers' outlooks and attitudes. For example, David Croteau's 1995 study of the apparently unbridgeable gulf between 'radical' and working-class politics shows that these (primarily white) workers' apparent dismissal of socialist ideas had little bearing on their endorsement of the prevailing ideology; in fact, as Croteau points out, the workers in his study were often considerably clearer as to the corrupt realities of present-day capitalism than were their 'radical' counterparts. Rather, workers' perceptions of society revealed a profound cynicism and fatalism, a sense that there is nothing you can do about these problems and that it is best simply to concen-trate on one's family and private concerns.[21]

This essentially abstentionist outlook confirms our hypothesis of an 'absence' of ideology or indeed any positive, coherent conception of social structure. Nevertheless, the fragile balance between 'pragmatic acceptance' and the underlying resentment indicated in the details of Croteau's study do not augur well for any prognosis of *stability* in the conduct of capitalist relations. While the issue of struggle is unexplored by Croteau, who leaves his workers as fatalistic and powerless as they began, such apparent resignation stands in sharp contrast to his inter-viewees' anger over issues of working time and labour intensification; issues which have propelled many similarly 'non-political' groups of workers into major industrial struggles in both Britain and America.[22]

The attempt to draw links between such material conditions and potentially subversive action has led in recent years to a revival of the old refrain about 'economic determinism'. Chantal Mouffe, for example, writes: 'How can it be maintained that economic agents can have interests defined at the economic level which would be represented *a posteriori* at the political and ideological levels? ... that amounts to stating that interests can exist prior to the discourse in which they are formulated and articulated'.[23] The problem with this kind of argument is that it in itself advocates a crudely 'deterministic' relationship between different levels of operation of capitalist production relations. Workers do not take part in resistance because of, or through, a 'discourse' which explicitly rejects capitalism in political and ideological terms. Such resistance, or disillusionment, occurs as a result of the material impact – on those who, because of their class position, have no alternative – of the contradictions operating within capitalist production.

Many of these are expressed in the collapse of the mythical 1980s 'prosperity' of Thatcherism, swallowed whole by British 'New Times' discourse theorists but cruelly undercut for workers by factors which were starkly, non-'hegemonically' economic. A 1992 study of British workers in the same 'Reagan Democrat' social stratum as those in Croteau's research (known as 'C2s' from their position in British socio-economic census categories) sheds light on the essential *instability* of skilled workers' adherence to the 'hegemony' of the Thatcher years.[24] Rather than the 'prosperity' and individualist 'consumerism' empha-sised in postmodernist analysis,[25] the overwhelming message that emerges from this research is one of widespread, and growing, economic insecurity. Respondents' 'perceptions' were only too well-founded on direct experience of redundancy, short-term contracts, house repossessions and the joblessness of their teenage children. The sense of insecurity and demoralisation conveyed in the words of these erstwhile working-class Tories – 'We are now going backwards ... struggling to survive' ... 'There's always that fear at the back of my mind' ... 'It's dire – we've hit the bottom and can't go any further' – is potent testimony to the lack of permanence of apparently impreg-nable hegemonic structures. Disillusionment with Thatcher's 'property-owning democracy', once acclaimed as the pinnacle of a new culture of 'individual aspiration', is compounded by the massive inten-sification of labour, alongside pay freezes and other pressures on living standards, experienced by those lucky enough to retain 'core' employment.[26]

But there is another side to the coin of this bewildered demorali-sation – the propensity of such economic factors to propel even the ideologically conservative 'C2's into action which challenges both capitalist production relations and the state. The relatively well paid and secure workers who, in addition to the much-vaunted 'self-employed', made up the subjects of the 1992 study were from the same stratum as those workers involved in key anti-employer struggles during the worst years of Thatcherism. The printworkers who fought the savage anti-Murdoch struggles at Wapping would fall almost entirely into the category hailed by post-modernist writers as swallowing whole the 'consumerist' bait of Thatcherism, as would Ford workers at Dagenham who staged a significant strike in the late 1980s which revealed the vulnerability of 'just-in-time' work arrangements. Many of the ambulance workers who took part in the protracted national dispute of 1989 were characteristic South-Eastern 'Tory waverers'.[27]

While the 'Reagan Democrats' and 'C2s' of our analysis so far, as predominantly white and (at least traditionally) 'privileged' workers, are generally presumed to be the most socially and politically conservative, the absence of coherent ideology and the presence of contradictory ideas is by no means exclusive to this stratum. In the face of very real fears of detention and/or deportation, immigrant workers such as farm labourers around the U.S. and Latino construction workers in Southern California have rebelled against their working conditions despite holding socially conservative ideas on reproductive rights, family 'values', and other 'hot button' issues. The point, however, is the same; struggles and confrontations based in class experience are seldom preceded by ideological clarity or 'political correctness'. If anything, it is the struggle that opens the way to new ideas and ways of viewing the world.

The lesson to be drawn would seem to be that no amount of conservative social ideology in the heads of workers is, ultimately, proof against their intermittent propulsion in an entirely different, and contradictory, direction. Yet it is the *economic circumstances* of these workers, rather than their initial consciousness, that propels them into resistance with the potential to challenge some of their most basic assumptions about the nature of the world. In this sense the struggle is not *chosen*, but neither is it, in certain circumstances, avoidable. Ideology may have lifted these workers out of their actual position in capitalist production relations; economic contradictions put them firmly back again.

Our focus on working-class consciousness or 'common sense' in terms of an *absence* of ideology, a 'pragmatic acceptance' of existing structures in contrast to any more positive endorsement of ruling-class ideology, needs to be complemented by a recognition of the impressive capacity of basic economic struggles for opening up, as it were, an 'epistemological break' in working-class consciousness. This has been testified to over and over, from the revolutionary upheavals of 1905, sparked by a dispute over compositors' piece-rates, to late 20th-century class insights gained by midwestern American workers through their involvement in struggles such as the strikes and lockouts at A.E. Staley in Decatur, Illinois, the Detroit Newspapers, and elsewhere.[28]

For well over a decade, a new 'common situation' (to borrow Marx's phrase in describing the formation of the early working class) has been experienced by ever wider sections of workers in both industrial and semi-industrial nations through drastic upheavals in the organization of work, labour markets, and even capital itself. Mergers, acquisitions, and transnationalization have produced ever more universal and visible organizations of capital. On the other hand, downsizing, contracting out, work intensification, and generally 'lean' norms of work organization now affect most working class people directly or indirectly across the world.[29]

This 'common situation' has had its impact in a measurable rise in class consciousness. A recent British survey showed the proportion assenting to the question 'Do you think there is a class struggle?' rising from 48% in 1964 to 81% in 1995.[30] In the U.S., the attitude toward strikes appears to have changed dramatically. While a 1984 poll showed that 45% of those questioned about strike situations supported management and 34% the strikers, in 1996 a nearly identical poll found a reversal of opinion as 46% sided with strikers and only 25% with management. More specifically, the recent wave of strikes at General Motors plants and, above all, the 1997 strike by 185,000 Teamsters against the United Parcel Service, gained majority 'public' support as more and more working people saw themselves in the same situation; polls indicated that 55% were for the UPS strikers and 27% for management. The fight for full-time jobs had become a social issue for much of the working class.

III

The story behind the successful 15-day strike at the United Parcel Service in August 1997 provides an almost laboratory-style example of the impotence of explicit capitalist ideology in one of its most contemporary and 'hegemonic' forms – when the company launched a concerted ideological offensive in preparation for 1997 collective bargaining – and, in contrast, of the impact of an *alternative* agenda of ideas and organization among rank and file activists.

The UPS workforce includes just about every level of the working class. The drivers, although not exclusively white or even male, are among the highly paid full-time workers described as 'Reagan Democrats' or 'C2s', while the sorters and loaders are racially diverse, mostly part-time, and fairly low-paid. The company believed that unity among these workers would collapse in the event of a strike, and large numbers of part-timers would cross the picket lines. What happened was the opposite. The strike was characterized by high levels of participation and mobilization, and a unity the company could not comprehend.

In the two years preceding the strike, the company mounted an ideological offensive meant to assure that disunity would be the order of the day. In 1995 they launched a new team concept programme, which like all such programmes was meant to win key sections of workers over to the company's ideology of 'competitive' goals – or at least to promote internalization of this piece of up-to-date bourgeois ideology among enough workers to head off an effective strike. The company overestimated the degree to which UPS workers would buy into this view of the world and the company, because they underestimated a process that had gone on among these workers for years – specifically, the long-term role of the Teamsters for a Democratic Union (TDU) and the more recent dynamic of reform within the Teamsters as a whole in preparing the workforce for a fight.

When it was formed in 1976, UPS workers were already a major constituency for TDU. The number of UPS workers who became active TDUers over the years was small in relation to the rapidly growing workforce, but the group provided a core of knowledgeable rank and file leadership among both full-timers and part-timers.[31] UPS workers were no less likely to accept the pro-company logic of team concept than any others; but they had access to an alternative 'common sense' in the form of the TDU activists, the regular publications of TDU, and the critical literature on the topic developed by *Labor Notes*, an independent trade union magazine and education centre in Detroit which was widely used by TDU and later the Teamsters Union. At the same time, the broader reform process, with TDU as its backbone, brought an entirely new leadership, headed by former UPS worker Ron Carey,[32] to power in the Teamsters and initiated a process of change across the union that affected many UPS workers. The new leadership was one of the few in the U.S. to explicitly reject team concept and the whole 'partnership' notion.

Mike Parker tells how TDUers reacted to the launch of the UPS team concept programme:

> In January 1995, UPS moved a trailer into its yard at the Ceres centre (outside Modesto, California) to be used for Total Quality Management (TQM) and self-directed work teams. Activists responded by getting *Labor Notes* and TDU material (which arrived promptly over-night via UPS, they point out) and prepared to deal with the programs from the beginning. Although the company controlled how the workers were divided up, the activists had sufficient numbers and training that they were able to effectively counter management in every team it set up.[33]

The union itself soon took up the TDU-initiated opposition to the team concept offensive. It directly confronted the pro-company ideological assumptions of team concept and in effect turned the entire company initiative around – *against* the goals of management. Teamster staffer Rand Wilson described the impact on the 1997 contract fight: 'The team concept campaign foreshadowed the contract campaign. UPS geared up its team concept activity as its preparation for the contract and by necessity we had to take them on as part of our preparation.'[34] Capitalist ideology not only failed to carry the day, it actually allowed or forced the union to campaign for a higher class consciousness.

The strike itself was not about team concept ideology, but about decidedly material issues and demands—above all the transformation of thousands of part-time jobs into full-time jobs, the reduction of the gap between part-time and full-time wages, and continued union influence over the pension plan. While there was a pay increase for the drivers, they had much less to gain in the most immediate sense than the part-timers who composed about 60% of the workforce. Yet they were as fervent as the part-timers.

Equally interesting in this respect was the more remote, yet sharply ideological fight over control of the pension plan. UPS workers in much of the country were part of a broader, multi-employer Teamster pension plan. UPS demanded its workers be taken out of the 'inefficient' union plan and put under a company-controlled plan, which, they claimed, would pay higher benefits. While the company's attempt to capture the pension plan may have been a bargaining ploy, the strikers took it seriously even though a certain leap in consciousness concerning the collectivist nature of the multi-employer plan was required. By the time the strike took place, that kind of collectivist consciousness was in place. UPS's attempt to convince them they could do a better job with the plan, because they were an efficient business, flopped completely. Union solidarity across company lines prevailed, a mini-triumph for working class collectivism.

The UPS strike victory was followed by a strong ideological reaction from the big business media and conservative politicians in the U.S. In the wake of the strike, the court-appointed officer who had overseen the 1996 election that put Carey back in office by a 52% vote declared the election invalid due to campaign funding irregularities she had uncovered earlier. Although Carey himself was not implicated, consultants he had hired had in fact broken the rules. For the *Wall Street Journal*, the *New York Times*, and other papers, this was a heaven-sent opportunity. They published a barrage of anti-Carey editorials and articles, often recycling the same news, in an attempt to discredit Carey and pressure the court into disqualifying him, thus in effect throwing the election to Hoffa. The media barrage was joined by pro-Hoffa Republicans in Congress – a chorus of ruling-class outrage at the effectiveness of a rank-and-file leadership that had actually been able to fight effectively for its own side. Yet, while the negative publicity was bothersome, it did not reverse the sense of achievement or the deeper class understanding which had been gained by many UPS workers over the past couple of years.

The argument here is not that workers are not susceptible to appeals for labour-management cooperation or the superiority of business efficiency. There are too many examples of company successes to deny that and, of course, these ideas abound across society as today's common sense. The point is, workers are no more possessed of these ideas than they are of the working class alternatives, which tend to already be present. When they are in struggle even over simply economic demands, the alternative ideas can make more sense. When, as in the unusual case of UPS, the ideas have an organized rank and file advocate and a leadership committed to them, it can be the working class 'common sense' that prevails. In this case, the working class 'common sense' became a counter-hegemony that allowed the union to buck what many thought to be an irreversible trend toward low-wage contingent work.

A similar scenario – or what, with conscious organisation, has the potential to become one – is suggested in the 1996 strike by British postal workers against the introduction of teamworking by their employer, Royal Mail. While these rank-and-file trade unionists fought the Royal Mail 'Employee Agenda' proposals with a tenacity that might suggest (as indeed much of the media darkly hinted) an explicit political agenda, the reality is that their struggle was rooted in basic material resistance to proposals which ultimately threatened their job security, working conditions and living standards.[35]

'Teamworking' (as team concept is usually called in Britain), along with many similar programmes, has of course been accepted by countless union leaderships despite these implications.[36] In the case of the postal workers, an unusually clearheaded and determined rank-and-file leadership, particularly in the London area, made a conscious effort to alert an already combative membership to the real meaning of the proposals in terms of their concrete effects on working conditions, in contrast to the 'empowerment' gloss invoked by management: 'The truth is it is not a case of workers having more control, but managers being in total control and workers just having to accept 'flexible' working but never having it really defined what they are accepting, because the parameters are so enormous and totally defined by the Business'.[37]

The series of strikes carried out by postal workers during the summer of 1996 succeeded, through a level of unity and cohesion similar to that at UPS, in removing every line of the 'Employee Agenda' from the bargaining table. The dispute is by no means over, of course; a management philosophy which has been in clear evidence since the 1980s suggests that temporary worker victories are now met by more concerted attacks, rather than consolidation. London Underground workers' combined resistance – uniting two normally rivalrous unions – to the company's 'Action Stations' plan in 1988 was followed by wave after wave of management offensive until the proposals were finally implemented – a melancholy example of the success of this retrenchment policy.

To maintain the kind of conscious class approach shown by the postal workers' local leadership in the face of such management aggression and strategic clarity[38] requires more than simple 'militancy', although the mobilisation of the membership and its willingness to fight are of course central elements. It also requires a level of awareness of the overall meaning and direction of management strategy which in effect exposes its roots in capitalist production relations centring on exploitation. Such a perspective is, of course, the opposite of the 'co-operation' and 'social partnership' approaches with which British and American trade union leaderships forlornly aspire to court the employers' non-existent benevolence. It denotes a sharp awareness of which sides you, and they, are on; an undeviating cleavage to *independent*, class-based forms of worker organisation.

This kind of explicit class perspective cannot be left to chance. It requires a *strategy* of grass-roots activist organisation of the kind which informs *Labor Notes* and similar projects in other countries and, more immediately, the sort of rank and file organisation exemplified in the TDU example above. But it is also important to be clear that the possibilities of class 'consciousness-raising' invoked in such activity are not the product of socialist wishful thinking, but of the material roots of resistance arising from class relations and conditions themselves. The political implications of 'everyday' working class struggle are not imposed from without, but are inherent.

Looked at from a purely 'political' perspective, the implications of the postal workers' resistance to teamworking, for example, are remarkable. Not only did they succeed in thwarting the goals of a multi-million pound 'corporation' in a struggle based on workers' rejection of supposedly all-powerful management ideology; they also resisted teamworking in direct defiance not only of their own union leadership but of the closely aligned 'modernist' perspectives of the (then) prospective Labour government.[39] The tradition of rank-and-file militancy which made this struggle possible was itself rooted in a series of spontaneous walkouts by postal workers which consistently flouted the draconian anti-union laws introduced by the Conservatives but stoutly backed by 'New Labour'. For workers supposedly colonised by (if not ruling-class then at least reformist) capitalist ideology, this stand must carry massive *potential* political significance. It remains to develop ongoing organisational vehicles through which such potential can be realised.

We have already referred to the impact of cataclysmic, long-fought struggles like the Staley dispute in transforming the consciousness of their participants – in a small number of cases, with permanent effect. Yet less prolonged and dramatic strikes like the postal workers', and more recently, that of British Airways cabin crew and catering workers, are linked to the same dynamic of detachment from both the material and ideological constraints of capitalism. Such 'breaks' in hegemony, which can be acknowledged to be an *ordinary* fact of capitalist class relations, do not stem from any pre-existing opening-up of consciousness amongst the workers concerned. Rather, in many ways they reflect the *ongoing* nature of working-class consciousness in its many-stranded character which both resists and admits the potential of a wider conceptualisation of existing socio-economic structures.

British Airways staff, particularly the cabin crew involved in one dimension of the dispute, are hardly the standard cast of working-class rebellion. Yet, like countless other groups of workers propelled into struggle, they were forced to transcend subjective conformity and conservatism by the brutal reality of (in their case) a 'Business

Efficiency Programme' based on a £1 billion cost-saving pay and conditions package which effectively freezes pay and removes overtime enhancements. In the words of one senior cabin crew member: 'We are being forced to strike for our basic rights'.[40]

The point here, then, is not that workers need to be 'incited' to resist capital by a corps of eager socialists. Rather, what is required of socialists is a commitment to focusing on and developing the implications of *existing*, contradictory, conflictual worker consciousness. The observation made by Lenin among others that the working class is ultimately far *more* revolutionary than any socialist 'vanguard' when it comes to fully- fledged struggle may seem absurd within today's round of undramatic, economically- motivated confrontations. But the point we are making here is that it is not the *readiness* of the working class to resist which is in question, but the understanding, channelling, development and sustaining of that readiness – and its potential for challenging labour movement reformism from within – by a socialist leadership locating itself within the class rather than reading that class politically-correct programmes from without.

IV

In making this point we are arguing for a reversal of standard left conceptions of socialist politics. Rather than proceeding from a carefully-worked out, analytically correct programme to the dissemination of such analysis to the masses (of one sort or another), this shift in perspective would abandon the pursuit of programmatic rectitude in favour of a focus on, and engagement with, existing levels of working-class consciousness and conflict.

The practical corollary is full adoption of a focus on working-class interests and struggle; a focus which has traditionally proved difficult for the left. The recent 'resurgence' of labour has been enthusiastically greeted by many socialists, perhaps particularly in the U.S., resulting in a welcome stimulation of debate between left union officials and radical intellectuals. Unfortunately, even this degree of left turn towards some aspects of working- class *realpolitik* may not be adequate for what we would define as the task in hand; that of building an alternative, explicitly class-based, current of resistance to capital within at least the 'advanced' sections of the class.

Such an approach calls for a consistent orientation towards the everyday 'economistic' demands and actions of a working class which may exhibit, for principled socialists, a discomfiting conservatism on many issues, or at least the kind of gulf between its own conceptions and those of middle-class socialism shown in Croteau's study. Where this gulf relates to issues such as racism or sexism, it must of course be confronted; but confronted in context. Even given such difficulties, the kind of 'sacrifice' of principles and programme required of socialists in starting from where the working class is, rather than where they might like it to be, is in our view indispensable if existing patterns of working class resistance are to realise their objective potential and meaning. Any such process requires from socialists the ability to see, and draw out, the political and class implications of what may appear on the face of it to be decidedly 'non-political' struggles.

Encouraging a process of *transition* from acting on basic economic demands to the explicit understanding of the class meaning of such demands may require forms of organisation which are themselves 'transitional'. The concept of transition is central in shaping a politics which, through its necessary roots in working-class concerns and conditions, can act to build a 'bridge' between the material conditions which continuously propel workers into struggle and a political perspective which can address and make sense of that process.

Historically, structures like *soviets* have been the most revolutionary forms of organisation that encapsulate this transitional dynamic in arising from basic mass strike movements, while pointing toward class power. Such structures are of significance not least in terms of their *spontaneous* eruption during major episodes of working-class struggle. As such, they have been a feature not only of the revolutionary era of the first world war period but also of more 'up to date' upsurges. In 1972, Chilean workers set up *cordones* to fight for the Allende government; in 1979, Iranian workers created *shoras* to safeguard the overthrow of the Shah. The Portuguese revolution in 1974 almost immediately threw up workers' commissions which united workers across union barriers within the workplace; these developed rapidly into *inter-empresa* (inter-factory) committees which clearly mirrored the Russian soviets, from necessity rather than conscious imitation.

There has also been a history of political attempts to create cross-union transitional formations along the lines of the Minority Movement of the 1920s in Britain (with the Comintern encouraging similar efforts in the U.S. and Canada in the Trade Union Educational League, and with less success in France through the 'friends of unity' in the CGT).[41] The Minority Movement explicitly saw itself as 'a "transitional" organisation, a means of broadening the political consciousness of discontented trade unionists . . .' The main idea was not immediately to push 'the union leadership into militant actions from below' but rather to relate the Communists' '. . .work in the trade unions directly to the creation of a revolutionary consciousness *in preparation for* the acute crisis which would arise with the outbreak of conflict in the mining industry'.[42]

Along similar lines, the need to build a class-conscious, independent leadership, rooted *within* the labour movement in *anticipation* of future upsurges, is now being explicitly taken up in a growing number of countries through cross-union formations of various kinds, usually based around a publication. One of the oldest of these is *Labor Notes* in the U.S., but to the list of such publications and cross-union centres has been added *Trade Union News* in Britain, *Solidariteit* in the Netherlands, *Trade Union Forum* in Sweden, *Labour Notes* in New Zealand, and *Labour* in Taiwan, alongside the Transnationals Information Exchange (TIE) networks in Germany, Brazil and North America among others.[43] Such publications set out to make coherent what rank and file union activists do less visibly day in and day out as they operate on the terrain of their members' basic interests and need for class organisation.

Projects like those listed above, by publishing reports of struggles and issues across the class, providing support contacts in other sectors for those in dispute, and bringing activists across employment together in schools and conferences, begin to demonstrate to rank-and-file trade unionists the class *meaning* of their everyday activity, without the need for principles and programmes dictated from above. Such initiatives cannot be sufficient to *complete* the transition to a 'class for itself' consciousness by the activists involved; but they are a necessary beginning for such a process.

The issue of membership control over even workplace union leaderships is another central focus of these cross-movement organisations, as indicated in the interactions between US *Labor Notes* and union rank-and-file caucuses like Teamsters for a Democratic Union.[44] The constant flux identified above between the bureaucratisation of unions as organisations, and the subversion of this by the concerns and demands of the membership, has been *consciously* confronted by rank-and-file union activists in such formations with the deliberate adoption of strategies structured to pull in the *opposite* direction – towards the creation of organic links between the workplace-based concerns of the membership and the policies and actions of their representatives. In a few cases, like the rank-and-file based involvement of Teamsters for a Democratic Union in the demands and organisation of the UPS strike, the threads come together with a powerful result.

We have seen that, with or without the support of socialists, workers will continue to organise on the basis of their own necessary, if sporadic, conflict with the system to create 'ramparts' of resistance and, whatever their apparently conservative consciousness, intermittently enter into outright confrontation with employers and the state. Socialists have never been required to *generate* class struggle and organisation; where they may be useful is in pointing out its class meaning and potential. Existing efforts to adopt this approach remain slight in comparison to the yawning gaps in consciousness and organisation they confront; yet they present a crucial perspective, and example, of *cross-movement* currents of opposition and resistance, rooted in the labour movement, which can begin to build towards a class response to the deepening social crisis.

NOTES

1. Karl Marx and Frederick Engels, *Manifesto of the Communist Party*, in David Fernbach (ed), *Karl Marx: The Revolutions of 1848*, New York, Vintage Books, 1974, p. 91.
2. Ibid., p. 95.
3. Ibid., p. 96
4. Hal Draper *Karl Marx's Theory of Revolution: The Politics of Social Classes*, New York: Monthly Review Press, 1978, p. 81.
5. Ibid., p. 82.
6. John Charlton, *The Chartists: The First National Workers' Movement*, London, Pluto Press, 1997.
7. Richard Hyman, *Marxism and the Sociology of Trade Unionism*, London, Pluto Press, 1971, pp. 4, 8.
8. John Kelly, *Trade Unions and Socialist Politics*, London, Verso, 1988, pp. 9–11 (author's emphasis).
9. Engels and Laura Lafargue, *Correspondence* Vol. 2, p. 330, 17.10.1889.
10. Marx and Engels, *Selected Correspondence*, Moscow, 1953, p. 490.
11. Hyman 1971 *Marxism*, pp. 14–17; Kim Moody *An Injury To All*, New York, Verso, 1988, pp. 52–53.
12. *Communist Manifesto*, p. 80.
13. Engels, *The History of the Communist League*, Marx and Engels *Selected Works* Vol. 3, p. 173.
14. *Communist Manifesto*, p. 79.
15. Marx 1973, *op. cit.*, *The Poverty of Philosophy*, Moscow, Progress Publishers, 1973, p. 150 (emphasis added).
16. Ibid., p.149 (emphasis added).
17. For example, Howard Newby, *The Deferential Worker*, London, Penguin, 1977, Martin Bulmer, ed., *Working Class Images of Society*, London, 1975.
18. Michael Mann, 'The Social Cohesion of Liberal Democracy', *American Sociological Review*, 1970.

19. Scott Lash, *The Militant Worker*, London, Heinemann, 1984.
20. P.K. Edwards and Hugh Scullion, *Shop Stewards in Action*, London, 1982, p. 198.
21. David Croteau, *Politics and the Class Divide: Working People and the Middle-Class Left*, Philadelphia, Temple, 1995, p. 139.
22. Kim Moody, 'A New American Politics: Who will Answer the Invitation?' *New Left Review* 216, 1996.
23. Chantal Mouffe, 'Working Class Hegemony and the Struggle for Socialism', *Studies in Political Economy* 12, 1983.
24. Giles Radice and Stephen Pollard, *Southern Comfort, More Southern Comfort* and *Any Southern Comfort?*, Fabian Pamphlets 555, 560, 568 (1992, 1993, 1994).
25. For example, Stuart Hall 'Gramsci and Us', *Marxism Today* June 1987 and Charles Leadbeater, 'Power to the Person', *Marxism Today* October 1988.
26. See London Hazards Centre, *Hard Labour: Stress, Ill-Health and Hazardous Employment Practices*, London, 1994.
27. John McIlroy, *The Permanent Revolution? Conservative Law and the Trade Unions*, London, Spokesman, 1991.
28. 'Before I got into this I thought socialists had horns on their heads'; 'Capitalism doesn't work'; 'I'm a socialist now': sample comments by Staley workers quoted in Marc Cooper, 'Harley-Riding, Picket-Walking Socialism Haunts Decatur', *Nation*, April 8, 1996.
29. Kim Moody, *Workers In A Lean World: Unions In The International Economy*, London, Verso, 1997, pp. 85–113, 180–195.
30. Brian Deer, 'Still Struggling After All These Years', *New Statesman* 23 August 1996, pp. 12–13.
31. For background on this period of the Teamsters and TDU see, Dan La Botz, *Rank and File Rebellion: Teamsters for a Democratic Union*, London, Verso, 1990.
32. Carey was president of Local 804 since 1968, a giant, mainly UPS-based local in New York City.
33. *Labor Notes*: No. 224, November, 1997.
34. Ibid.
35. Cohen, Sheila, ed., *What's Happening? The truth about work, and the Myth of 'Partnership'*, London: Trade Union Forum, 1998.
36. Parker, Mike and Slaughter, Jane *Working Smart: A Union Guide to Participation Programmes and Reengineering*, Detroit: Labor Notes, 1994.
37. Ward, Dave 'Postal Workers Unite Against Teamworking' in *What's Happening? op.cit.*
38. Danford, Andy, 'The "New Industrial Relations" and Class Struggle in the 1990s', *Capital and Class* 61, Spring 1997.
39. Lucio, Miguel Martinez and Stewart, Paul, 'The Paradox of Contemporary Labour Process theory: The Rediscovery of Labour and the Disappearance of Collectivism', *Capital and Class* 62, Summer 1997.
40. Quoted in *The Guardian*, p. 5, 2nd July 1997.
41. M. Woodhouse and B. Pearce, *Communism in Britain*, New Park, 1975, p. 87; Roderick Martin, *The National Minority Movement* Oxford, Blackwell, 1974, p. 174.
42. Roderick Martin, *The National Minority Movement*, Oxford, Blackwell, 1974, p.179.
43. Moody, *Workers*, pp. 249–267.
44. La Botz, *Rank and File*.

THE PASSAGES OF THE RUSSIAN
AND EAST EUROPEAN LEFT

Peter Gowan

Between the two poles of Blairite accommodation to neo-liberalism and nationalist populist accommodation to xenophobia lies a socialist left of many millions in the former Soviet Bloc in search of socialist advance. These people can be found in the parties from the Ukrainian left in the East to the Czech Communist Party and the German PDS in the West, from the Lithuanian left in the North to the Bulgarian and Albanian Socialist Parties in the south. Throughout the region, the left and the labour movements have now experienced almost a decade of what Michael Ellman has aptly called Katastroika. They have watched the impoverishment and humiliation of tens of millions of people suffering the degrading consequences of what the pitiless Western powers call Economic Reform, while in the former Soviet Union and parts of South Eastern Europe barbarism itself remains in sight.

In such conditions, brought about in the first place by the far from inevitable failure of the Soviet project to offer a sustainable and credible alternative civilisational model to the advanced capitalist countries, it is hardly to be expected that the left in Central and Eastern Europe could quickly turn forward to the task of offering a new perspective of advance towards social progress and emancipation. What is at issue is, *rather*, its longer-term potential, which we can only begin to assess through a sober analysis of its most recent trajectory. This is what this article seeks to provide, concentrating on three main themes.

First, we must track the many differing political and ideological trends and configurations of trends in the different Communist Party leaderships in the 1980s for these profoundly shaped the subsequent course of left politics during and after the collapse of the Soviet Bloc. The initiative for actually dismantling the political systems of the Bloc actually came from within some of these leaderships, in other words 'from above'. Popular movements from below against Communist rule played some part, notably in Bohemia and the GDR, but their role has often been greatly exaggerated in the West.

Secondly, and the other side of the coin of Western images of 'civil society' against 'totalitarianism', we must examine the degree to which large parts of civil society remained attached to the values of socialism and indeed (though to a lesser extent) to the Communist Parties within the region. This has, on the whole, been widely under-rated. While electorates overwhelmingly rejected the authoritarian political system of single party rule, significant and in many cases large parts of the electorates retained perceptions of the former 'single parties' which were much more sympathetic to their record than 'totalitarian' theory could allow for. The interactions between these parties, the new Western-backed Social Democrats and the sections of electorates still oriented towards socialist values have demonstrated just how many links have been maintained between the former ruling parties and their societies: only in the Czech Republic out of all the countries of the former Bloc has a Western-backed social democratic party become stronger amongst parties to the left of centre than the former Communists.

And thirdly, the directions taken by the various post-Communist Parties have also been shaped quite strongly by the parties' perception of the new geopolitical situation in which they have found themselves. We will explore all these themes with reference to three sub-regions in what used to be called Eastern Europe: East Central Europe, known often today as the Visegrad countries; South Eastern Europe, particularly Bulgaria and Romania (leaving to one side the tragic special case of Yugoslavia); and Russia and Ukraine amongst the former Soviet Republics.

I. THE LAST ATTEMPT AT REFORM COMMUNISM

The collapse of 1989–91 and the subsequent evolution of the post-Communist Parties was shaped, of course, by the Soviet Communist Party leadership's attempt to reform the political and economic systems of the Soviet Bloc between 1985 and 1990. Gorbachev gained allies for the political aspect of his reform project from powerful groups in the Polish PUWP leadership and in the Hungarian HSWP leadership.[1] When these latter two groups gained majorities in their respective central committees at the start of 1989 a political opening towards liberal democratic pluralism was initiated within the Soviet Bloc.

These steps in turn destabilised the Communist Party leaderships in the GDR, Czechoslovakia, Romania and Bulgaria, all of whom had been resisting the Soviet leadership's programme of political democratisation. Moreover, unlike Gorbachev, the Hungarian democratisers were already committed to introducing capitalism along with liberal democracy and by 1989 this was also largely true of the Polish Communist leaders as well.

Gorbachev's reform project could be summarised in terms of three main planks: ending the party's political monopoly and moving towards political pluralism arbitrated by free elections; attempting to end the conflict with NATO, replacing it with what might be called a cosmopolitan liberalism; and scrapping the doctrine of the Bloc as an autonomous economic system, seeking to integrate it into the institutions of the capitalist world economy.

Ending the Party's Political Monopoly

By the mid-1980s the Stalinist political model of the single party system had long since lost its legitimacy, even within the party nomenklaturas themselves. During the collapse of 1989 no significant sections of the Communist Parties continued to try to justify a single party system. At best the political monopoly was justified as an instrument both to preserve the Soviet Bloc – the argument for stability – and to maintain the socialist economic system.[2]

The CPSU leadership had come to the conclusion that the lack of free discussion and circulation of information was crippling Soviet development, and between 1985 and 1989 Gorbachev gradually dismantled the vertical political control mechanisms through the campaigns first for 'glasnost', then for 'democratisation'. In June 1988, the 19th Party Conference of the CPSU scrapped the Stalinist constitutional principle of the 'leading role of the party' – by agreeing that the CPSU would have to *achieve* leadership by gaining popular support, instead of having it guaranteed constitutionally.

In Hungary competitive elections had been initiated in 1985, though without allowing full party pluralism; early in 1989, the HSWP Central Committee decided to move towards full-scale liberal democratic competitive politics. In Poland minor elements of subordinate pluralism had existed within the political system since 1956 (notably the small, independent Catholic political groups, represented in parliament and the media) but the PUWP's dominance had been underwritten constitutionally since the mid-1970s. It had then been challenged by the rise of Solidarity in 1980-81, followed by martial law and the suppression of Solidarity in the early 1980s. In attempting to re-engage the population with the regime, the PUWP leadership had resorted to trying to use referenda and had liberalised the media, but these methods were judged to have failed by 1988 and from the autumn of 1988 parts of the PUWP leadership were openly calling for radical change within the political order. This wing of the leadership then triumphed in early 1989 when the Central Committee decided to hold round table negotiations with the remnants of the Solidarity leadership in order to pave the way for free though partial parliamentary elections in the early summer of 1989.

Although other party leaderships sought to resist the dismantling of the 'leading role of the party' and the turn to liberal democratic pluralism, it is striking that only one of these leaderships had the confidence or energy to try to resist the democratic challenge in practice through the use of significant force: that was the nationalist Ceausescu in Romania. Even in the USSR, the attempted coup of August 1991 against the loosening of the bonds of the USSR was a feeble, lethargic effort.[3]

The Break with the Primacy of Power Politics

A second fundamental pillar of Stalinism was the primacy which it gave to state force and great power politics in the international arena. Both Lenin and Trotsky were acutely aware that the triumph of Communism was ultimately dependent upon the power of international Communism as a social movement and they sought to rebuild the energies of this movement both within Russia itself after the civil war and internationally. But under Stalin, the primacy of state power politics over all other values became fundamental, both in domestic and international affairs. While in the second world war this emphasis on the military aspect of Communism seemed eminently justified, its continuation and even accentuation during the post-war period was to have catastrophic consequences, leading to Soviet 'overreach' in East Central Europe, locking the USSR and its allies into trying to compete militarily with the USA and its allies instead of competing on the central front of social and cultural models of development, distorting Soviet economics and undermining the attractiveness of Soviet society.

The break with this Stalinist legacy was the most dramatic and obvious side of the politics of the Soviet leadership under Gorbachev: its ending of the Brezhnev doctrine its increasingly unilateral measures of disarmament and military disengagement and its adoption of new military ideas of minimum sufficient defence. All these changes were allied to a downgrading of state force for dealing with opposition in domestic life. This aspect of Gorbachev's programme, of course, profoundly affected the thinking of the Communist Party leaderships. The lesson drawn in much of the literature is that this is what led them to open their regimes to political democracy rather than attempting to resist popular pressures. But this aspect is almost certainly exaggerated as far as Czechoslovakia and the GDR is concerned.[4] They realised that their entire geopolitical context was being transformed and thus also, in the case of the East-Central European Visegrad countries, their relationship with West European capitalism.

From Autonomous Economic System to Integration in the World Economy

During the Stalin period the Soviet leadership had convinced itself that it could develop limitlessly on the basis of its own resources and internal division of labour without significant participation in the international capitalist economic system (a position which, of course, Zinoviev and Trotsky disputed). This belief continued to be a central tenet of official Soviet Bloc thinking right through the Khrushchev period and into the early 1970s. The nomenklatura of the Bloc believed that on the basis of their own autonomous economic system they could overtake the capitalist world and thus ultimately triumph, provided only that the Bloc was not once again subject to external attack. But at least from the early 1970s, confidence in this idea was progressively undermined with the Communist Party leaderships themselves. The USSR itself could not even feed its own population without importing grain from the capitalist world. During the 1970s various East Central European party leaderships sought to integrate their economies more deeply in the capitalist market, and when their policies failed, some of them (notably the Polish, Hungarian and East German leaderships) felt unable to draw back from even deeper international integration.

From the very start of his General Secretaryship this became a central pre-occupation of Gorbachev and his team. The strategic concept was to make Soviet integration into the institutions of the world economy possible by destroying the ability of the Western powers to continue branding the USSR as an enemy state rather than just a social competitor. Domestic political democratisation and the

turn away from power politics were to help to make this drive for international integration more possible.

For the reform Communists in the CPSU, this turn towards international economic integration was not supposed to be accompanied by
the social integration of the USSR into capitalism. Gorbachev hoped
for one world economy with two social systems, and indeed he hoped
that international economic integration would revive the socialist
project within the USSR itself. The Hungarian party leadership, on the
other hand, were committed by the late 1980s to Hungary's return to
capitalism. The Polish PUWP's nomenklatura was also increasingly
convinced that this was the only possible path for a Poland in which
the industrial working class had lost allegiance to the Communist
Party. This Hungarian and Polish view was not accepted by the
majority of the leaderships in the other East Central and South East
European Communist parties. While the Czechoslovak Communist
Party was ready to accept political pluralism, it remained committed to
preserving a socialised economy. The PDS leadership and government
in the GDR took a similar stance until, in February 1990, it felt unable
to resist the collapse of the socialised economy. Similar resistance to
capitalist restoration was maintained both by Iliescu in Romania after
Ceausescu's overthrow, and by the Bulgarian Socialist Party during
1990.

At the same time, these parties resisting capitalist transformation
lacked any common economic policy platform. This was equally true
of the Gorbachev leadership of the CPSU, which signally failed to
produce any coherent strategy for economic reform and whose
economic policies simply plunged the economy into deeper crisis. In
these circumstances large parts of the managerial nomenklaturas of the
Soviet bloc abandoned their efforts to maintain the socialised
economies and began a scramble for property rights, leaving the
Communist parties in their tens of thousands or using their party
connections for largely illegal transfers of property.

II. THE COMMUNIST PARTIES' ELECTORAL BASE AFTER
THE COLLAPSE

East Central and South East Europe.

Opinion surveys during the 1980s in the Visegrad countries and the
GDR showed that significant minorities of the population supported
the ruling parties. Even after the imposition of martial law in Poland,

polls in 1984 showed that 25% supported the Communist Party leadership, 25% were hostile to it and 50% either had no opinions or did not wish to express them.[5] Furthermore, the 25% supporting the party tended to hold socialist social values, particularly egalitarianism and nationalised property, while those hostile tended to be anti-egalitarian and in favour of the free market: Polish society was thus politically polarised on a left-right basis, with the PUWP supporters occupying the left. The same poll evidence shows majorities of the population supporting various central aspects of the social principles of state socialism.

Similar evidence is available for neighbouring countries. From 1985, competitive elections were taking place in Hungary, and these demonstrate that as late as 1989, the Hungarian Communists were gaining 30% or more of the vote[6] and such votes were indicative of support for left-wing political and social values. Polling in the GDR tells a similar story. Polls conducted there between 20th November and 27th November, 1989, showed the Socialist Unity Party (SED) as having the largest percentage of support of any party – 31%.[7] In Czechoslovakia polling in December 1989 showed majority support not only for socialised property but for central planning.[8] This pattern was equally evident in the Soviet Republics and in South Eastern Europe.

A further very important feature of political developments in the late 1980s and early 1990s has been the survival of the official unions of the State Socialist period as the dominant trade union confederations during the transition to capitalism.[9] They survived despite concerted efforts to weaken them on the part of governments of the Right, and of Western bodies like the ICFTU and the AFL-CIO. In Hungary, the main trade union centre, MSzOSz, retained some 3 million of its 4.5 million 1988 membership in 1991.[10] The Polish official union, OPZZ, emerged with 4.5 million members in comparison with Solidarity's 2.3 million members. The same pattern held in Czechoslovakia where the official federation, CSKOS, predominated.[11] In Bulgaria the official unions faced the most serious challenge with the emergence of an initially strong new union centre, Podkrepa, but after rising from about 350,000 at the end of 1990 to over 600,000 at the end of 1991, Podkrepa's membership declined to about 225,000 by the start of 1993. The old official federation's membership also declined, from 3 million at the end of 1990 to 2.5 million at the end of 1991 and only 1.6 million at the end of 1992, but its dominance within the trade union field was maintained. In Romania, the official unions also remained the strongest, although they fragmented into competing centres in the early 1990s. The continuing role of official trade unions has also been evident in the former USSR.

The official unions of the Communist period thus turn out not to have been mere transmission belts for a 'totalitarian' state without a significant social base; there was a substantial trade union constituency remaining in these organisations to be won by parties of the left if they were prepared to orient themselves towards it.[12] The strong showing of the socialist parties during the first part of the 1990s is thus scarcely surprising. Indeed, the puzzle is why these parties did not do much better in the first post-1989 elections than they did – why their votes were lower in the GDR and the Visegrad zone than polling evidence from the 1980s would have suggested. One explanation could be that erstwhile Communist supporters were temporarily swept up in the wave of enthusiasm for a transition to capitalism in 1989-90 and switched their support to the parties of the free-market right. This does seem to have been an important factor in the GDR elections of March 1990. Polling in early 1990 showed over 60% of the GDR electorate holding social democratic or socialist opinions, yet Kohl's campaign promises swung a big majority for the Right precisely in the traditional social democratic Saxon strongholds, leaving the PDS with only 16.3% and the SPD with only 21.8%.

On the face of it the same effect seems to have operated elsewhere. In 1990 and 1991 opinion polls showed large majorities in favour of so-called 'market economies' in Poland, Hungary, the Czechoslovakia and Bulgaria, with a majority the other way only in Romania. This support had dropped massively by 1994 (except in Romania where there was a reverse trend).[13] But this evidence of enthusiasm for the market among large parts of the electorate does not explain why the still large minorities hostile to the introduction of the capitalist market did not fully turn out for the 'post-Communists'. The reality is that there were large numbers of abstentions; many of those who told pollsters they favoured a market economy must have decided not to vote. In the 1989 Polish elections, less than 50% of the electorate voted for Solidarity: the turn-out was low. In 1991 when the first full parliamentary elections in Poland were held, total turn-out was 43%. In the 1993 Parliamentary elections both the turnout (52%) and the vote for the SDPR went up substantially and detailed analysis has shown that this correlation was central to the SDPR's success.[14] Parties of the Centre and Right in Hungary also failed to gain support from over 50% of the electorate on a low turnout, and the party that called fairly explicitly for free market capitalism, the Alliance of Free Democrats, gained only 21% of the votes cast.

The high abstention rate in Poland and Hungary suggests another puzzle: why was it that in the only two countries where the ruling Communist Party leaderships took autonomous decisions (in February 1989) to move towards pluralist democratic political systems, and where they had been campaigning for years for 'market reform', did the Communists perform worst of all the Communist parties in the region? If the great issue of these elections was freedom (and the free market) against totalitarianism, why did these two parties perform worse than the two parties that resisted democratic change and the market – the East German and Czechoslovak parties?[15]

This points to the possibility that the poor performance of the Polish and Hungarian parties had nothing to do with freedom versus totalitarianism, but was linked to another feature that distinguished these two parties from the Czechoslovak and East German parties. This was the fact that their party leaderships had for some years been vigorously promoting policies which tended to contradict the socially egalitarian ideologies of their parties - policies of increasing marketisation and increasing social differentiation - with increasingly negative effects on those sections of the population in whose name they ruled: policies which were not being promoted by the Czechoslovak and East German parties whose economies were more successful under centralised planning.[16] Evidence from the results gained by smaller parties in the Hungarian elections tends to confirm this view that the HSP's low vote was partly the result of its pro-Market orientation. While the HSP gained 10.9% of the vote a further 8.8% of votes went to small parties, mainly further to the left on the issue of marketisation. The HSWP gained 3.7%, but more significant is the fact that a group of Agricultural Technicians stood on the single issue of opposing the break up of agricultural co-operatives and gained 3.2% of the vote; and some local political leaders from the HSWP days stood separately from the HSP as a network of local leaders and gained 1.9%.

Research on all these issues still needs to be undertaken. What has been offered here is nothing more than a set of hypotheses based upon some empirical pointers. But it would certainly explain the rather general revival of the fortunes of these parties as the 1990s progressed: their levels of support were returning to the trend of the 1980s. And they did so despite strenuous efforts by anti-Communist parties and the media to delegitimise these parties. It would also suggest another conclusion: that a significant minority of electorates may have held social values to the left of the post-Communist Party leaderships and may indeed still do so.

Meanwhile in what may be called, in a broad sense, the Balkans, the 'post-Communists' tended to emerge from the first elections as the strongest parties. This occurred in Romania, Bulgaria, Serbia, Montenegro, and later Albania.[17] These initial successes were not momentary: these parties retained strong support even if they were, in Bulgaria and Albania, subsequently to go into opposition.

Russia and Ukraine

In the Soviet case far more than in East Central Europe, the populations experienced the collapse of both the single party system and of the Union itself as something external to them and traumatic. After 5 years of growing economic crisis under the auspices of the reform Communists' 'perestroika' there was great disillusionment with the Gorbachev leadership, and the elections for the Congress of Peoples Deputies showed hostility on the part of voters towards candidates from the party apparatus. But popular political allegiance was transferred to other leaders and groups within the CPSU nomenklatura, particularly those at Republican level offering republican rather than all-Union solutions to daily problems. This was true both in Russia, where former Politburo member Yeltsin sought to build his base as a leader of the Russian federation, and in Ukraine where the party leader Kravchuk championed the idea that Kiev could solve problems better than Moscow.[18]

These developments have often been viewed as the rise of ethnic nationalism against Communism but outside the Baltic States and parts of the Caucasus this view is very misleading.[19] At the time of the Soviet Union's collapse, ethnic nationalism was a very minor force in the three big Slav republics and in Kazakhstan. And republican nationalism, though hostile to 'Moscow' as the all-Union centre, was not necessarily anti-Communist. This picture appeared to be transformed utterly by the failed coup of August 1991, which was followed by the banning of the Communist Parties of Russia, Ukraine and Belarus in the autumn of that year.[20] But these prohibitions were ambivalent steps which by no means signified a unified popular hostility to the Communists. On the other hand the last two years of the CPSU had been a drawn out and increasingly chaotic fragmentation and paralysis which undoubtedly did much to undermine public support. The banning of the CPSU at the same time enabled the Communist nomenklatura groups in power at republican level to free themselves from political constraints and maintain their positions of power, while also freeing themselves from All-Union party disciplines. And it enabled hundreds of thousands of members of the managerial nomen-klatura to easily turn their backs on Communism and throw themselves into the scramble for private wealth.

Continuing support for the Communist Party in Russia could not be tested until the party was refounded in February 1993 with a declared membership of about half a million. Over the next three years its support grew rapidly from 12.4% (6.7 million votes) in the December 1993 elections to 22.3% (15.5 million votes) in the December 1995 elections (to which should be added another 5 million votes of other basically Communist forces). In the first round of the Presidential elections in June 1996 the Communist candidate Zyuganov gained 24 million votes and this figure climbed to just under 30 million, or 40.4% of the electorate, in the second round.

In Ukraine the Communist Party leadership responded to the ban of August 1991 by forming a Socialist Party of Ukraine in October of that year. Its relationship to the former Communist Party of Ukraine was ambiguous: its leader refused to declare it the legal successor of the Communist Party but most of its members considered it as such. Its membership rose from a mere 29,000 in 1991 to 80,000 in 1994, making it by far the largest party in Ukraine.[21] When the Communist Party of Ukraine was able to re-emerge legally in the summer of 1993, at least half of the membership of the Socialist Party left to join the Communists, who claimed a membership of over 130,000 in October 1993. In the parliamentary elections in the spring of 1994 the Socialists, Communists and Agrarian parties formed an alliance which gained a substantially larger share of the vote than any other party. The official first round result overall for the alliance was 21.78% but this seriously underestimates left support because the electoral system encouraged many to stand as 'independents', including many successful candidates allied to these left parties.[22] Within the left alliance the Communists gained by far the largest share of the votes – 14.84% as against 3.7% for the Socialists and 3.24% for the Agrarians.

At the same time, both in Russia and Ukraine, public opinion's continued support for collectivist economic and social values and for social egalitarianism and social security is far more extensive than its support for the post-Communist Parties themselves. In 1996, opinion polls continued to show, for example, an absolute majority of the population preferring big industrial enterprises to be state owned rather than privatised.[23]

The failure of Western-backed social democratic parties to mount a significant challenge to the former Communists anywhere in the region apart from the Czech Republic is due above all to the fact that these parties failed to demonstrate any serious commitment to social egalitarianism and social welfare: they were simply too far to the right in their social programmes to gain an audience.[24]

III. DIVERGENT PATHS FROM SOVIET ORTHODOXY

If there has been a general pattern of continuing electoral support for socialist parties throughout the former Soviet Bloc, the directions in which the parties have travelled since the start of the 1990s have varied greatly. The different parties' directions were influenced by four main factors: where the parties stood electorally in the aftermath of the collapse; the geopolitical position of their country in the new international situation; the dominant trend in the party leadership after the collapse; and the party's location within the national political system.

The Parties in East Central Europe

In the Visegrad countries, the former Communists all were ousted from power in the first general elections, while at the same time their countries were being rapidly drawn into the Western alliance's sphere of influence. In both Poland and Hungary, the dominant groups within the new 'post-Communist' parties were firmly committed to becoming the dominant centre-left parties very much along the lines of the Party of the Democratic Left (PDS) in Italy. They also re-oriented themselves towards support for the European Union and NATO, eventually championing their countries' membership in both. The Polish Socialists did, however, include supporters of a traditional social-democratic persuasion, seeking privatisations and to limit the erosion of social welfare provision. The Hungarian Socialist Party has a small Marxist left with some intellectual influence, as well as a more pronouncedly neo-liberal wing even than the Polish socialists.

The Czechoslovakian Communist Party leadership, on the other hand, attempted to maintain a Marxist orientation, while accepting a liberal-democratic political framework. It refused to change its name and opposed the capitalist transformation of the country, adopting a stance somewhat like that of the French Communist Party under its present leadership. With the division of Czechoslovakia, the Czech Communists have maintained this course, while the Slovak Communists have divided, one branch being prepared to co-operate with nationalist formations hostile to the free market while the other has sought alliances with social democratic formations.

In Bulgaria, the post-Communists won the first elections and have been the ruling party for much of the 1990s, though currently in opposition. The consequence of their electoral victory was that many of the linkages between the party and state economic management groups, broken in countries where the former ruling parties were placed in opposition, remained strong. At the same time, Bulgaria's geopolitical position placed the party in an unusual international environment: it was not earmarked by the West European states to be drawn rapidly into their sphere, while for the USA, preoccupied with the Yugoslav wars, the most important goal for Bulgaria was political stability rather than Shock Therapy. In consequence, the BSP retained a leadership which, though internally divided, was much more concerned with handling the economic crisis of a country strongly tied economically to the former USSR than with engaging in rapid social engineering towards capitalism. The party continued to include strong Marxist currents and to retain strong attachments to collective forms of property both in the countryside and in the industrial sector, despite the leverage offered to the West by Bulgaria's very heavy debt burdens and extremely fragile financial system. With the Dayton Accords and manoeuvring between the USA and Russia over NATO enlargement, however, Bulgaria became a target of intense Western interest and its financial difficulties were used by the IMF powers to destabilise the BSP government, leading to a continuing grave crisis within the party itself.

The Romanian political transition was carried through by a combination of potentially radically opposed forces: a popular uprising against the Ceausescu dictatorship and a palace coup by Ceausescu's formidable praetorian guard. Political leadership was seized by the pro-Soviet wing of the Communist Party under Iliescu. This group then successfully stabilised a new regime by simultaneously banning the Communist Party and transferring its forces into a new National Salvation Front (NSF). In 1992 the NSF split into two separate movements, one led by Iliescu, the other by his former Prime Minister, Petre Roman. The Iliescu group then formed a Party of Social Democracy of Romania (PSDR) in 1993, while another group, led by Verdet, established a Socialist Labour Party, claiming allegiance to the traditions of Romanian Communism. The Iliescu group remained the dominant party in all elections up to the autumn of 1996, when it lost power to the Centre Right.[25]

With the Soviet collapse at the end of 1991, Iliescu's new Party oriented itself towards the introduction of capitalism, though initially of a strongly ' national-capitalist' rather than 'globalised' variety and with a declared commitment to continued welfare provision. The PSDR's privatisation programme was geared towards passing the ownership of the bulk of enterprises into Romanian hands rather than offering large scope for foreign buyers. Since the Ceausescu government had paid off Romania's debts, the IMF had little leverage against this orientation in the early 1990s.[26]

But Iliescu's orientation shifted in an increasingly Europeanist direction; signalled and reinforced by Romania's acceptance into the Council of Europe in November 1993.[27] The government gave up its earlier attempts to re-annex Moldova. In October 1995 the PSDR broke its alliance with the extreme right Greater Romania Party and during a visit to Washington Iliescu called the leader of this party and the leader of another allied far right party 'Romania's Zhirinovskies'.[28] Hand in hand with this has been Iliescu's positive response to the election of the HSP in Hungary in 1994, expressed in his desire to settle disputes with Hungary over minority and territorial issues, through an 'historic reconciliation' treaty between the two countries.[29]

The Post-Soviet Parties in Russia and Ukraine

The collapse of the USSR, and way it collapsed, profoundly shaped the new parties of the left in both countries from 1992. The reform Communists around Gorbachev accepted the banning of the CPSU in August 1991 and lacked the energy or cohesiveness to form a new party. When they did try to establish a presence they did so on the basis of accepting a capitalist transformation, while trying to insist that this capitalism should be humanised by social democratic values. They were thus swiftly marginalised as a serious force in Russian politics. Although various efforts were in fact made to create social democratic parties, support at the polls for groups roughly equivalent to Western social democratic parties has been insignificant: not more than 1%. Those prepared to maintain the networks of the banned Communist Party and to rebuild it when it was re-legalised were therefore overwhelmingly those who had opposed the Gorbachev reform effort of the second half of the 1980s. This leading group also bitterly opposed the break-up of the USSR and Yeltsin's programme for restoring capitalism. And they were able to draw upon the networks already established within the Russian Federation section of the CPSU before the collapse, networks with a strong traditional Stalinist stance.

Led from its foundation in 1993 by Gennadi Zyuganov, the Communist Party of the Russian Federation (CPRF) leadership has proved tactically astute and sophisticated in building a formidable coalition against the Yeltsin government. When the leadership of the Russian Parliament was goaded by Yeltsin's break with the constitution into trying to seize control of Moscow television by force, Zyuganov opposed this as a trap. Despite the extensive evidence of the Yeltsin government's fraud in the 1993 referenda and elections, the CPRF stuck to a strictly electoral strategy. It also sought to claim the mantle of patriotism for itself while repudiating links with the quasi-fascist party of Zhirinovsky. It thus displaced Zhirinovsky as the main opposition to the government until by 1996 Russian political life was polarised between the Communist Party and a government camp including Zhirinovsky's party. And while strongly championing the reconstruction of the USSR, Zyuganov also criticised from the start Yeltsin's military attack on Chechnya and holds that the recreation of the Union should be on a voluntary basis (although other prominent figures within the CPRF were more positive towards Yeltsin's military adventure).

At the same time, the CPRF's definition of Russia's predicament and of its own tasks sets the party apart from any other of the post-Communist Parties of the former Soviet Bloc. It presents the catastrophe which has overcome the country as if Russia has been the victim of something akin to a Western invasion and colonisation. The party's programmatic task is thus defined as a kind of national liberation struggle by all patriotic forces in all classes against imperialist capitalism and its anti-patriotic and largely criminal Russian stooges. The CPRF must then lead a national democratic struggle, drawing in not only workers and intellectuals but also patriotic capitalists. As Zyuganov explained in his speech to the CPRF Congress in April 1997, the restoration of 'rampant capitalism' is resulting, in practice 'in the progressive colonisation of Russia. Or rather, it is a qualitatively new form of waging war against our country. The dirty money, lies and provocations with which the fifth column arms itself have proved no less devastating to Russia than the incursions of Batu, Napoleon, and Hitler put together. In essence the Third Patriotic War is already raging in the wide territories of our country. . . .'[30]

The CPRF's economic programme calls for taking the commanding heights of the economy back into state hands, especially 'income-generating enterprises', and renationalising the banking sector, without excluding a role for private 'national capital' and small private businesses. It aims to crack down on capital flight, squeeze the dollar out of the domestic economy, restore the state monopoly of foreign trade in strategic sectors, 'strike resolutely' at criminal structures and corruption and increase taxation on non-productive property while easing taxation on commodity production. The party's political programme is centred first on returning power from the Presidential executive to parliament. But the party also champions the ultimate aim of reconstructing Soviets, to which labour collectives will nominate their representatives, and Soviets are counterposed to the liberal conception of the division of powers. As Zyuganov put it to the 1997 Party Congress, '[The Soviets] shape unity of action among power structures.' These goals are supplemented by a distinctive set of ideological themes and symbols, stressed by the Zyuganov group. These have been well brought out by Jeremy Lester,[31] who stresses that for Zyuganov the ethnos is the main 'agent of history'. And the Russian ethnos is integrally connected to Russian Communism. So too is the Russian orthodox Christian tradition.

These ideas are by no means universally shared within the CPRF. Although dominant since the party's founding, the Zyuganov group, which is most closely associated with the nationalist themes, is probably an ideological minority within the party. There are strong currents much closer to the outlooks of West European communists and there are also currents closer to Western social democratic ideas.

The Ukrainian post-Communist Parties provide an interesting contrast with the CPRF. After being a conservative bastion of opposition to the Gorbachev leadership in Moscow the Ukrainian Communist Party split before the break-up of the USSR, with the dominant group led by Kravchuk adopting a statist republican nationalism against the Gorbachev leadership in Moscow. This generated two currents of opposition to the Kravchuk wing of the CPU within the Party: conservative Communist opponents both of Gorbachev and of Kravchuk's nationalism, who favoured a return to Brezhnevite principles within a single Soviet Union; and a modernising current, led by Oleksandr Moroz, the leader of the Communist deputies in the Ukrainian parliament, which also favoured the separation of the Communist party of Ukraine from the CPSU.

Unlike Yeltsin, Kravchuk made no attempt to introduce Shock

Therapy into Ukraine. He declared that there were two main problems for Ukraine to solve: economic reform and state building, but that the priority was state building. This orientation appealed both to right-wing Ukrainian nationalists in the Western Ukraine and to the Communist-oriented Eastern Ukraine which was strongly hostile to the introduction of capitalism. Behind this position, large parts of the former nomenklatura proceeded to pillage the country's assets in ways very similar to those in Russia, with Kravchuk turning a blind eye. Against this background, Moroz sought to rally the Communist constituency in the country to the Socialist party formed in October 1991 while the CPU remained banned. He tried to develop a left socialist platform for economic modernisation, the development of a private sector but retaining a large state sector and a strong social security policy.

With the reappearance of the Ukrainian Communist party, Moroz's Socialist Party lost much of its base and membership to the reformed party. The latter expressed strong solidarity with the CPRF and declared its aim to be the restoration of the USSR, seeking a return to the status quo ante of the Brezhnev years. At the same time, it did not subscribe to the messianic Russian nationalist themes of the Zyuganov group and in its Eastern and Southern Ukrainian heartlands it was much more directly and strongly a champion of the cause of the industrial workers against their managements and against the local and regional bosses linked to first, Kravchuk, and then his successor Kuchma. And in national politics the CPU was prepared to seek alliances with Moroz's Socialist Party.

Thus the main themes on the Ukrainian left were much closer to the language of the Western Communist and left socialist movements than was the case in Russia, where the CPRF appears, in European terms, to be sui generis.

IV. CONCLUSION: DIVERGENT PATHS OF RETREAT

The main political fact throughout the region during the 1990s has been the terrible blow delivered to the self-confidence, organisation, living conditions and health of the great bulk of working people in all the countries concerned. This shock has thrown the post-Communist parties into ideological and programmatic retreat. Only the Czech Communists have felt able to hold onto a perspective of both transcending capitalism and retaining the democratic and working class commitments familiar to Communists in Western Europe.

Similar currents exist in nearly all the other parties and amongst socialist intellectuals throughout the region, but these other parties have tended either to attempt to follow the path already trodden by the Italian PDS towards a strategic accommodation with current capitalist dynamics, or have tended to attempt a nationalist appeal against the drive eastwards by Western state and business interests.

The Polish and Hungarian post-Communist Socialists are not *just* accommodators to casino capitalism. They are also important defenders of secular and democratic, anti-nationalist traditions. The Polish socialists have also avoided some of the more extreme versions of capitalist deregulation and privatisation. But what neither of these parties has been prepared to do has been to take a stand in defence of the principles of social citizenship and at least a minimal social egalitarianism. In this they have been to the right of their own electorates, very much in the mould of Blairite politics in Britain.

In Romania and Russia, on the other, hand the successors of the ruling Communist parties have sought to develop a nationalist-populist resistance to Western capitalist expansion eastwards. In the Romanian case this type of politics was launched by the state executive itself after the overthrow of Ceausescu and its aims were as much to do with attempting to stifle deeply antagonistic tendencies within the ranks of the National Salvation Front and Romanian society as with attempting to develop a project based on socialist values. The Iliescu government's attempts to manipulate extreme right, quasi-fascist groups for its own political advantage brought great dangers for Romania's Romany population and its flirtation with irredentist projects towards Moldova had nothing to do with any form of socialism. The Iliescu government was subsequently prepared to sign a Treaty with Hungary designed to settle the potentially explosive issues of border recognition and Hungarian minority rights. But its very capacity to exploit xenophobia at one moment and repudiate it the next was symptomatic of the fact that both the NSF and its successor PSDR were less like stable political formations and more bands of followers of a state leader.

In Russia, the CPRF leadership's nationalist political stance also takes it very far from either the Socialist or the Communist traditions of the West European left. Its definition of the situation facing the Russian people is basically false. Russia has been destroyed not by the force of a Western imperialist invasion but by the demoralisation and corruption of the ex-CPSU nomenklatura. While the weak, open economies of the Visegrad countries were brusquely subordinated to the diktat of the main Western capitalist powers, the West had very little coercive leverage over Russia when the USSR collapsed in 1991. The Yeltsin government had no need of the IMF credits offered in the summer of 1992, unlike its Polish or Hungarian counterparts. Alone amongst the countries of the region, Russia could have avoided dependence on the IMF/World Bank, despite the defaults of many of the countries which owed it debts. Western capitalist penetration of Russia was the result of the free choice of the Yeltsin regime, with, of course, powerful inducements from Western capital to allow themselves to be bought. And this decision to open Russia to Western capital was in turn the result of the utter demoralisation of the Soviet nomenklatura inherited from the Soviet period. No longer believing in the Soviet project, these bureaucrats have engaged in an orgy of criminal asset-stripping, with disastrous consequences for the economy and the Russian people.

The IMF's role in Russia has been more or less unprecedented in IMF history: it has supplied billions of dollars to the Yeltsin government largely regardless of that government's previous compliance with IMF conditionality in order that the government can use the money to sustain domestic political support. The IMF has done this in order to help secure a central objective of the Clinton and Kohl governments – preserving Yeltsin in power. While Western governments encouraged the dollarisation of the economy and facilitated capital flight, responsibility for these developments must still lie with the Russian government.

It is, of course, also true that the activities of Western financial operators in Russia and the policies of Western governments have been immensely destructive of Russia's economic assets. Western governments have wanted to weaken Russia and have also wanted to gain control of its energy and raw material resources. And the economic programme of the CPRF does address a great strategic choice as to the future of Russia: because of the exportability of the country's vast energy and raw materials, the Russian state could take what might be described as a Nigerian path in which the development of Russia's internal market and of the domestic industry to serve that market is ignored in the interests of a small group of compradors controlling a state which survives through the revenues derived from exporting energy and raw materials. That path would lead to the end of any democratic development in the country and to the long-term contin-uation of the present impoverishment of the Russian people. By emphasising national economic development, a strong state industrial sector and a nationalised banking sector, the CPRF does offer a progressive alternative development strategy for the country. All of this means that the CPRF would be justified in saying that it is defending the Russian nation as a whole from the slide into impoverishment and peripheralisation. Back at the end of the 1920s Trotsky warned: 'The Soviet system with its nationalised industry and monopoly of foreign trade, in spite of all its contradictions and difficulties, is a protective system for the economic and cultural independence of the country. This was understood even by many democrats who were attracted to the Soviet state not by socialism but by a patriotism which had absorbed some of the lessons of history.'[32] Trotsky added that a restored Russian capitalism 'would be a dependent, semi-colonial capitalism without any prospects' which would occupy a position somewhere between the third-rate position of Tsarist Russia and the position of India.

The CPRF also has to its credit the enormously important fact that it is a party of legality and a defender of constitutional government, in stark contrast to the Yeltsin government which has repeatedly shown itself ready to flout constitutional norms and the most elementary standards of legality, practising electoral fraud and chicanery in its drive to hold onto power and enrich the families of its ministers and their retinues. In short, the CPRF is the main bastion of constitutionalism within Russia today. It also has to its credit the fact that it has pushed the quasi-fascist so-called Liberal Democratic Party of Zhirinovsky, which in 1993 was the main opposition to the Yeltsin government, to the margin of the Russian political system. It has also fought the authoritarian demagogy of General Lebed.

Yet the CPRF's Zyuganov leadership promotes ideas which have nothing in common with any tradition of the socialist Left and which cannot be excused by the need to seize the patriotic banner from the Right. Zyuganov himself seems attached to some of the very worst aspects of the intellectual heritage of the Stalin years and to mark an ideological regression in comparison even with Brezhnev. His nationalism suggests a Russian spiritual superiority over other nations and it also contains disturbing suggestions of some sort of inner, organic unity of the Russian nation. Zyuganov's vision of the Soviets as expressing this supposed unity and as being superior to a supposedly destructive division of powers is very far from the conceptions of socialist democracy advanced by Lenin. If in the political field the CPRF has combatted the fascist Right, in the field of ideas and symbols, the Zyuganov leadership has made concessions to a Russian obscurantic mysticism which has nothing to do with the left. The party also has more than its share of people who hanker after a revival of Russian power politics. Within the CPRF itself there are, however, also many who utterly reject such themes and it is to be hoped that those who oppose Zyuganov's nationalism will grow in influence and help to reconnect the Communist movement in Russia with the Left in the rest of the world.

NOTES

1. The Polish United Workers Party later wound itself up and created the Social Democrats of the Polish Republic (the SDPR). The Hungarian Socialist Workers Party majority later formed the Hungarian Socialist Party (HSP) while the minority formed what is now the Hungarian Workers' Party.
2. In the early 1990s in the Czechoslovakian Communist Party a small neo-Stalinist group tried to advance the idea of a return to a single party system: they were swiftly expelled from the party. This lack of legitimacy was far less evident in the Slav and Asian republics of the USSR, except, increasingly, within the CPSU itself, as well as in liberal, democratic, Western-oriented sections of the intelligentsia.
3. During the August 1991 coup the CPSU leadership neither supported nor opposed it, remaining completely silent.
4. Even if the Soviet leadership had combined its democratisation programme with the maintenance of the Brezhnev doctrine, it is extremely unlikely that the governments of Prague or East Berlin would have attempted to use large scale force against the broad popular opposition movements in the autumn of 1989. Those who think that such a response would have been automatic should take note of the response of the Polish government in 1980 to the August strikes.
5. Lena Kolarska-Bobinska: 'Myth of the Market: Reality of Reform' in S. Gomulka and A. Polonsky (ed.): *Polish Paradoxes* (Routledge, 1991).
6. Bill Lomax: 'Hungary' in Stephen Whitefield (ed.): *The New Institutional Architecture of Eastern Europe,* (St. Martin's Press, 1993).
7. Dieter Segert: 'The SPD in the Volkskammer in 1990: A New Party in Search of a Political Profile.' in Michael Waller, Bruno Coppieters and Chris Deschouwer (eds.): Social Democracy in Post-Communist Europe (Frank Cass, 1994).
8. Sharon Wolchik, *Czechoslovakia in Transition,* (Pinter, 1991), and James P. McGregor: 'Value Structures in a Developed Socialist System: the Case of Czechoslovakia' *Comparative Politics,* Vol. 23, No. 2, 1991.
9. See the special issue of the *Journal of Communist Studies*: 'Parties, Trade Unions and Society in East-Central Europe', Vol 9, No. 4, December, 1993.
10. See Ruth A. Bandzak: 'The Role of Labour in Post-Socialist Hungary' in the *Review of Radical Political Economy,* Vol. 28, No. 2, June 1994.
11. For a valuable analysis of the Czech trade unions, see Anna Pollert: 'From Acquiescence to Assertion? Trade Unionism in the Czech Republic 1989 to 1995' Paper Presented to 2nd Conference of the European Sociological Association, Budapest, August 1995.
12. See *Labour Focus on Eastern Europe*, 49, Autumn 1994 and 55, 1996 for surveys

of trade unions in the region. See also Michael Waller (ed.): *Parties, Trade Unions and Society in East Central Europe* (Frank Cass, 1994) and Kirill Buketov: 'Trade Unions and Politics in Russia 1994' in *Labour Focus on Eastern Europe*, 50, Spring 1995.

13. In 1994 the proportion of electorate who said that they had previously supported the market economy but now rejected it were as follows: 21% in Poland; 28% in the Czech Republic; 29% in Slovakia; 32% in Hungary, and 47% in Bulgaria. See European Commission: *Eurobarometer Survey*, 1994.

14. Wade et al. stress that the higher turnout 'was perhaps the most important political reason for the strong emergence of the left in 1993.' See Larry L. Wade, et al.: 'Searching for Voting Patterns in Post-Communist Poland's Sejm Elections' *Communist and Post-Communist Studies*, Vol. 28, No. 4, 1995.

15. The Polish and Hungarian parties did worse than the PDS and the Czechoslovak Communists: respectively 10.9% and 12% as against 16% for the PDS and 14% for the Czechoslovak Communists.

16. A further factor in Poland may have been the fact the partial character of the June 1989 election: the electorate seemed to have a chance to protest against the PUWP government without facing the possibility of that government being removed.

17. In Macedonia the Communists were the largest party but were not able to form the government.

18. See Jonathan Steele: *Eternal Russia* (Faber and Faber, 1994) for the best account of the collapse of the USSR.

19. In the Baltic Republics and in Georgia strong ethnic nationalist parties did challenge the local Communist Parties.

20. Strictly speaking the CPSU and the Russian Communist Party were not banned in August 1991: their activities were suspended.

21. See Andrew Wilson: *The Ukrainian Left: In Transition to Social Democracy or Still in Thrall to the USSR?*

22. Thus although only 15 deputies were elected on an openly socialist party ticket, 27 joined their parliamentary faction; 19 deputies were elected on the official agrarian party ticket but 28 joined their faction in parliament.

23. See Renfrey Clarke: 'Public Opinion in the East', *Labour Focus on Eastern Europe*, 50, Spring 1995. See also Eurobarometer annual reports on the Central and East European Countries.

24. For a fuller analysis of these Social Democratic Parties and for the sources of Czech exceptionalism, see Peter Gowan: 'The Post-Communist Socialists in the East' in D. Sassoon: *Looking Left* (I. B. Tauris, 1997).

25. On the early development of the NSF see Tom Gallagher: 'Romania: The Disputed Election of 1990', *Parliamentary Affairs*, Vol. 44, No. 1 January 1991 and Mark Almond: 'Romania since the Revolution', *Government and Opposition*, January 1991. Petre Roman's Democratic Party-National Salvation Front has now set up an electoral alliance with the small Social Democratic Party of Romania. The Alliance is called the Social Democratic Union.

26. The IMF did insist upon the opening of a stock market, but the result was a stock exchange with 12 quoted companies only one of which was fully private. See Dan Ionescu: 'Romania's Stand-By Agreement with the IMF' *RFE/RL Research Report*, Vol. 3, No. 18, 6th May 1994.

27. See Dan Ionescu: 'Romania Admitted to the Council of Europe', *RFE/RL*

Research Reports, Vol. 2, No. 44, 5th November 1993.

28. On the vituperative dispute which followed these remarks, see Michael Shafir: 'Anatomy of a Pre-Election Political Divorce' *Transition*, 26th January, 1996

29. In the foreign policy field, the turn by Iliescu in 1993 has been equally marked. The PSDR government has declared membership of the EU and NATO to be its 'strategic goal' and has worked vigorously to try to ensure that Romania is allowed to enter NATO at the same time as any Visegrad countries. The government evidently has two serious fears: first that the first enlargement of NATO may also be the last, with the result that Romania will be left in a security void that Russia would seek to fill and that would in turn pull the country away from being able to join the EU; secondly, the government fears that Romania's exclusion from NATO's first enlargement at the same time as Hungary is included could generate a new and perhaps serious deterioration of relations with Hungary over Transylvania which could also make Romanian entry into NATO and the EU much more difficult. See Dan Ionescu: 'Hammering on NATO's Door' *Transition*, 9th August 1996.

30. Translation from *Sovyetskaya Rossiya*, 22nd April 1997 in *Socialist Action Review* Vol. 2, No. 7, June/July 1997.

31. See Jeremy Lester: 'Overdosing on Nationalism: Gennadii Zyuganov and the Communist Party of the Russian Federation', *New Left Review*, No. 221, January-February, 1997.

32. Trotsky: 'Is parliamentary democracy likely?' in *Writings, 1929* (Pathfinder Press, New York, 1975) p. 55, cited in *The Choices for Russia* (Socialist Action, 1991).

MARX AND THE PERMANENT REVOLUTION IN FRANCE: BACKGROUND TO THE *COMMUNIST MANIFESTO*

by Bernard H. Moss

To those who believe in fifty year Kondratieff cycles, those long waves of growth and deflation repeated in history, it is not accidental that the sesquicentennial of the *Communist Manifesto* comes after a quarter of a century in which its basic condition, the polarization of classes, has been realized. For just as in 1848, the year of its publication, the sesquicentennial falls after a long period of deflation during which wages and conditions have deteriorated and income inequality risen to unprecedented levels. Indeed, it is perhaps truer today than in 1848 that the condition of workers has sunk 'deeper beneath the level of existence of their class.' The sinking has taken different forms in Europe and America, with mass unemployment in the first – an eleven per cent average in the European Union – and disguised unemployment or low-wage unproductive jobs in the second. During the period 1973–93 in which GDP per capita rose 29% in the USA, annual male incomes fell 11%.[1] Never before in the history of capitalism have workers faced such a long-term impoverishment, which has enriched the owners of capital, more than quintupling the number of those earning more than a million dollars a year. More than ever, the factor determining life chances is not gender, race, educational attainments or even occupation, but access to capital.

The polarization between wage-earners and capitalists has not gone unnoticed. The last few years have seen signs of increasing awareness of the contraction of opportunity in capitalist society. 'Downsizing' and 're-engineering' have caused insecurity in both the working and the middle class. Despite the euphoria over prices on Wall Street the American dream of each generation doing better than its parents is fading.[2] Disillusionment with government has produced growing electoral abstentionism among workers in the U.S., France and Britain.

147

In France rising unemployment has produced a loss of faith in private business and the governing elite, and a demand for more state intervention that resulted in the election of the red-rose-green government of Lionel Jospin in June 1997.[3] It is not accidental that the only Western working class that has so far offered serious resistance to the exploitative pressures of capital is the one in the background of the *Manifesto*, so deeply rooted are political traditions that can be recharged and redeployed to meet new challenges.

As in 1848, France today is ruled by a social democratic coalition representing the working and middle classes with a programme for wage reflation, reduction of hours and job creation that is not explicitly anti-capitalist. As Marx foresaw, the experience of 1848 showed that capitalist resistance to even minimal reforms like hours reduction could lead to intensified conflict and even civil war. Jospin is likely to compromise his programme before approaching that point. Today as in 1848, when Marx was the lone Communist in a Parisian republican club, there are no mass vanguard parties, the Communists having abandoned the goal of socialism and dissolved into multiple currents; for the first time Left Trotskyists, Communists, Socialists and Greens have more in common with each other than they have with their respective parties. The striking absence from the movement today is that of intellectuals and the utopian imagination. As in 1850 when Marx first decided on the formation of a working-class Communist Party, time will tell whether its absence makes a crucial difference.

Marx's positions and analyses shifted with circumstances. He made three successive different interpretations of the revolution of 1848 and the Paris Commune, but that does not make his politics merely circumstantial.[4] There are contradictions between texts and within texts, but some explanations are more robust, some determinations more fundamental, and some historical formulations more balanced than others. His texts must be read as part of a corpus and understood in historical context, particularly in relation to the working-class movement that gave unity to his life and thought, for it is in the texts and formulations that engage with the working-class movement that Marx is the most illuminating. Conversely, it is when he loses touch with the movement – either when he takes up an ultra-revolutionary position, as in 1849–50 or, in reaction to its failure, a detached objectivism as in 1851–52 – that his vision becomes skewed and distorted. The first of these mistakes was subjectivist – the belief that all was made possible by political will; the second was objectivist – the belief that human action could not change the immutable laws of history.

These deviations occurred because of the disintegration of the social democratic movement with which Marx identified, particularly in Germany; but the subjectivist one, amazingly enough, prefigured the future, both the Paris Commune and 1917.

THE POLITICS OF THE COMMUNIST MANIFESTO

A sketchy pamphlet written for a small sect, the mostly German League of Communists, the *Manifesto* is nevertheless the most complete and balanced expression of Marx's politics, largely because of its engagement with the larger democratic movement. One reason it was not much noted in 1848 was that most of the ideas it contained were commonplace among working-class democrats, certainly in France.[5] The greatness of the work lies in the synthesis. The history of society is the history of class struggle that tends to polarize between workers and employers under capitalism. Communism is seen arising from a double movement, the economic development of capitalist society, polarizing classes and stimulating class struggle and organization, and the activity of the Communists, the most advanced and resolute section of the working-class party, who push it forward, understanding the goal and line of march and need for unity across industries, localities and nations. As in the past, the outcome of the struggle is open-ended; it could result in the revolutionary re-constitution of society or the common ruin of the contending classes.

According to the *Manifesto* the Communists do not form a separate party but act as a vanguard in the democratic working-class movements of different countries: Chartists in England, agrarian reformers in America and Poland, radicals and social democrats under middle-class leadership in Switzerland and France, and democrats supporting the bourgeois revolution in Germany. Marx recognized that the bourgeoisie helped to organize the proletariat through its own struggles against feudalism. The success of the bourgeois democratic revolution would, he argued, clear the way for direct class struggle and organization against the bourgeoisie. Communists in Germany should support the bourgeoisie so long as it acted in a revolutionary way, even to the extent of restraining their own demands; yet they should never cease to instil antagonism to it into the workers, so as to be able use the political and social conditions it must necessarily introduce as so many weapons in the fight against it that would begin immediately with the fall of the reactionary classes.

The aim of the Communists was to make the proletariat the ruling class by winning the battle for democracy. By 'democracy' Marx meant not a formal system of parliamentary governance, but a class coalition of workers, peasants, and petty bourgeois, the movement of the immense majority in the interest of the immense majority. For them he proposed a transitional programme of political and social democracy, including measures of gradual nationalization that would be too radical for the system to absorb and which, outstripping themselves, would lead to socialism. Marx and Engels hoped that the proletariat with its revolutionary momentum would be able to lead this process, but realized that the middle class might be able to exploit the parliamentary system for its own purposes in order to stabilize capitalist relations and halt progress toward socialism. The proletariat had a better chance of assuming leadership in the course of armed struggle than in electoral contests and parliamentary debates. Thus, a second revolution might be needed. The actual course of the 1848 revolutions demonstrated, however, that the bourgeoisie could not stand the risk of parliamentary democracy, and that the real choice lay between worker-led revolution and reaction.[6]

In the *Manifesto* the purpose of working-class rule, which Marx in 1850 called the dictatorship of the proletariat, was to wrest by degrees all capital from the bourgeoisie, to centralize all means of production in the hands of the state and increase the total of productive forces as rapidly as possible. The dictatorship was a transitional regime that exercised coercion against the capitalists, expropriating them, rapidly increasing the productive forces and thereby sweeping away the bases of class antagonism and of its own rule.[7] When Marx talked of the need to centralize and rapidly increase production he was thinking of less industrialized nations like France and Germany that had to catch up with Britain. In these countries the dictatorship would also have to prosecute the civil and international war that it would provoke, eventually carrying the revolution to the leading capitalist nation, Britain. Reform in one country could not be sustained unless the revolution triumphed on a world-wide scale. This was a rather extreme apocalyptic scenario that anticipated the dilemma of the Soviet revolution. What if the necessary conditions for the success of world revolution were beyond the political and economic possibilities of the moment?

Previously Marx had thought that the revolution would first come to the country that had the largest proletariat and most clear-cut class division. But in *The Class Struggles in France*, written in 1850, he recognized the revolutionary advantages of backwardness, what

Trotsky in 1905 was to call 'combined and uneven development.'[8] In France, conflicts among factions of the bourgeoisie, the subordination of peasants, petty bourgeois and industrialists to finance capital, and of the latter to English capital, are all superimposed upon the conflict between workers and employers. The proletariat, focusing the grievances of all the subordinate classes, leads them in a coalition against the bourgeoisie. In a revolution that combines democratic and socialist reforms the ideas of the French Revolution spur on the subordinate classes, carrying even a section of the bourgeoisie beyond the economic limits of their class interest. The revolutionary process makes up for economic and social backwardness.

LEGACY OF THE FRENCH REVOLUTION AND MARX'S POLITICS

The fundamental background to Marx's thinking and action in 1848–1851 was the French Revolution of 1789. Marx, a German philosopher, was ambivalent about the value of this heritage, at times regarding it as a spur, and at others as a barrier, to materialist class consciousness ('a nightmare that weighs on the minds of the living'[9]). At all events he was careful about making his own theoretical demarcation. Marxists have tended to take their distance from the French Revolutionary tradition; social democrats because of its association with dictatorship and terror,[10] and Communists because of their pretension to theoretical closure.[11] Conservatives since Edmund Burke have better understood the subversive potential of 1789 and 1792, 'the 'living and unbroken tradition'[12] running from Jacobinism to Marxism, but their analyses remained ideological, abstracted from social context.

As the French Socialist leader and historian of the Revolution Jean Jaurès declared, with only a bit of exaggeration, 'the French Revolution contains the whole of socialism.... Socialism was contained from the outset within the republican idea.'[13] Moreover, the Revolution was a whole, a 'bloc', as the radical-socialist Georges Clemenceau said in 1891. It cannot be separated into an antiseptic liberal phase and a bloody Jacobin one; the raging populace were present in the first just as a fraction of the bourgeoisie carried through the second. It includes the 1796 communist conspiracy of Babeuf, the most advanced point of the popular movement, as well as the arch-conspirator of the nineteenth century, Auguste Blanqui, whose politics were much closer to Marx's than tradition allows.

By background and reading Marx was steeped in the Revolution. He came from a part of the Rhineland that had been transformed by it. His father, and his philosophical mentor Hegel, were both enthusiasts for it. He spent most of 1843 in Kreuznach and Paris reading the *philosophes* and the history of the Revolution, both the bourgeois historians Adolphe Thiers and Auguste Mignet and the Robespierrist *Mémoires of R. Levasseur*, Philippe Buchez's *Histoire parlementaire de la Révolution française*, and possibly Filippo Buonarroti's *Conspiracy of the Equals*. From Rousseau, with his concept of the 'general will' overcoming the particular barrier of private property, he drew communist conclusions.[14] Obviously fascinated by the Jacobins, he was planning a history of the Convention.[15]

Marx alternated between bourgeois and Robespierrist interpretations without achieving a synthesis. From the liberal historians he learned of a class struggle of the bourgeoisie against the aristocracy for the abolition of feudalism. According to this reading, the bourgeoisie, faced with the resistance of the king and aristocracy, who came to represent all the injustices of the old regime, was able to arouse the enthusiasm of the masses in the name of the universal Enlightenment ideal of freedom. The Terror was a necessary instrument of the bourgeoisie to defend liberty against internal subversion and foreign invaders and to abolish the last remnants of feudalism and royalism.

From the Robespierrist historian Buchez, on the other hand, Marx would have gotten a different view of the Terror as an attack on bourgeois egoism and attempt to found an egalitarian community. Levasseur also saw the Jacobin republic as a sharp break with monarchy; from him Marx learned that it arose from the popular will, expressed in clubs and municipalities, smashed the monarchist state apparatus, and elected a unitary working body, the Convention, which combined legislative, executive and judicial powers.[16] This strong, coercive, unitary state, emanating from the popular will, prosecuting civil and international war and serving as a transition to a constitutional republic, became for Marx the archetype for the dictatorship of the proletariat.

The truth was multi-faceted. The Jacobin dictatorship did represent the bourgeois revolution at its most advanced point, but its alliance with the smallholding *sans culottes* was inspired by the egalitarian and communitarian ideals of Rousseau.[17] Arising from popular demands, measures of food requisition, price control, forced loans, state provision of work or welfare, and the distribution of the land of convicted traitors to the poor, all pointed toward a more regulated egalitarian society.[18] This was expressed in Robespierre's Declaration of the Rights of Man and of the Citizen, which defined property as a social convention subordinate to the rights of existence. But Marx and later historians found it hard to admit that this Robespierrist vision could be so subversive of the propertied order.

Yet it was only natural that its spirit would inspire a communist insurrection after the fall of Robespierre left the *sans culottes* without bourgeois allies or succour for their hunger. The ideal of smallholding democracy had been sustained by the alliance of the Jacobin fraction of the bourgeoisie with the masters and shopkeepers of the *sans culottes*. With the disappearance of bourgeois allies and return of dire hunger, the centre of popular gravity moved to the wage earners, who were one half of Parisian society. The proletarianization of the *sans culottes* prepared the way for the communisation of Robespierrism by Gracchus Babeuf.

Babeuf's conspiracy was preceded by two spontaneous uprisings, those of Germinal and Prairial, which demanded bread and the appli-cation of the Jacobin Constitution of 1793.[19] It arose out of recog-nition that for a popular uprising to succeed it needed the planning, offensive initiative and secrecy that only a small, tight-knit leadership could provide. The conspirators were agreed that only common, not equal, ownership, could prevent a return to inequality. Since the people did not yet understand what they required for happiness, the conspir-ators proposed to establish a temporary dictatorship, supported by the people in arms, that would eliminate its armed enemies, undertake measures of re-distribution to show the benefits of equality, and guide the people back to the Constitution of 1793. The conspiracy was not an isolated, eccentric plot by extremists, but had popular support from below and tentative links with the army and the government. It was the last expression of the popular democracy unleashed by the Revolution.[20]

From the history of the Revolution Marx could thus derive almost all the elements of his politics: class struggle and hegemony; the need to smash the old state; the necessity for a popular dictatorship to prosecute civil and international war, and as a transition to a more egalitarian order; and the process of permanent revolution. The revolution was permanent because it was continuous, uninterrupted, never stabilized. It followed an ascending line of radicalization, and a descending line of democratic participation, with each phase growing out of the preceding one. From the Constitutionalists to the Girondists and the Jacobins, each faction leaned on its more progressive neighbour for support. As soon as it had brought the revolution far enough to be unable to follow it further, each faction was thrust aside by the bolder ally that stood behind. As more and more radical strata came to dominate the scene, the springs of society, overloaded by the strain, snapped back to make the revolution conform to historical possibilities.[21] In fact, the revolution had left the classes so fissured that the bourgeoisie, threatened by both the aristocracy and working classes, had to rely on an expansionist Napoleonic dictatorship to establish stable rule.

Marx initially regarded the Revolution as a philosopher rather than a historian, in the light of a Feuerbachian critique of Hegel. According to this reading it had achieved merely a political emancipation that consecrated the sanctity of private property, creating through the legal equality of the liberal state an illusory community that masked the reality of propertied inequality. Jacobinism was but the extreme example of the political illusion that human will was sufficient to create equality, an illusion that led to violence and terror and ended with the reassertion of bourgeois society under Thermidor. Napoleon conducted the last battle of terror against bourgeois business interests by glorifying the state and 'substituting permanent war for permanent revolution.'[22]

In this Feuerbachian vein Marx saw the state as an independent power rising above social classes: the absolutist monarchy arbitrated between bourgeoisie and aristocracy,[23] the Napoleonic state was an end in itself, and the bureaucracy was a closed corporation oppressing society.[24] Marx also returned to this state-centred analysis to explain the Second Empire of Louis Napoleon. The revolution against feudalism had produced a bureaucratic state that was nonetheless infected by feudalism, by its spirit of hierarchy and domination. It provided sinecures for political adventurers and the propertied elite, usurped social and economic functions, and taxed the peasantry. In this light the Paris Commune of 1871 was initially perceived not as a socialist revolution, but primarily as a revolt against the centralized Napoleonic state.

But Marx rejected the idealism of this state-centred explanation of history, which became the basis for the Tocquevillian school, in *The German Ideology* and the *Theses on Feuerbach* of 1846. Here he abandons Feuerbach's contemplative materialism for an engaged one. There is no 'essence of man' to be realized in communism, but only the open-ended development of humans in their productive relations. The proletariat is to be transformed through revolutionary practice, without the help of theoretical anticipation and guidance; the only role of leaders and theory is to clarify existing consciousness. From the materialist viewpoint the state is merely a reflection of civil society and an instrument of the ruling class, the aristocratic monarchy, the bourgeois Napoleonic state. The French Revolution remained bourgeois, the Terror representing the plebeian way for the bourgeoisie to eliminate feudalism, Napoleon the military way of securing its interests.

This materialist view, while basic, was one-dimensional, leaving little room for political activity, theory and the relative autonomy of the state. The bourgeois revolution in its Rousseauistic phase had anti-bourgeois consequences. The working class did not immediately develop its own materialist consciousness, but in the nineteenth century stormed heaven with ideas borrowed from the bourgeois democratic revolution that preceded it.

THE FRENCH REVOLUTIONARY TRADITION AND SOCIALISM: 1830–48

These ideas were taken over and translated into socialism and communism after the July days of 1830 overthrew the restored monarchy with Parisian workers in the lead.[25] The outbreak of worker protest that followed was accompanied by a revival of republican and Robespierrist idealism. The school-teacher aristocrat Albert Laponneraye[26] opened courses for workers on the history of the Revolution that criticized Robespierre for not going far enough in the redistribution of wealth. Using the Saint-Simonian concept of exploitation, republicans focused on the plight of wage earners, proposing trade or producers' associations as the way to achieve worker ownership of the means of production. Blanqui, condemned to prison for trying to arm the workers, already saw history as a struggle of the oppressed against property-owning exploiters. The only way to resolve the duel between profits and wages was through common ownership in producers' associations. Workers, however, needed the guidance of 'intellectual pariahs' like himself.[27]

Young students and intellectuals organized skilled workers into revolutionary sections that adopted Robespierre's Declaration of the Rights of Man as their credo. The significance of the credo, which divided working-class from middle-class republicans, was that it implied at least a redistribution of wealth if not common property. The German section that adopted the credo, the League of the Outlaws, was the origin of the League of Communists. Like its French parent the German league had a programme for collectivization through state-aided producer cooperatives.[28] The mass organization of the *Droits de l'homme* – 3000 workers in 162 Parisian sections led by an elected committee of students and intellectuals – was outlawed and suppressed in 1834, but from its ruins came the secret societies and communism.[29]

To survive the suppression of press, freedom of association and jury trials, activist republicans needed organizations that were tighter and more disciplined, with secret, self-selected leaders. The Blanquist secret society, led by a triumvirate, kept its members in a state of readiness for a blow against the symbols of state power that would spark a general insurrection. This action would 'derive its legitimacy and force from the consent of the armed population who will represent the will of the great majority of the nation.'[30] Like the dictatorship of Babeuf, this one would also liquidate the enemy, satisfy workers' demands and gradually expropriate capitalists through the formation of workers' cooperatives, after which it would tend to wither away.[31] The similarity to Marx's conception is striking.

The League of Outlaws, renamed the League of the Just, participated in the abortive Blanquist uprising of May 1839. Blanqui paid the price of voluntarism and secrecy, always striking when the iron was not hot. 'The profound secrecy of the conspiracy had the effect that republicans were neither less surprised nor more prepared than the government.'[32] The secret society was a response to the suppression of public political life but one that severed its connection with neighbourhood sections and public opinion. When the revolution came in 1848 secret societies were in the vanguard, but only after a long depression had provoked popular protest and a middle-class banquet campaign for electoral reform had brought hope in the form of a public demonstration on the streets of Paris.

The secret societies that succeeded Blanqui's, like the *Société des travailleurs égalitaires*, which was divided into trades, workshops and factories, were explicitly working-class and communist.[33] The election campaign of 1840 set off five months of strikes and political agitation in Paris that saw the first public communist banquet and also the publication of Etienne Cabet's *Voyage en Icarie* and Louis Blanc's *Organisation du travail*. Blanc's programme for the gradual collectivization of industry through state-aided trade cooperatives became the panacea of social republicanism. Cabet, advocated a peaceful communism in which an elected parliament would act through wage increases and a progressive income tax gradually to collectivize property. Cabet had 200,000 working-class supporters.

Other communists like Théodore Dézamy, criticizing him for his reliance on the bourgeoisie, thought a violent revolution against the monarchy was required but did not exclude a parliamentary transition to communism. In the *Code de la Communauté*, which Marx, however, found infected with private property, Dézamy foresaw an industrialized communist society of abundance and 'generous equality.'

This, then, was the background to Marx's discovery, when he arrived in Paris in the Fall of 1843, that workers were communists, that sociability and 'the brotherhood of man' were 'no mere phrase with them,' and that 'theory and propaganda [were] their first end.'[34] Engels similarly discovered a revolutionary class among the Chartists in London. It was not without reason that they concluded that a majority of democrats, certainly working-class democrats in the major centres, were communists. 'Nowadays democracy is Communism. . . . Democracy has become a proletarian principle, the principle of the masses. The masses may be more or less clear about this, the only correct meaning of democracy, but all have at least an obscure feeling that the social equality of rights is implicit in democracy,' wrote Engels in 1846.[35] Moreover, in practice little separated him and Marx from middle-class radicals like Alexandre Ledru-Rollin, who with their programme of cooperative socialism were 'communists without knowing it.'[36] Engels wrote for Ledru-Rollin's daily *La Réforme*. The Jacobins of 1793 were the communists of today, Marx concluded on the eve of the 1848 revolution.[37]

Marx criticized French republicans for their 'phrases and illusions handed down from the Revolution,'[38] but theoretical differences were of little immediate consequence. The French republicans may well have had a better understanding of early industrial society than Marx. Though they acknowledged the class struggle that was just emerging between workers and employers, they focused on secondary forms of exploitation by landholders and financiers – the 200,000 electors of the July Monarchy – in the form of rent, interest and taxes. On the other hand they conceived of socialism as a final goal, rather than as a transition to communism made possible by the growth of productive forces. And they expected to succeed within the boundaries of France, whereas Marx asserted that socialism could not survive in one country without conquering Britain, which dominated the world market.[39]

MARX AND THE MID-CENTURY REVOLUTION: 1848–51

The working-class revolution that broke out in February 1848 in Paris installed a provisional coalition government that included the socialists Ledru-Rollin, Blanc and Albert, a metal worker and one of the first conspiratorial communists. Marx was invited as a guest of honour by the socialist minister Ferdinand Flocon. He joined the *Droits de l'homme*, one of 250 clubs formed by the working classes to pressure the government against bourgeois influence and push it towards the socialist 'organisation of labour.' He proposed sending delegates to the provinces to organize a demonstration calling for the deferral of elections. The government needed time to educate the public and demonstrate to it the benefits of equality, particularly to peasants under the thumb of local gentry. He marched 'in the shadow of Robespierre,' he said.[40] Alongside Blanqui he wanted to arm the workers in order to protect public liberties and to make sure ministers kept their promises. He also spoke on behalf of small manufacturers. His politics were indistinguishable from those of Blanqui who, apparently trusting to the ballot box, walked away in disgust from the ridiculous *coup de main* of 15 May that nonethelesss put him in prison.[41]

Marx and Engels returned to Germany and worked to build a social democratic coalition in support of the bourgeois revolution. For that purpose they had issued a seventeen-point programme. The demands were limited, so as to attract some bourgeois support: free education, limitations on inheritance, a national bank. Marx dispatched Communists to form workers' associations all over Germany. He joined the Cologne Democratic Association, was elected president of the local Workers' Association and launched the *Neue Rheinische Zeitung* as the advanced working-class organ of social democracy.[42]

But the bourgeois democratic coalition in Germany would not hold. The *Manifesto* had excoriated the German petty bourgeoisie as reactionary, helplessly dependent on the princes. Engels was surprised by the depth of popular unrest in Germany and the wide gulf separating workers and peasants from middle-class democrats. As regards bourgeois leadership of the revolution, Marx's pessimistic analysis of 1843 was vindicated. Frightened by the popular upheaval, the bourgeoisie refused to break with the old regime. Only the working class was in a position to carry on the movement, but German workers, dispersed over many states and divided by craft and guild affiliations, lacked the experience of a national struggle for power. It was too late for the bourgeoisie and too early for the working class to take up the struggle.[43]

The disintegration of the bourgeois democratic front in Germany conditioned Marx' analysis of the situation in France.

In June 1848 the dismissal of workers from the jobs scheme known as the national workshops provoked a mass uprising in Paris that lasted three days. Marx interpreted this spontaneous uprising, which lacked leadership and organization, as the working class breaking free from the petty bourgeois social democrats. After this Marx and Engels would interpret social democracy through a prism that fractionated it into proletarian and petty bourgeois components. This described a potential, rather than an actual, break between workers, organized in clubs and secret societies, and the parliamentarians of the Mountain like Ledru-Rollin. The latter made a huge advance in the elections of May 1849, gaining one-third of the peasant vote, perhaps half of the army and raising the spectre of a 'red' presidential victory in the election of 1852. They were committed to leading a rebellion in the event that Louis Napoleon used force against the Roman republic in violation of the Constitution. On 13 June 1849 Ledru-Rollin led a demonstration against the violation and called the people to arms. The uprising failed not because of the lack of will and 'parliamentary cretinism' of the petty bourgeoisie, as Marx claimed in *Class Struggles*, but for lack of revolutionary organization, coordination and initiative. The remnants of the Mountain in parliament after June were torn between real hopes of electoral victory in 1852, and workers and peasants in secret societies who had given up on constitutional processes.[44]

Marx and Engels hoped that a second revolution in France would save the faltering German revolution. The June Days in 1848 had demonstrated the futility of relying on social democracy and the need for a workers' party capable of leading any second revolution. After the failure of the military campaign to save the Reich Constitution in April 1849 Marx resigned from the Rhenish Committee of Democratic Associations and undertook to organize a congress of workers' associations and a working-class party.[45]

From friends in Paris he heard that workers were turning away from the Mountain to the secret societies. 'Blanqui has become their real leader, the permanent Revolution their goal.'[46] The peasants, weighed down by taxes and mortgages, were joining workers in opposition to the bourgeoisie. This was the context for *Class Struggles* in which Marx explained why uneven and combined development is a stimulus to revolution. The model is that of the permanent revolution, the armed workers pushing the petty bourgeois democrats forward in February 1848, but being abandoned by them in June. The fiasco of the demonstration of 13 June frees them from their last illusions and they rally around the revolutionary socialism of Blanqui. When the government restricted the suffrage in May 1850, disenfranchising the poorest third of the electorate, Marx and Engels urged the Blanquists to launch an insurrection that would establish a long-term dictatorship of the proletariat to confront the prospects of civil and world war.[47]

This ultra-revolutionary turn by Marx in 1850 is perhaps understandable in view the suppression of public political activity, but it went beyond the possibilities of the moment. On the other hand, it brilliantly prefigured the future – the Paris Commune and the Soviet revolution. The League of Communists in Germany was re-formed as a working-class party. In the March *Address* of its Central Committee Marx outlined a strategy of dual power in which the German working class would help bring the petty bourgeoisie to power and then, armed and organized in municipal governments and committees, push it forward to make maximum inroads on property before taking power itself, simultaneously with the next revolution in France. Marx's eagerness for action was seen in the international alliance he formed in London with Blanquists and other putschists. Called the Universal Society of Revolutionary Communists, it was organized as a self-selected party of combat dedicated to overthrowing the privileged classes, the dictatorship of the proletariat, and permanent revolution leading to the realization of communism–a remarkable anticipation of the Third International.[48]

By June 1850, however, Marx had concluded from the absence of response in France and from the evidence of world-wide recovery that the era of revolution was over. Ensconced in the British Museum, he set out to win intellectual victories with his work on economics while his politics languished. He turned disillusioned from revolutionary optimism to an ironic detached pessimism. The Hegelian abstractions of *Kapital*, from which workers' struggle is conspicuously absent, are a product of this period.[49] Marx had lost touch with workers and peasants, driven underground by repression. Nothing more, he thought, could be expected from workers exhausted by defeats and peasants incapable of social initiative. With the threat of proletarian revolution averted, the ruling class could settle the question of power amongst themselves, overcoming parliamentary division by strengthening executive power.[50]

This was the approach Marx adopted in the *Eighteenth Brumaire of Louis Bonaparte*, written in December 1851. Engels believed bourgeois press reports of peasant atrocities and called Louis Napoleon a mediocrity, his coup a farce. He urged Marx to write from 'the standpoint of world history,' of the inexorable Hegelian world spirit, 'a diplomatic non-committal epoch-making article.'[51] The resulting narrative is full of appearances, shams, illusions, ridiculous postures and the spirit of paradox. The model of permanent revolution is run in reverse as restoration *en permanence*. The revolution begins deceptively at its highest point with the proletariat in the lead, posing solutions which could not be realized, and proceeds in descending order. The victory of Louis Napoleon is not that of the bourgeoisie over the proletariat, but that of the executive over the legislative and the bureaucratic state over society. His juggling of contradictory interests, being all things to all men, produces instability that will lead to his downfall. The lumpenproletariat get spoils of office, the bourgeoisie get social order and public contracts, the peasantry get mortgage banks and nationalism, the working class get public works and promises of association. The account is, as Engels recommended, 'prolix,' over-complex and sophisticated, too contradictory, detached and ironic, missing the central tendency.

Missing is the centrality of class struggle that previously aroused Marx' hopes: the crises of January 29, March 21, June 13 now seen as merely rehearsals for Louis Napoleon's coup and the polarization of classes that took place in 1849 described in *Class Struggles*. Marx does not identify the main cause and consequences of the coup: the bourgeois fear of an electoral revolution in May 1852[52] and the uprisings of more than 100,000 peasants and workers from 900 communes, followed by the arrest of 26,884 mostly working-class republicans, the first mass political purge in history, that ended opposition and grounded political stability.[53] The description of the peasantry as an atomized 'sack of potatoes,' subsistence farmers needing state representation, is distorted. Smallholding peasants living together in villages, victims of market fluctuations and open to socialist propaganda, were the very people who carried out insurrections against the coup. If some – not all – approved the coup in the referendum, it was because they were terrorized. Marx foresees a revolution against Louis Napoleon that will do away with bureaucracy, infected with feudalism, while preserving necessary centralization, but he seems to regard state intervention of all sorts, for education, credit, bridge and railway building, as a usurpation of self activity. In his disengagement from class Marx retreats to his early Feuerbachian state-centred analysis.

THE FIRST INTERNATIONAL AND THE COMMUNE: BREAK OR CONTINUITY?

Marx did not return to an engagement with the actual workers' movement until 1864 and the formation of the First International, of which the most important product was the Paris Commune of 1871. Some writers have tried to distinguish between the 'Blanquist' Marx of 1848-1850, with his recognition of the need for vanguards and dictatorship, from a more accommodating procedurally democratic Marx of this later period.[54] This distinction is more than questionable. Marx's engagement with the labour movement of the 1860s was not essentially different from that of the democratic movement in 1848. In each case he was prepared to violate procedural norms and to break with the existing movement in order to accelerate the formation of the revolutionary party.

In the International Marx acted from behind the scenes to push it toward socialist conclusions, framing them '*fortiter in re, suaviter in modo* (bold in matter, mild in manner)' to make them acceptable to the existing labour movement.[55] Little pushing was at first required since the key group, the French Proudhonians, were being radicalized under the impact of strikes and the revival of republicanism. Marx had to exercise control over the British sections because the English lacked the necessary spirit of generalization and revolutionary passion.[56] Marx was drawn by the success of the German socialists to the importance of electoral politics as a means of organization and propaganda. The failure of the Commune and the repression that followed also pointed to the need for the formation of disciplined national parties that could contest elections.

This evolution was blocked by Michael Bakunin, the anarchist antagonist to state socialism, and his allies in the International, who rejected electoral action.[57] Following the fall of the Commune, Marx used his authority to convene a secret conference that extended his powers to combat the Bakuninists and passed a resolution, rewritten by him, that 'the proletariat can only act as a class by forming itself into a distinct political party opposed to the old parties formed by the propertied classes.'[58] Through his authoritarian methods Marx lost the support of nearly all the national sections and decided to transfer the headquarters to New York rather than allow the triumph of the federalist majority. The willingness to break with procedural norms to accelerate the movement was repeated in France in 1880 when Marx supported the split of the bourgeois intellectual Jules Guesde, a centralist, from the majority of federalists in the workers' party.[59]

Nor is it true that the Commune forced a revision of the *Manifesto*. The Commune proved that the working class could not simply lay hold of ready-made state machinery and wield it for its own purposes.[60] But from the time of his early notes on the French Republic Marx was aware of the need to break with the old state apparatus, which encapsulated the power of the ruling class, and for a new state arising from the working class. This idea was implicit in the *Manifesto* and explicit in the 1850 *Address*. French workers adopted a communalist strategy because they were strongest in the disenfranchised cities and because they were battling against a highly centralized and bureaucratic repressive apparatus.

Marx initially perceived the Commune not as a socialist revolution, but primarily as a revolt against the centralized state. It attacked the incubus of 'parasitic' bureaucracy, paying public officials a workman's wage (actually much more) and making them elective and revocable, reducing taxes for peasants and providing a free and unencumbered space for the class struggle. In the final draft of *The Civil War in France*, however, Marx came to appreciate that the Commune had more directly socialist objectives and that the Napoleonic state was attacked not as a parasitic excrescence, but primarily as the repressive apparatus of the bourgeoisie. The Commune, with its programme for trade cooperatives, was a lever for economic emancipation or expropriation. It did not merely reduce taxes, but reached out to peasants who were being ground under by capital. It did away with excessive bureaucracy but not with the necessary centralization of social and economic functions in the hands of the state. He did not regard it as a final transition to communism, but as the beginning of a long series of struggles and processes following capitalist development.[61]

While recognizing it as a workers' government, Marx in fact criticized it for not being enough of a dictatorship of the proletariat.[62] He was aware that, surrounded by French and Prussian troops, it faced insurmountable problems of survival. The first duty was military – to intimidate and repel the enemy. The National Guards had not taken advantage of the disarray in government ranks to launch an offensive against Thiers, but had instead conducted elections in which sworn enemies had been allowed to stand. Three months after the fall of the Commune Marx suggested that it did not meet the conditions for a

successful transition to communism of an armed proletariat constituting a revolutionary dictatorship.[63]

The Commune had more features of such a dictatorship than Marx
imagined. He never appreciated the revolutionary role played by his
own internationalists in preparing the ground, notably in the insurrection of 18 March that brought the Commune to power[64] – perhaps
because he did not control them and was surprised by their action. He
minimized the degree of political coordination and control that
actually existed through the action of the revolutionary socialist party
arising from neighbourhood committees, the creation of the
Committee of Public Safety in imitation of the Jacobins, and the use
of force against internal enemies, the banning of opposition press and
meetings, a show of strength that swung opinion behind the
Commune.[65] Marx does not discuss the contradiction between the
forms and content of democracy – he was never interested in forms of
governance and constitutional constraint – but the Bolsheviks also had
to sacrifice Soviet democracy in the Civil War in order to survive.

CONCLUSION: NEW ROADS TO SOCIALISM?

This essay has looked at the permanent revolution in France as
background to Marx's politics and the *Manifesto*. The French Revolution
was a violent resolution of the contradiction between forces and relations
of production, protocapitalist forces bursting through their feudal
integument, that combined bourgeois and democratic reforms.[66] The
key to its permanence was the resistance of the king, church and
aristocracy to the new political and juridical arrangements necessary for
the development of capitalism. To break that resistance the bourgeoisie
had to appeal to the peasantry and working classes, who pushed the
Revolution further than it wanted to go toward the abolition of
feudalism and under the Jacobins toward an egalitarian social democratic
state that was incompatible with bourgeois society. Faced with the
hostility of both aristocracy and populace, the bourgeoisie finally had to
rule by means of an expansionist Napoleonic dictatorship.[67]

The short cycle of permanent revolution was repeated in France over
the course of the nineteenth century with the working class emerging
out of the populace and communism out of social democracy. Worker
radicalism resulted from the popular depth of the anti-feudal bourgeois
revolution.[68] The French Revolution provided a model of social
democracy for the working class and of monarchist or Napoleonic
reaction for the propertied. The democratic revolution of 1848 could

not be accomplished without socialism. Rather than terror without end under parliamentary democracy the bourgeoisie chose an end to terror with another Napoleonic dictatorship.

Marx's politics were revolutionary because framed in the context of continental states in which the combination of feudal resistance to liberalization and the radicalization of the working class made peaceful transition and parliamentary government impossible. Here the proletarian revolution required the violent smashing of the old state and the establishment of a strong coercive government in the context of civil and world war. In countries with long constitutional traditions–and completed bourgeois revolutions–like the U.S., Britain and perhaps Holland a peaceful transition to socialism, he said in 1872, might be possible.[69] Of course, the absence of permanent revolution in these countries deprived workers of the spirit of generalization and revolutionary passion. But if reformism triumphed in the labour movements of these countries, it was because capitalism was able to provide expanding opportunities for higher wages and social mobility.[70]

These opportunities may now be closing. One of the features of the present situation reminiscent of 1848 is that even reformist campaigns in defence of the welfare state are fiercely opposed by business in the name of globalization and competition. The socialism of the *Manifesto* may once again appear on the agenda, but the path will not be the same. In societies in which wage-earners constitute the immense majority, there may not be a leading role for the manual working class or of a vanguard party. The 1848 revolution was preceded by an efflorescence of the utopian imagination, which made socialism seem practical and possible. Today a generation of intellectuals who once found the labour movement too reformist for their consideration are paralyzed by a belief in the 'world spirit' of globalization, not realizing that like Bonapartism it is partly the result of political defeats and resignation.[71] In the absence of socialist leadership, popular movements against capitalism may stray as in France into right-wing extremism or a self-defeating social democracy. The *Manifesto* warns us that without a historical theory and a vision of the future these struggles will end not in the 'revolutionary reconstitution of society' but in 'the common ruin of the contending classes.'

NOTES

1. Jeffrey Madrick, 'In the Shadows of Prosperity,' *New York Review of Books*, 14 Aug. 1997.

2. Andrew Sullivan, *The Sunday Times*, 4 Feb. 1996. *International Herald Tribune*, 6 March 1996, p. 1.

3. Bernard H. Moss, 'France: Economic and Monetary Union and the Social Divide,' in *The Single European Currency in National Perspective: A Community in Crisis?*, eds. B. Moss and J. Michie (London: Macmillan, 1998).

4. Cf. Alan Gilbert, *Marx's Politics: Communists and Citizens* (Oxford: Robertson, 1981).

5. See Karl Marx and Frederick Engels, *Le Manifeste Communiste*, ed. C. Andler, 2 vols. (Paris: SNLE, 1901).

6. Bernard H. Moss, 'Marx and Engels on French Social Democracy: Historians or Revolutionaries?' *Journal of the History of Ideas* 46(1985): 542.

7. Hal Draper, *'The Dictatorship of the Proletariat' from Marx to Lenin* (London: Monthly Review, 1987), minimizes its coercive character.

8. Michael Lowy, *The Politics of Combined and Uneven Development: The Theory of Permanent Revolution* (London: Verso, 1981), pp. 2–8.

9. Karl Marx and Frederick Engels, *Collected Works* (London: Lawrence and Wishart, 1975) 11:103, hereafter *CW*.

10. The revisionist Eduard Bernstein regarded Marx's politics in mid-century, particularly his address of 1850, as Blanquist. George Lichtheim, *The Origins of Socialism* (London: Weidenfeld and Nicolson, 1969), who stressed continuity with the French Revolution, also regarded 1850 as an aberration.

11. Exceptional are Roger Garaudy, *Les Sources françaises du socialisme scientifique* (Paris: Hier et aujourd'hui, 1948), and articles by R. Huard, C. Mainfroy and K. Halszapfel and M. Zeuski in *Cahiers d'histoire de l'Institut de recherches marxistes*, no. 21 (1985).

12. J.L. Talmon, *The Origins of Totalitarian Democracy* (London: Praeger, 1952), p. 249 and *passim*. See also, François Furet, *Revolutionary France, 1770–1880* (London: Blackwell, 1992).

13. Cited in Ian Birchall, *The Spectre of Babeuf* (London: Macmillan, 1997), p. 102.

14. Marx and Engels, *CW* 3:29–31, 142–4. Shlomo Avineri, *The Social and Political Thought of Karl Marx* (London: C.U.P., 1968), pp. 33–4.

15. Jean Bruhat, 'La Révolution française et la formation de la pensée de Marx,' *Annales historiques de la Révolution française* 38(1966): 125–70. Maximilien Rubel, 'Les Cahiers de lecture de Karl Marx,' *International Review of Social History* II(1953): 392–420.

16. Bruhat, 'Révolution,' pp. 140–1. *Mémoires de R. Levasseur* (Brussels: L. Hauman, 1830), I, 72–75, 113–5.

17. See Ellen M. Wood, 'The State and Popular Sovereignty in French Political Thought: A Genealogy of Rousseau's "General Will,"' *History from Below: Studies In Popular Protest and Popular Ideology in Honour of George Rudé*, ed. F. Krantz (Montreal: Concordia U.P., 1985).

18. Cf. Jean-Pierre Gross, *Fair Shares for All: Jacobin Egalitarianism in Practice* (London: C.U.P., 1997).

19. *Levasseur*, IV, 241, 256, V, 12–17.

20. Birchall, *Babeuf*. Filippo Buonarroti, *Conspiration pour l'Egalite dite de Babeuf* (Brussels: Librairie romantique, 1828).

21. Marx, 'The Eighteenth Brumaire of Louis Bonaparte,' *CW* 11:124.

22. Marx, 'The Holy Family,' cited in François Furet, *Marx and the French Revolution* (London: The University of Chicago Press, 1988), p. 139, and *passim*.

23. See Perry Anderson, *Lineages of the Absolutist State* (London: New Left Books, 1974), pp. 8–23.
24. Hal Draper, *Karl Marx's Theory of Revolution, vol I: State and Bureaucracy* (New York: Monthly Review Press, 1977), adopts this view.
25. Bernard H. Moss, 'Parisian Workers and the Origins of Republican Socialism, 1830–1833,' *1830 in France*, ed. J. Merriman (London: Franklin Watts, 1975).
26. *Cours public d'Histoire de France depuis 1789, en 1830* (Paris: Rouanet, 1832).
27. Samuel Bernstein, *Blanqui and the Art of Insurrection* (London: Lawrence and Wishart, 1971), pp. 59–62.
28. Marx and Engels, *Manifeste*, II, 16–17.
29. Moss, 'Parisian Workers,' pp. 210–14.
30. Cited by Jacques Grandjonc, *Communisme/Kommunismus/Communism: Origine et développement international de la terminologie communautaire prémarxiste des utopistes aux néo-babouvistes, 1785–1842* (Trier: Karl-Marx-Haus, 1989), p. 167.
31. Bernstein, *Blanqui*, pp. 81–3.
32. Cited in *ibid.*, p. 93.
33. Grandjonc, *Communisme*, pp. 159, 210–12.
34. Marx and Engels, *CW* 3:313.
35. *Ibid.* 5:5.
36. *Ibid.* 38:168.
37. *Ibid.* 5:545.
38. *Ibid.* 5:518.
39. Bernard H. Moss, 'Marx and Engels on French Social Democracy: Historians or Revolutionaries?' *Journal of the History of Ideas* 46(1985): 543.
40. Samuel Bernstein, 'Marx in Paris, 1848: A Neglected Chapter,' *Science & Society* III(1939): 347.
41. *Ibid.*, pp. 343–58. Moss, 'Marx and Engels,' pp. 545–6.
42. Hal Draper, *Karl Marx's Theory of Revolution, vol. II The Politics of Social Classes* (London: Monthly Review, 1978), pp. 212–14.
43. Moss, 'Marx and Engels,' pp. 543–6.
44. *Ibid.*, pp. 545–50. Also, my 'June 13, 1849: The Abortive Uprising of French Radicalism,' *French Historical Studies* 14(1984): 390–414.
45. Moss, 'Marx and Engels,' pp. 546–7. Draper, *Social Classes*, pp. 237, 247–9, 665.
46. *Der Bund der Kommunisten: Dokumente und Materialien*, Band 2, 1849–51 (Berlin, 1982), p. 513.
47. Moss, 'Marx and Engels,' pp. 551.
48. Norman Plotkin, 'Les Alliances des Blanquistes dans la proscription,' *1848: revue des révolutions contemporaines*, no. 189(1951), pp. 120–1.
49. See articles by J. Mepham, K. Tribe, and J. O'Malley in *Karl Marx's Social and Political Thought: Critical Assessments*, ed. B. Jessop, 4 vols. (London: Routledge, 1989).
50. Moss, 'Marx and Engels,' pp. 551–3.
51. Marx and Engels, *CW* 38:505, 516.
52. Thomas Forstenzer, *French Provincial Police and the Fall of the Second Republic: Social Fear and Counter-revolution* (Princeton, N.J.: Princeton U.P., 1981).
53. Ted Margadant, *French Peasants in Revolt: The Insurrection of 1851* (Princeton: Princeton U.P., 1979). J. Merriman, *The Agony of the Republic: The Repression of the Left in Revolutionary France, 1848–1851* (New Haven: Yale U.P., 1978).
54. G. Lichtheim, *Marxism: An Historical and Critical Study* (London: Routledge and

Kegan Paul, 1961), ch. 4. Cf. Monty Johnstone, 'Marx and Engels and the Concept of the Party,' *Socialist Register 1967*, pp. 12–58.

55. Marx and Engels, *Correspondence, 1846–1895* (London: Martin Lawrence, 1934), pp. 159–63 (Marx to Engels, 4 Nov. 1864).

56. Henryk Katz, *The Emancipation of Labour: A History of the First International* (New York: Greenwood Press, 1992), p. 65.

57. *Ibid.*, chs. 7–10. Bernard H. Moss, *The Origins of the French Labor Movement: The Socialism of Skilled Workers, 1830–1914* (Berkeley: University of California Press, 1976), pp. 71–82.

58. Cited in *ibid.*, p. 77.

59. *Ibid.*, pp. 106–21.

60. K. Marx and F. Engels, *Writings on the Paris Commune*, ed. H. Draper (London: Monthly Review Press, 1971), p. 226.

61. *Ibid.*, p. 76.

62· Cf. Monty Johnstone, 'The Commune and Marx's Conception of the Dictatorship of the Proletariat and the Role of the Party,' *Images of the Commune*, ed. J. Leith (Montreal: McGill-Queens U.P., 1978), pp. 204–05.

63. Marx and Engels, *Commune*, pp. 221(Marx to Kugelmann, 12, 17 Apr.), 224–5 (speech at London Conferenc, 1871), 233(Marx to Nieuewenhuis, 22 Feb. 1881).

64. Moss, *French Labor*, pp. 48–62, 73–5. Martin Phillip Johnson, *The Paradise of Association: Political Culture and Popular Organization in the Paris Commune of 1871* (Ann Arbor: The University of Michigan Press, 1996).

65. *Ibid.*, pp. 53–60, 116–22.

66. Ricardo Duchesne, 'The French Revolution as a Bourgeois Revolution: A Critique of the Revisionists,' *Science & Society* 54(1990): 321–50.

67. Despite torrents of revisionist abuse the best history is still Albert Soboul, *The French Revolution, 1789–1799: From the Storming of the Bastille to Napoleon* (London: Unwin Hyman, 1989). As Albert Mathiez remarked about Jaurès, the best historians of the Revolution have been political activists. An excellent commentary is Paul McGarr and Alex Callinicos, *Marxism and the Great French Revolution* (Paris: International Socialism, 1993).

68. For comparisons see Bernard H. Moss, 'Republican Socialism and the Making of the Working Class in Britain, France and the United States: A Critique of Thompsonian Culturalism,' *Comparative Studies in Society and History* 35(1993): 390–413.

69. Katz, *Labour*, p. 136.

70. See Neville Kirk, *The Growth of Working-Class Reformism in Mid-Victorian England* (London: Croom Helm, 1985).

71. See *Single Currency in National Perspective*, eds. Moss and Michie.

THE COMMUNIST MANIFESTO AND THE ENVIRONMENT

John Bellamy Foster

The rise of environmental issues to the forefront of contemporary political life over the last few decades has sparked a searching reexamination of the entire history of social thought. In a context set by a widening ecological crisis that now seems to engulf the entire planet, all of the great traditions of modern thought – liberalism, socialism, anarchism, feminism – have sought to reexamine their intellectual forerunners, dropping some ideas and picking up others in an effort to 'green' their understandings of society. As a result an impressive array of thinkers from Plato to Gandhi – have all had their work scrutinized in relation to ecological analysis.[1]

It is in connection with the work of Marx, however, that one finds by far the most voluminous and controversial body of literature in this regard. This of course is to be expected since Marx remains the preeminent critic of capitalist society. The extent to which his general critique (and that of the various traditions to which he gave rise) can be integrated with an ecological critique of machine capitalism is therefore of great importance. Indeed, much more is involved here than a mere question of 'political correctness' (understood in green terms). The overriding question is rather whether Marx's critique of political economy plays an essential part in the reconstruction of social theory in an age of planetary crisis. Further, how far does he offer insights that are crucial to our understanding of the contemporary ecological malaise?

The participants in this debate have fallen into three camps: those who argue that Marx's thinking was anti-ecological to its core, and directly reflected in Soviet environmental depredations; those who contend that Marx provided 'illuminating asides' on ecology in his work, even if he chose in the end to adopt a 'Promethean' (pro-technological, anti-ecological) viewpoint; and those who insist that Marx had a deep awareness of ecological degradation (particularly with respect to questions of the earth or soil), and that he approached these issues systematically, to the point that they entered into his basic conceptions of both capitalism and communism, and led him toward a notion of sustainability as a key ingredient of any future society.[2]

Most of the debate about Marx's relation to environmental thought has focused on the early philosophical critique of capitalism in his *Economic and Philosophic Manuscripts of 1844* and on his later economic critique embodied in *Capital* in the 1860s – since in both of these works he had a great deal to say about human interactions with nature. Nevertheless, the *Communist Manifesto* has often been invoked as presenting a view that was anti-ecological – some would say the very definition of anti-ecological modernism.

Indeed, the *Manifesto* is customarily viewed as a work that is at best oblivious to environmental concerns, at worst 'productivist' – even 'Promethean' – in character, steeped in notions of progress and the subjection of nature that are deeply anti-nature. This is important because the *Manifesto* is generally viewed as lying at the heart of the Marxian system and whatever flaws are to be found in the overall analysis are seen as having their roots there. Yet the question of the relation of the *Manifesto* to the environment is one that has never been addressed systematically. In our time this is no longer adequate, and it is necessary to ask: To what extent is the *Manifesto* – arguably the most influential political pamphlet of all time – compatible with ecological values, as we understand them today? Moreover, how is the *Manifesto* to be situated within the rest of Marx and Engels' thought in this respect?

THE SEARCH FOR A SMOKING GUN

One might suppose that compelling textual evidence that Marx and Engels were anti-environmentalist in orientation would not be hard to find. They wrote at a time when most thinkers embraced a mechanistic world view in which nature and human beings were seen as diametrically opposed to one another. Indeed, much of the European view of science from the sixteenth and seventeenth centuries on was governed by the notion that science had allowed humanity to escape nature's dominance and to become dominant in turn; and Marx and Engels certainly referred frequently – as did nearly all nineteenth century (and most twentieth century) thinkers – to the 'mastery', 'domination', 'conquest' and 'subjection' of nature.

But they did so almost invariably in contexts which refrained from making nature the enemy. Rather, the domination of nature was seen by them as a phase of historical development – part and parcel of the whole self-alienation of human society, which also meant its alienation from nature – which would necessarily have to be transcended under communism. There are innumerable passages strewn throughout their writings where Marx and Engels demonstrate enormous sensitivity to environmental issues. For example, the 23-year old Engels, in his first work on political economy, published in 1844, wrote: 'To make the earth an object of huckstering – the earth which is our one and all, the first condition of our existence – was the last step toward making oneself an object of huckstering.'[3] For his part Marx observed in 1844, in his *Economic and Philosophical Manuscripts*, that 'Man lives from nature, i.e., nature is his *body*, and he must maintain a continuing dialogue with it if he is not to die.' In this same work Marx complained that under the alienated existence of capitalism, 'Even the need for fresh air ceases to be a need for the worker. Man reverts once more to living in a cave, but the cave is now polluted by the mephitic and pestilential breath of civilization.'[4]

In his more mature works, from the 1860s on, Marx became increasingly concerned about signs of ecological crisis, particularly with respect to the degradation of the soil, which induced him to envision future communist society to a very large extent in terms of sustainability. Writing in volume one of *Capital*, Marx argued that 'the destruction' under capitalist agriculture 'of the eternal natural condition of the lasting fertility of the soil' – of the basic elements of 'the metabolic interaction between man and the earth' – through the disruption of the soil nutrient cycle, compelled 'its systematic restoration as a regulative law of social production, and in a form adequate to the full development of the human race.'[5] So dialectical (in the sense of many-sided) was this kind of analysis that William Leiss concluded in his pioneering study, *The Domination of Nature*, that taken together, the writings of Marx and Engels, 'represent the most profound insight into the complex issues surrounding the mastery of nature to be found anywhere in nineteenth century thought or *a fortiori* in the contributions of earlier periods.'[6]

Still, none of this has kept critics from attempting to find a 'smoking gun' to demonstrate beyond all doubt that Marx and Engels adopted a one-sided, exploitative view of nature. But in order to do so green critics have had to go to quite extraordinary lengths. In attempting to demonstrate (against all the evidence to the contrary) that the early

Marx was insensitive to nature, the social ecologist John Clark lays stress on the fact that Marx, while frequently referring to nature as 'man's body,' also referred to it as an 'inorganic' bodily link. He ends his critique by stating that 'Marx's Promethean and Oedipal 'man' is a being who is not at home in nature, who does not see the Earth as the 'household' of ecology. He is an indomitable spirit who must subjugate nature in his quest for self-realization.' But as evidence to back up this charge Clark is only able to offer some stanzas from Marx's youthful and not very remarkable poetry (written when he was 19 years old in 'The Book of Love, Part II,' dedicated to Jenny) in which he wrote,

> I am caught in endless strife,
> Endless ferment, endless dream;
> I cannot conform to Life.
> Will not travel with the stream.[7]

For Clark this is definitive proof that, 'For such a being [Marx], the forces of nature, whether in the form of his own unmastered internal nature or the menacing powers of external nature must be subdued.'[8] One cannot but wonder how many youthful poets Clark might not condemn based on like evidence. Who has never wanted to go 'against the stream'?

Other green critics have pointed, with more *prima facie* justice, to a passage by Engels in *Anti-Dühring* on the growing mastery of nature that will ensue once human beings have transcended social alienation:

> The conditions of existence forming man's environment, which up to now have dominated man, at this point pass under the dominion and control of man, who now for the first time becomes the real conscious master of Nature, because and in so far as he has become master of his own social organisation. The laws of his own social activity, which have hitherto confronted him as external, dominating laws of Nature, will then be applied by man with complete understanding, and hence will be dominated by man. . . . It is humanity's leap from the realm of necessity into the realm of freedom.[9]

Ted Benton criticizes Engels on the grounds that such a view 'presupposes control over nature' and hence 'an underlying antagonism between human purposes and nature: either we control nature, or it controls us!'[10] In other words, Engels is said to have adopted an extreme anthropocentric rather than ecocentric perspective. But is Engels' argument here really vulnerable to such criticism? Despite the use of such terms as 'master of Nature' the intent of this passage ought to be quite clear. It is that a revolution in social organization is necessary to allow human beings to avoid being simply prey to natural forces (or forces that purport to be 'natural,' as capitalist economic forces are represented in bourgeois political economy). In fact, what is being celebrated here is not human mastery of nature so much as the human mastery of the making of history, which gives humanity the capacity to reorganize its relation to nature, under conditions of human freedom and the full development of human needs and potentials. There is nothing here to suggest an underlying antagonism toward nature in Engels' notion of the realm of freedom. Communism, Engels observed elsewhere, was a society in which people would 'not only feel, but also know, their *unity* with nature.'[11]

The same response may be given to criticism of Marx's closely related discussion of the 'realm of necessity' and 'the realm of freedom' in volume 3 of *Capital*. 'The true realm of freedom, the development of human powers as an end in itself,' commences where the realm of necessity ends, 'though it can only flourish with this realm of necessity as its basis. The reduction of the working day is the basic prerequisite.'[12] The full development of human freedom and the human relation to nature, for Marx, therefore requires the transcendence of a bourgeois order which makes labour – the means by which the metabolic relationship between human beings and nature is expressed – simply a matter of bare, material necessity for the workers, even as the accumulated wealth and the combined powers of society grow. As Paul Burkett writes: 'The expansion of free time and collective-democratic control over the social use of the conditions of production in Marx's communism' establishes the fundamental basis for sustainability in social and ecological relationships because it creates 'conditions conducive to noninstrumental valuation of nature (i.e., to the further development of ecological needs and capabilities among the society of producers).'[13]

In the most revolutionary phase of human development, Engels along with Marx always insisted, the object would be to transform the human relationship to nature in ways that went beyond the childish notion of having 'conquered' nature. 'At every step,' Engels wrote near the end of his life, 'we are reminded that we by no means rule over nature like a conqueror over a foreign people, like someone standing outside nature – but that we, with flesh, blood, and brain, belong to nature, and exist in its midst, and that all our mastery of it consists in the fact that we have the advantage over all other beings of being able to know and correctly apply its laws.' One of the basic principles in relating to nature was in fact reciprocity, leading Engels to argue that one could view as a natural necessity the 'demand . . . that man shall give back to the land what he receives from it.'[14]

It is true that Marx and Engels focused on human needs rather than on those of nature and thus can be accused of being 'anthropocentric' rather than 'ecocentric.' But this is, from Marx and Engels' own standpoint, a false dualism. Nature and society, in their perspective, cannot be viewed as diametrically opposed categories, but evolve in relation to each other as part of a dynamic process of 'metabolic' interaction. This was similar in its broad outlines to what is now called the 'coevolutionary' perspective, in which it is argued that nature and human society each coevolve in a complex process of mutual dependence. The complexity of the interaction between nature and society envisioned by coevolutionary theory leaves little room for such ideas as 'anthropocentric' and 'ecocentric' since even in defending nature we are often defending something that was reshaped by human beings.[15]

RURAL SOCIETY AND AGRICULTURE

The difficulty of finding anything that would even today be considered a strongly anti-ecological statement in the work of Marx and Engels has meant that critics have often been compelled to quote the reference to 'the idiocy of rural life' in Part I of the *Manifesto* as their main textual 'evidence' (frequently their only such evidence) of the alleged anti-environmental orientation of the founders of historical materialism. For example, Victor Ferkiss states: 'Marx's attitude toward nature can in large measure be inferred from his numerous remarks about such things as 'the idiocy of rural life.' He was a notorious critic and indeed an enemy of the peasantry . . . Such an attitude is hardly compatible with idealization of unspoiled nature.'[16] The deep ecologist Gary Snyder adopts a similar view, claiming that within the U.S. today we are seeing 'an alliance of Capitalist Materialists and Marxist Idealists in an attack on the rural world that Marx reputedly found idiotic and boring.'[17]

There is a host of questions raised by these statements. What did Marx and Engels mean by 'the idiocy of rural life?' Is this to be regarded as an anti-ecological statement? Was Marx really 'an enemy of the peasantry'? In order to be an environmentalist is it necessary to idealize unspoiled nature? Was Marx a one-sided advocate of urbanism in opposition to rural existence, as some critics like Ferkiss and Snyder have suggested? Such questions are best addressed not in the abstract but through an examination of the *Manifesto* itself, along with Marx's other writings. The reference to 'the idiocy of rural life' comes in the midst of the paean in Part I of the *Manifesto* to the bourgeoisie's revolutionary historical role.

> The bourgeoisie has subjected the country to the rule of the towns. It has created enormous cities, has greatly increased the urban population as compared with the rural, and has thus rescued a considerable part of the population from the idiocy of rural life. Just as it has made the country dependent on the towns, so it has made barbarian and semi-barbarian countries dependent on the civilized ones, nations of peasants on nations of bourgeois, the East on the West.[18]

This is a very compressed statement which needs sorting out. In the first place, Marx had a classical education and we may presume knew that the meaning of 'idiot' in classical Athens derived from 'Idiotes', a citizen who, unlike those who took the trouble to participate in the assembly, was cut off from public life and who viewed it from the parochial, privatized standpoint. Pre-capitalist Europe – tribal, feudal – made peasants necessarily 'idiotic' in this sense. And while primitive accumulation only made things worse in this respect, there seems no reason to doubt that Marx thought the long-run effect of capitalism was to 'rescue' people from this by driving them into cities and new forms of association with each other. Like nearly all nineteenth century European intellectuals Marx and Engels saw the forces of enlightenment and civilization in their time as emanating principally from the towns. But their recognition of the way in which the bourgeoisie had made the 'country dependent on the towns' should not be seen as uncritical support for this social arrangement, since the best that could be said for it from their point of view (at least at this stage in their thought) was that it was a necessary part of the whole bourgeois revolution, inseparable from the general achievements of the latter.

Marx and Engels saw the dependence of the country on the towns as a product in part of the enormous 'agglomerations of population' that emerged within cities during the bourgeois era – an issue that they discussed in the paragraph immediately following the above quotation. Hence included in their vision of revolutionary change, as depicted in Part II of the *Communist Manifesto* (which was devoted to the historically specific demands of proletarians and communists) was an insistence on the need to carry out 'a gradual abolition of the distinction between town and country, by a more equable distribution of population over the country.' Indeed, throughout their writings – and with increasing emphasis in the later works such as Engels' *The Housing Question (1872)* – Marx and Engels insisted on the need for the abolition of the antagonism between town and country, whereby the latter became dependent on the former. They saw this antagonism as one of the chief contradictions of capitalism and a principal means through which a double exploitation of the urban proletariat and the rural worker (in England no longer a peasant) was carried out. 'The abolition of the antithesis between town and country,' Engels wrote in *The Housing Question*, 'is no more and no less utopian than the abolition of the antithesis between capitalists and wage-workers.'[19]

This sense of the contradiction between town and country was not a mere slogan inherited from the utopian socialists but was seen as taking the form of a rupture in the necessary 'metabolic' relation between human beings and nature. Thus in *Capital* Marx was to contend that by agglomerating the population in large urban centres capitalism: (1) 'prevents the return to the soil of its constituent elements consumed by man in the form of food and clothing; hence it hinders the operation of the eternal natural condition for the lasting fertility of the soil'; and (2) 'destroys at the same time the physical health of the urban worker, and the intellectual life of the rural worker.'[20]

It was the combined action of the emigration of all culture to the city, the dispersal of a shrinking rural labour force over a wider countryside, and the annihilation of traditional connections both to the soil and to human community, that Marx saw as the source of 'the idiocy of rural life' within bourgeois civilization. Thus he took seriously (though not without offering some criticism) David Uruquart's observation that society was increasingly divided into 'clownish boors' and 'emasculated dwarfs' as a result of the extreme division between rural and urban existence, which deprived one part of the working population of material sustenance, the other of intellectual sustenance. The point was not that nature was to be despised but rather that the antagonism between town and country was one of the chief manifestations of the alienated nature of bourgeois civilization.[21]

In their reference to the 'idiocy of rural life' Marx and Engels, who already saw capitalism as evolving largely along the lines of England, were not referring only to the peasantry, since one of the things that most distinguished the English political economy was the thoroughness with which the expropriation of peasant lands had taken place, leaving behind a landless rural proletariat (as well as landed proprietors and tenant farmers). Nevertheless, it is worth noting – in the face of Ferkiss' criticisms – that Marx's view of the peasantry was always complex – because historically nuanced. It is true that he saw the French peasantry as a class playing a reactionary role by the time of

Napoleon III's Second Empire, yet he also distinguished the revolutionary from the conservative peasantry. The former he described in heroic terms as 'the peasant that strikes out beyond the condition of his social existence, the smallholding.' The revolutionary peasant, for Marx, was characterized by 'enlightenment' and represented the future, the 'modern Cévennes.'[22]

In *Anti-Dühring* Engels argued that large landholders have almost invariably been more destructive in their relation to the land than peasants and free agricultural labourers. The Roman Republic in Pliny's day replaced tillage with stock raising and thereby brought 'Italy to ruin (*latifundia Italiam perdidere*)'; in North America 'the big landlords of the South with their slaves and their improvident robbery of the land, exhausted the soil until it could only grow firs' – thereby representing a much more destructive relation to the earth (as well as to society) than the labour of free farmers.[23]

Moreover, the whole question of peasant societies (and peasants within capitalist societies) should not be confused with the issue of pristine nature – as Ferkiss seems to do. Peasant agriculture is non-industrial in character and 'closer to the earth,' but it is already well down the road of the human transformation of nature, including 'man'. If one looks back far enough there were subsistence economies – i.e. not defined by market relations – but one should be careful not to idealize them. Long before primitive accumulation generated capitalist social forms genuine communal agriculture had been largely eliminated under noncapitalist modes of production in most of Europe. In some of these societies the majority of human beings were, as Raymond Williams observes, 'working animals, tied by forced tribute, forced labour, or 'bought and sold like beasts'; 'protected' by law and custom only as animals and streams are protected, to yield more labour, more food, more blood.'[24]

For Marx and Engels nature was intertwined with human history and on these grounds they sharply attacked those conservative romantics of their day who sought to root themselves and society in a conception of unspoiled nature – as an adequate basis for a revolt against capitalism. Hence, in criticizing idealizations of a rural order emanating from feudal times, they were not thereby rejecting 'unspoiled nature' – though they carefully avoided any idealization of pristine nature. Indeed Marx thought it important to remark in volume 1 of *Capital* that, 'Everyone knows there are no true forests in England. The deer in the parks of the great are demure domestic cattle, as fat as London aldermen.' While in Scotland the so-called 'deer-forests' that were being established for the benefit of the huntsmen (at the expense of rural labourers), contained deer but no trees. 'The development of civilization and industry in general,' Marx wrote in volume 2 of *Capital*, 'has always shown itself so active in the destruction of forests that everything that has been done for their conservation and production is completely insignificant in comparison.'[25]

SUSTAINABILITY AND THE EARTH

In the *Communist Manifesto* Marx and Engels included in their ten-point programme for revolutionary change not only '1. Abolition of property in land and application of all rents of land to public purposes,' and (as previously mentioned) '9 . . . gradual abolition of the distinction between town and country, by a more equable distribution of population over the country,' but also '7 . . . the bringing into cultivation of waste lands, and the improvement of soil generally in accordance with a common plan.'[26] At this point in the development of their thought they adopted what might be thought of as an early conservationist approach in relation to such issues as the 'improvement of soil.' They had been influenced early on (as early as 1843 in the case of Engels) by the pioneering research of the great German soil chemist Justus von Liebig. From Liebig, whom they considered to be the greatest representative of bourgeois science in the area of agriculture, as well as from other figures like the Scottish political economist James Anderson, Marx and Engels learned of the necessity of returning to the soil the nutrients that had been taken from it. Their insistence on the 'improvement of [the] soil generally in accordance with a common plan' is then to be understood in this sense.[27]

Marx saw the bourgeoisie engaging in the utmost exploitation of the earth or soil on the same basis as every other element of commerce. For the bourgeoisie, he wrote in 1852, 'the soil is to be a marketable commodity, and the exploitation of the soil is to be carried on according to the common commercial laws. There are to be manufacturers of food as well as manufacturers of twist and cottons, but no longer any lords of the land.'[28]

Beginning in the 1860s, when he was completing *Capital*, Marx was influenced by the widespread concern that emerged in Europe and North America over the crisis of the earth or soil, resulting from the forms of exploitation applied by capitalist agriculture – a crisis that was given definitive expression in the work of such thinkers as Liebig, the

Scottish agricultural chemist James F.W. Johnston, and the U.S. economist Henry Carey. By 1859 Liebig was arguing that the 'empirical agriculture' of the trader had given rise to a 'spoliation system' in which the 'conditions of reproduction' of the soil were violated. Soil nutrients (such as nitrogen, phosphorous and potassium) were 'carried away in produce year after year, rotation after rotation.' Both the open system of exploitation of American farming and the so-called high farming of European agriculture were forms of 'robbery.' 'Rational agriculture,' in contrast, would give 'back to the fields the conditions of their fertility.[29]

Marx's concern over the condition of agriculture and the crisis of the soil led him toward a much more sophisticated understanding of environmental problems from the 1860s on, focusing on the issues of ecological degradation (disruption of the soil nutrient cycle), restoration, and sustainability – all of which were linked in his analysis to changing social relations. 'Large landed property,' he wrote at the end of his critique of capitalist ground rent in volume 3 of *Capital*,

> reduces the agricultural population to an ever decreasing minimum and confronts it with an ever growing industrial population crammed together in large towns; in this way it produces conditions that provoke an irreparable rift in the interdependent process of the social metabolism, a metabolism prescribed by the natural laws of life itself. The result of this is a squandering of the vitality of the soil, which is carried by trade far beyond the bounds of a single country.[30]

Sustainable development has been defined in our time by the Brundtland Commission as 'development which meets the needs of the present without compromising the ability of future generations to meet their needs.'[31] It was the need for sustainability in precisely this sense that Marx came to emphasize as a result of his research into the crisis of the earth or soil under capitalism, and which became an integral part of his conception of a future communist society. As he himself put it, 'The way that the cultivation of particular crops depends on fluctuations in market prices and the constant changes in cultivation with these price fluctuations – the entire spirit of capitalist production, which is oriented towards the most immediate monetary profits – stands in contradiction to agriculture, which has to concern itself with the whole gamut of permanent conditions of life required by the chain of successive generations.'[32]

Indeed, for Marx, who understood that transcending the ecological contradictions of capitalist agriculture was an absolute necessity for communist society, the question of sustainability was central to the future development of humanity. 'A conscious and rational treatment of the land as permanent communal property,' he wrote, was 'the inalienable condition for the existence and reproduction of the chain of human generations ... '[33] In this sense, ecological sustainability could be viewed as a nature-imposed necessity for human production. The implications of this as understood by Marx were truly global in scope:

> From the standpoint of a higher socio-economic formation, the private property of particular individuals in the earth will appear just as absurd as the private property of one man in other men. Even an entire society, a nation, or all simultaneously existing societies taken together, are not owners of the earth. They are simply its possessors, its beneficiaries, and have to bequeath it in an improved state to succeeding generations, as *boni patres familias* [good heads of the household].[34]

Devising a sustainable alternative to the destructive ecological tendencies of capitalist society was thus not merely a technical problem for Marx, but one that required a far-reaching transformation of society. The basic change needed was a shift to a society controlled by the associated producers, characterized by the expansion of free time and collective-democratic organization, and hence by a non-instrumentalist approach to nature and human society. Among the revolutionary changes necessary to bring this about was an end to 'the monopolized earth' of private property. 'Private property,' Marx contended, referring to James Johnston's analysis of the impoverishment of the soil in the mid-nineteenth century, 'places insuperable barriers on all sides to a genuinely rational agriculture.'[35]

WAS MARX 'PROMETHEAN'?

In his *Contemporary Critique of Historical Materialism* Anthony Giddens contends that those passages in Marx's writings which suggest that 'nature is more than a medium through which human history unfolds' are mostly confined to his 'early writings' and that overall a 'Promethean attitude,' in which the technology of production is praised while nature is treated simply in instrumental terms, 'is pre-eminent' in Marx's work. Indeed, for Giddens, Marx is to be sharply criticized because 'his concern with transforming the exploitative human social relations expressed in class systems does not extend to the exploitation of nature.'[36] The foregoing discussion, however, has shown that Giddens' condemnation of Marx on the first and third counts (abandoning his ecological insights after his 'early writings,' and failing to acknowledge the exploitation of the earth) are both contradicted by a mass of evidence. Marx referred again and again to the exploitation of the earth or soil and he did so in his later writings even more than his earlier works. Indeed, as Massimo Quaini noted, Marx 'denounced the spoliation of nature before a modern bourgeois ecological conscience was born.'[37]

But what of the other charge that Giddens levels at Marx; that of advocating a 'Promethean' (in the sense of productivist or instrumentalist) attitude to nature? This same broad criticism – so broad and all-encompassing that it is usually thought unnecessary to provide any evidence to support it – has been voiced not only by Giddens but by numerous others, including such varied thinkers as Ted Benton, Kate Soper, Robyn Eckersley, John Clark and Victor Ferkiss.[38]

If what is meant by this charge of 'Prometheanism' is that Marx, in line with the Enlightenment tradition, placed considerable faith in rationality, science, technology, and human progress, and that he often celebrated the growing human mastery over natural forces, there is no denying this to be the case. Here we only have to turn to the *Communist Manifesto* itself where Marx wrote his panegyric to the bourgeoisie:

> The bourgeoisie, during its rule of scarce one hundred years, has created more massive and more colossal productive forces than have all preceding generations together. Subjection of Nature's forces to man, machinery, application of chemistry to industry and agriculture, steam-navigation, railways, electric telegraphs, clearing of whole continents for cultivation, canalization of rivers, whole populations conjured out of the ground. What earlier century had even a presentiment that such productive forces slumbered in the lap of social labour?[39]

It would be a mistake, however, to conclude from this that Marx and Engels suspended all critical judgment where science, technology and the idea of progress were concerned. Marx and Engels were well aware of the fact that science and technology could be misused and distorted by bourgeois civilization, a form of society which, they note in the *Communist Manifesto*, 'is like the sorcerer, who is no longer able to control the powers of the nether world whom he has called up by his spells.' The whole giant apparatus of modern relations of production, exchange, and property, backed up by science and technology, that constituted the creative power of capitalist society, was, Marx and Engels argued, vulnerable to its own achievements, leading to economic crises and the rise of the modern working class or proletariat as the gravedigger of the system. Moreover, as Marx and Engels were to emphasize again and again, the same productive forces resulting from the coupling of capitalist market society with modern science and technology resulted in the exploitation not only of human beings but of the earth itself, in the sense of violating the conditions of its sustainability.

Robyn Eckersley in her influential book *Environmentalism and Political Theory* has written that, 'Marx fully endorsed the . . . technical accomplishments of the capitalist forces of production and . . . thoroughly absorbed the Victorian faith in scientific and technological progress as the means by which humans could outsmart and conquer nature.'[40] Yet in his 'Speech at the Anniversary of *The People's Paper*,' delivered in April 1856, Marx observed that

> In our days, everything seems pregnant with its contrary. Machinery, gifted with the wonderful power of shortening and fructifying human labour, we behold starving and overworking it. The new-fangled sources of wealth, by some strange weird spell, are turned into sources of want. The victories of art seem bought by the loss of character. At the same pace that mankind masters nature, man seems to become enslaved to other men or to his own infamy. Even the pure light of science seems unable to shine but on the dark background of ignorance. All our invention and progress seem to result in endowing material forces with intellectual life, and in stultifying human life into a material force. This antagonism between modern industry and science on the one hand, modern misery and dissolution on the other hand; this antagonism between the productive powers and the social relations of our epoch is a fact, palpable, overwhelming, and not to be controverted.[41]

Despite the faith that they generally placed in 'the pure light of science', Marx and Engels exhibited a complex view of science, technology and human progress, as can be seen in their analysis of the exploitation of the soil. With the introduction of machinery and large scale industry into agriculture under capitalist conditions, Marx argued, 'a conscious, technological application of science replaces the previous highly irrational and slothfully traditional way of working;' but it is precisely this science and technology in capitalist hands, Marx goes on to observe, that 'disturbs the metabolic interaction between man and the earth' by being turned into a force for the exploitation of both the worker and the soil.[42]

Marx has often been accused of devaluing nature and justifying the extreme human exploitation of nature through his economic value analysis, which, since it attributed all value to labour, thereby denied – so the critics have charged – any 'intrinsic value' to nature, which was treated as a 'free gift' to capital.[43] It is here, some have contended, that his 'Prometheanism' is most evident. Such criticisms, however, are misplaced. Marx didn't invent the notion that nature was a 'free gift' to capital. This conception was developed by the classical liberal political economists themselves and was emphasized in particular by Malthus and Ricardo in their economic works. Even today neoclassical economic textbooks present the same notion. For example in the 10th edition of the widely used introductory economics text by Campbell R. McConnell we find the following: 'Land refers to all natural resources – all "free gifts of nature" – which are usable in the production process.' And later in the same text we read: 'Land has no production cost; it is a "free and nonreproducible gift of nature."'[44]

Marx agreed that under the law of value as developed by capitalism nature was accorded no value. As he put it, 'The earth . . . is active as agent of production in the production of a use-value, a material product, say wheat. But it has nothing to do with producing the *value of the wheat*.'[45] The value of the wheat or any commodity under capitalism was derived from labour. This, however, expressed the narrow, limited character of capitalism and of its conception of wealth, which was restricted simply to exchange values. For Marx, genuine wealth consisted of use values – the characteristic of production in general. Hence, nature, which contributed to the production of use values, was just as much a source of wealth as human labour – indeed, judged in physical terms, labour, as Marx was wont to observe, could only alter the form of what nature had initially provided. 'Labour,' he wrote at the beginning of *Capital*, 'is not the only source of material wealth, i.e. of the use-values it produces. As William Petty says, labour is the father of material wealth, and the earth is its mother.'[46] Marx actually railed against socialists of his time who attributed '*supernatural creative power* to labour' by conceiving it as the sole source of wealth and disregarding the role of nature. Wealth under communism, he argued, would need to be conceived in more universal terms, allowing for the full development of human creative powers, expanding the wealth of connections allowed for by nature, and in accord with natural conditions.[47]

REVOLUTIONARY IMPERATIVES

As Joseph Schumpeter emphasized,[48] one of the most original and profound insights of the *Communist Manifesto* was Marx and Engels' perception of the technological dynamism of capitalism which, to an extent never before seen in world history, demanded the 'constant revolutionizing of production' in order to survive. It was this understanding of the inner dynamism of production under capitalism which led Marx, in fact, to his most comprehensive assessment of the impact of capitalism on nature, and on everything that appeared external to itself. Thus in the *Grundrisse* Marx wrote:

[J]ust as production founded on capital creates universal industriousness on one side . . . so does it create on the other side a system of general exploitation of the natural and human qualities, a system of general utility, utilising science itself just as much as all the physical and mental qualities, while there appears nothing *higher in itself*, nothing legitimate for itself, outside this circle of social production and exchange. Thus capital creates the bourgeois society, and the universal appropriation of nature as well as of the social bond itself by the members of society. Hence the great civilizing influence of capital; its production of a stage of society in comparison to which all earlier ones appear as mere *local developments* of humanity and as *nature-idolatry*. For the first time, nature becomes purely an object for humankind, purely a matter of utility; ceases to be recognized as a power for itself; and the theoretical discovery of its autonomous laws appears merely as a ruse so as to subjugate it under human needs, whether as an object of consumption or as a means of production. In accord with this tendency, capital drives beyond national barriers and prejudices as much as beyond nature worship, as well as all traditional, confined, complacent, encrusted satisfactions of present needs, and reproductions of old ways of life. It is destructive towards all of this, and constantly revolutionizes it, tearing down all the barriers which hem in the development of the forces of production, the expansion of needs, the all-sided development of production, and the exploitation and exchange of natural and mental forces. But from the fact that capital posits every such limit as a barrier and hence gets *ideally* beyond it, it does not by any means follow that it has *really* overcome it, and since every such barrier contradicts its character its production moves in contradictions which are constantly overcome but just as constantly posited.[49]

The drive to unlimited accumulation, the incessant revolutionizing of the means of production, the subjugation of all that was external to itself to its own commodity logic – all of this, Marx argued, was part of the juggernaut of capital. Capital sees nature purely as an object, as an external barrier to be overcome.[50] Commenting on Bacon's great maxim that 'nature is only overcome by obeying her' – on the basis of which also Bacon proposed to 'subjugate' nature – Marx, as we have seen, replies that for capitalism the discovery of nature's autonomous laws 'appears merely as a ruse so as to subjugate it under human needs.'[51] He thus decried the one-sided, instrumental, exploitative relation to nature associated with contemporary social relations. Despite its clever 'ruse,' capital is never able to transcend the barrier of natural conditions, which continually reassert themselves with the result that 'production moves in contradictions which are constantly overcome but just as constantly posited.' No other thinker in Marx's time, and perhaps no other thinker up to our own day, has so brilliantly captured the full complexity of the relationship between nature and modern society.

Much of the criticism that has been levelled at Marx and Engels in the area of ecology stems, in fact, from a post-materialist or postmodernist ecology which is no longer so influential today, displaced by the growth of materialist ecology. The social ecology of the 1960s, '70s and early '80s was often built around the 'post-materialist thesis' that environmental issues arose only in conditions of affluence. Emphasis on the limits of growth, which were viewed as positing an absolute conflict between economic growth and the environment, often contributed to a neglect of the political economy of environmental degradation. Instead the principal focus was on cultural factors, frequently abstracted from material conditions – such as the question of anthropocentric vs. ecocentric culture. Over the past decade, however, we have witnessed growing concern about the future of the biosphere, with the rise of such problems as global warming, the destruction of the ozone layer and the worldwide extinction of species to the forefront of the ecological discussion. Among analysts of social ecology attention has shifted to issues of sustainable development, environmental injustice (or the intersection of environmental degradation with class, race, gender and nation-state divisions), and coevolution.[52]

In this changing context it is not surprising that Marx's approach to the question of the natural conditions underlying human society – emphasizing as it did sustainability, the connection between the exploitation of the earth and other forms of exploitation, and the interdependent, 'metabolic' character of the evolving human-nature interaction – should now be exciting new interest. In all of these respects Marx was well ahead of most contemporary environmental thought.

Nevertheless, Marx's approach to environmental issues was inadequate in one very important respect, most evident in the *Communist Manifesto*. The *Manifesto* was first and foremost a revolutionary document, but ecological contradictions, though perceived by Marx and Engels even at this early stage in their analysis, play little or no role in the anticipated revolution against capitalism. Marx and Engels clearly thought that the duration of capitalism would be much shorter than earlier modes of production, brought to a relatively rapid end by the intensity of its contradictions and by the actions of the proletariat – the gravedigger of the system. As a result, they tended to view the ecological problems that they perceived as having more bearing on the future of communist than capitalist society.[53] This is why ecological considerations enter much more explicitly into their programme for communism in the *Manifesto* than into their assessment of the conditions leading to the demise of capitalism.

Today it is obvious that this approach is inadequate, in that the ecological contradictions of capitalism have developed to the point that they will inevitably play a large role in the demise of the system – with ecology now constituting a major source of antisystemic resistance to capitalism. Our whole notion of the revolt against capitalism has to be reshaped accordingly. Marx's conception of a sustainable society, in which the earth would be bequeathed 'in an improved state to succeeding generations,' in the context of a reconstituted social order organized around the collective realization of human needs, is perhaps the most complete vision of a feasible utopia – judged in social and ecological terms – that has yet been developed. It therefore constitutes the essential starting point for the articulation of a truly revolutionary social ecology. Today we must give a much fuller meaning than originally intended to the famous lines of *The International*:[54]

> The earth shall rise on new foundations,
> We have been naught, we shall be all.

NOTES

1. For references to this large and rapidly expanding body of literature see John Bellamy Foster, 'The Crisis of the Earth: Marx's Theory of Ecological Sustainability as a Nature-Imposed Necessity for Human Production,' *Organization & Environment*, vol. 10, no. 3 (September 1997), p. 278.

2. The first of these three positions can be seen in the interpretations of such thinkers as Victor Ferkiss and John Clark; the second in the work of Anthony Giddens, Ted Benton, Kate Soper, Robyn Eckersley, Murray Bookchin, and David Goldblatt (the reference to 'illuminating asides' can be found in Goldblatt's book *Social Theory and the Environment* [Boulder, CO: Westview, 1996], p. 5); the third in the writings of Elmar Altvater, Paul Burkett, Michael Perelman, Michael Lebowitz, David Harvey, and the present author. For more specific references see the discussion below.

3. Frederick Engels, 'Outlines of a Critique of Political Economy,' in Karl Marx, *Economic and Philosophical Manuscripts of 1844* (New York: International Publishers, 1964), p. 210.

4. Marx, *Early Writings* (New York: Vintage, 1974), pp. 328, 359–60.

5. Marx, *Capital*, vol. 1 (New York: Vintage: 1976), p. 638.

6. William Leiss, *The Domination of Nature* (Boston: Beacon Press, 1975), pp. 85, 198. Ecologists have often claimed John Stuart Mill as a forerunner of modern

ecological thought, but it is much easier to nail him as anti-nature: '[T]he ways of Nature are to be conquered not obeyed . . . her powers are often towards man in the position of enemies, from whom he must wrest, by force and ingenuity, what little he can for his own use.' John Stuart Mill, *Nature, the Utility of Religion, and Theism* (London: Longman's, Green, Reader, and Dyer, 1924), pp. 20–21.

7. Karl Marx, 'Feelings,' in Karl Marx and Friedrich Engels, *Collected Works*, vol. 1 (New York: International Publishers, 1975), p. 525.

8. John Clark, 'Marx's Inorganic Body,' *Environmental Ethics*, vol. 11, no. 3 (Fall 1989), p. 258.

9. Friedrich Engels, *Anti-Dühring* (New York: International Publishers, 1939), pp. 309–310.

10. Ted Benton, 'Marxism and Natural Limits,' *New Left Review*, no. 178 (November–December 1989); p. 75. For other green criticisms of Marx and Engels in this respect see Robyn Eckersley, *Environmentalism and Political Theory* (Albany: State University of New York Press, 1992), pp. 80–81; and Murray Bookchin, *Toward an Ecological Society* (Montreal: Black Rose Books, 1980), pp. 204–06.

11. Friedrich Engels, *The Dialectics of Nature* (New York: International Publishers, 1940), p. 293 (emphasis added).

12. Marx, *Capital*, vol. 3, p. 959.

13. Paul Burkett, 'Nature in Marx Reconsidered,' *Organization & Environment*, vol. 10, no. 2 (June 1997), p. 172.

14. Friedrich Engels, *The Dialectics of Nature* (New York: International Publishers, 1940), pp. 291–92, and *The Housing Question* (Moscow: Progress Publishers, 1975), p. 92.

15. See René DuBos, *The Wooing of the Earth* (New York: Charles Scribner's Sons, 1980); David Harvey, 'The Nature of Environment,' in Ralph Miliband and Leo Panitch, ed. *The Socialist Register, 1993* (New York: Monthly Review Press, 1993), p. 26; Richard B. Norgaard, *Development Betrayed* (New York: Routledge, 1994). For an example of the dualistic approach to environmental problems focusing on the 'anthropocentric' vs. 'ecocentric' distinction and criticizing Marx and Engels for belonging allegedly to the former rather than the latter camp see Robyn Eckersley, *Environmentalism and Political Theory* (Albany: State University of New York Press, 1992).

16. Victor Ferkiss, *Nature, Technology, and Society* (New York: New York University Press, 1993).

17. Gary Snyder, 'Nature as Seen from Kitkitdizze is No "Social Construction," ' *Wild Earth*, vol. 6, no. 4 (Winter 1996/97), p. 8.

18. Marx and Engels, *The Communist Manifesto* (New York: Monthly Review Press), p. 40.

19. Engels, *The Housing Question*, p. 92.

20. Marx, *Capital*, vol. 1, pp. 636–39.

21. *Ibid.*, pp. 637–38.

22. Karl Marx, *The Eighteenth Brumaire of Louis Bonaparte* (New York: International Publishers, 1963), p. 125; Cévennes, a mountainous region in France, was the site of a large uprising of Protestant peasants at the beginning of the eighteenth century. Teodor Shanin, ed. *Peasants and Peasant Societies* (New York: Blackwell, 1987), pp. 336–37.

23. Engels, *Anti-Dühring*, pp. 195–96.

24. Williams, *The Country and the City* (London: Hogarth Press, 1973), p. 37.
25. Karl Marx, *Capital*, vol. 1 (New York: Vintage, 1976), pp. 892–93; Karl Marx, *Capital*, vol. 2 (New York: Vintage, 1978), p. 322. In *Anti-Dühring* Engels too complained of how large landowners in Scotland 'robbed' the peasants of their common land and turned 'arable land into sheep-runs and eventually even into mere tracts for deer hunting.' Engels, *Anti-Dühring*, p. 196. Marx's approach to nature tended to emphasize the fact that much of what we call nature has been socially constructed. As he and Engels wrote in *The German Ideology* in response to the abstract, ahistorical notion of nature propounded by Feurbach: '[N]ature, the nature that preceded human history, is not by any means the nature in which Feurbach lives, it is nature which today no longer exists anywhere (except perhaps on a few Australian coral islands of recent origin), and which, therefore, does not exist for Feurbach either.' Marx and Engels, *Collected Works*, vol. 5, pp. 39–40.
26. Marx and Engels, *The Communist Manifesto*, p. 40.
27. The meaning given in Marx and Engels' day to the notion of the 'improvement' of the soil was well expressed in their time by the U.S. agriculturist (and later sanitary engineer) George Waring in his *Elements of Agriculture* in which he states 'From what has now been said of the character of the soil, it must be evident that, as we know the *causes* of fertility and barrenness, we may by the proper means improve the character of all soils which are not now in the highest state of fertility.' Waring, *Elements of Agriculture* (New York: D. Appleton and Co., 1854), p. 88.
28. Karl Marx, 'The Chartists,' in Marx and Engels, *Collected Works*, vol. 11 (New York: International Publishers, 1979), p. 333.
29. Justus von Liebig, *Lectures on Modern Industry* (London: Walton and Mabery, 1859), pp. 171–83, 220.
30. Marx, *Capital*, vol. 3, p. 950.
31. World Commission on Environment and Development, *Our Common Future* (New York: Oxford University Press, 1987), p. 43.
32. Marx, *Capital*, vol. 3, p. 754.
33. Marx, *Capital*, vol. 3, p. 948–49. The continuing relevance of the ecological analysis of the soil nutrient cycle and its relation to the development of capitalist industry can be see today in the work of the following: Kozo Mayumi, 'Temporary Emancipation from Land,' *Ecological Economics*, vol. 4, no. 1 (October 1991), pp. 35–56; Fred Magdoff, Les Lanyon and Bill Liebhardt, 'Nutrient Cycling, Transformations and Flows: Implications for a More Sustainable Agriculture,' *Advances in Agronomy*, vol. 60 (1997), pp. 1–73.
34. Marx, *Capital*, vol. 3, p. 911.
35. *Ibid.*, pp. 754, 963.
36. Anthony Giddens, *A Contemporary Critique of Historical Materialism* (Berkeley: University of California Press, 1981), p. 59–60.
37. Massimo Quaini, *Marxism and Geography* (Totowa, New Jersey: Barnes and Noble Books, 1982), p. 136.
38. See, for example, Kate Soper, 'Greening Prometheus,' in Ted Benton, ed., *Greening Marxism* (New York: Guilford, 1996), pp. 81–99.
39. Marx and Engels, *The Communist Manifesto*, p. 10.
40. Eckersley, *Environmentalism and Political* Theory, p. 80.
41. Karl Marx, 'Speech at the Anniversary of *The People's Paper*,' in Karl Marx and Friedrich Engels, *Collected Works*, vol. 14 (New York: International Publishers,

1980), pp. 655–56.

42. Marx, *Capital*, vol. 1, p. 637.

43. For examples of this common but mistaken criticism of Marx see Ward Churchill, *From a Native Son* (Boston: South End Press, 1996), pp. 467–68; J. Deléage, 'Eco-Marxist Critique of Political Economy,' in Martin O'Connor, ed. *Is Capitalism Sustainable?* (New York: Guilford, 1994), p. 48; Michael Barratt Brown, *Models in Political Economy* (Harmondsworth, Middlesex, U.K.: Penguin, 1995), pp. 171–73; and Nicholas Georgescu-Roegen, *The Entropy Law in the Economic Process* (Cambridge, Mass.: Harvard University Press, 1971), p. 2. For a useful discussion see Paul Burkett, 'On some Misconceptions about Nature and Marx's Critique of Political Economy,' *Capitalism, Nature, Socialism*, vol. 7 (September 1996), pp. 64–66.

44. Campbell R. McConnell, *Economics: Principles, Problems and Policies*, 10th edition (New York: McGraw Hill, 1987), pp 20, 672.

45. Marx, *Capital*, vol. 3, p. 955.

46. Marx, *Capital*, vol. 1, p. 134.

47. Karl Marx, *Critique of the Gotha Programme* (Moscow: Progress Publishers, 1971), p. 11.

48. Joseph A. Schumpter, *Essays* (Cambridge, Massachusetts: Addison-Wesley Press, 1951), pp. 293–4.

49. Karl Marx, *Grundrisse* (New York: Vintage, 1973), pp. 409–410.

50. The reference to 'general barriers' to capital is taken from Michael Lebowitz, who has demonstrated that Marx pointed to two kinds of barriers to capital, leading to contradictions in capital, accumulation and crises: general barriers common to production in general, and thus having to do with natural conditions, and more specific historical barriers immanent to capital itself. See Lebowitz, 'The General and Specific in Marx's Theory of Crisis,' *Studies in Political Economy*, no. 7 (Winter 1982), pp. 5–25.

51. Francis Bacon, *Novum Organum* (Chicago: Open Court, 1994), pp. 43, 29.

52. On the shift from post-materialist to materialist ecology see Juan Martinez-Alier, 'Political Ecology, Distributional Conflicts and Incommensurability,' *New Left Review*, no. 211 (May–June 1995), pp. 70–88.

53. The relation of sustainability to communism, as conceived in the work of Marx and Engels, can be seen in the young Engels' response to the Malthusian issue of overpopulation. 'For even if Malthus were completely right, this transformation [i.e. social revolution] would have to be undertaken on the spot, for only this transformation and the education of the masses which it alone provides makes possible the moral restraint of the propagative instinct which Malthus himself presents as the most effective and easiest remedy for over-population.' Engels, 'Outlines of a Critique of Political Economy,' in Marx, *Economic and Philosophic Manuscripts*, p. 221.

54. Eugene Pottier, 'The International,' in John Bowditch and Clement Ramsland, ed. *Voices of the Industrial Revolution* (Ann Arbor: University of Michigan Press, 1961), p. 187.

REMEMBER THE FUTURE?
THE COMMUNIST MANIFESTO AS HISTORICAL AND CULTURAL FORM

Peter Osborne

The *Communist Manifesto* is without doubt the most influential single text written in the nineteenth century, in any language, by some considerable way. Indeed, it may stand as a metonym for the desire called 'history' which coursed through that century in the wake of the French Revolution. Situated at the hinge between Hobsbawm's ages of revolution and capital (1789–1848 and 1848–1870), as described in the first two volumes of his great trilogy on the long 19th century, from the French Revolution to the First World War,[1] the Manifesto presents the historical dialectic between these two terms ('revolution' and 'capital') in two equally extraordinary, though no longer equally convincing, ways: from the standpoint of the prospectively successive revolutionary historical roles of the social classes of the bourgeoisie and the proletariat, respectively. It is in the disjunction between these two presentations that the meaning of the text must be sought today. For with the disappearance of the horizon of proletarian revolution, and the retreat to the spirit world of the famous 'spectre' of communism, the text has undergone a profound transformation. In short, the *Manifesto* appears to have been transformed from an eschatological *tour de force*, in which the end of capitalism was assured ('What the bourgeoisie . . . produces, above all, is its own gravediggers'), into what Marshall Berman has notoriously described as a 'lyrical celebration of bourgeois works':[2] a celebration, more specifically, of the *revolutionary temporality of capitalism*; a capitalism which – without a fundamental countervailing force – appears now as open-ended. From the standpoint of the philosophy of history, communism as the eschatological absolute has given way to the 'bad infinity' of capitalism – 'the affirmation as negation of the finite'[3] – capitalism without end, amen.

Or at least, so it would seem. But does the rest of the *Manifesto* belong unambiguously to a shape of life grown old? Or is there another sense in which it is still a 'living' text, after the fall of historical communism? Is there, perhaps, *new* life in it today? What lives in the *Communist Manifesto*? In particular – and this is the question I shall address here – what is the temporal character of its address to us, citizen-subjects of Western capitalist democracies? How does it inscribe us into historical time, today?[4]

1. THE POETRY OF TRANSITION

Let me quote what is probably – in the wake of Marshall Berman's path-breaking work – the most cited passage from the *Communist Manifesto*, in a Western academic context, over the last 15 years:

> The bourgeoisie, historically, has played a most revolutionary part. The bourgeoisie, wherever it has got the upper hand, has put an end to all feudal, patriarchal, idyllic relations. It has pitilessly torn asunder the motley feudal ties that bound men and women to their 'natural superiors', and has left remaining no other nexus between people than naked self-interest, than callous 'cash payment'. It has drowned the most heavenly ecstasies of religious fervour, of chivalrous enthusiasm, of philistine sentimentalism, in the icy waters of egotistical calculation. It has resolved personal worth into exchange value, and in place of the numberless indefeasible chartered freedoms, has set up that single, unconscionable freedom – Free Trade. In one word, for exploitation, veiled by religious and political illusions, it has substituted naked, shameless, direct brutal exploitation. [. . . The bourgeoisie] has been the first to show what human activity can bring about. It has accomplished wonders far surpassing Egyptian pyramids, Roman aqueducts, and Gothic cathedrals; it has conducted expeditions that put in the shade all former Exoduses of nations and crusades.

And now, what is for Berman the most important part:

> The bourgeoisie cannot exist without constantly revolutionising the instruments of production, and thereby the relations of production, and with them the whole relations of society. Conservation of the old modes of production in unaltered form, was, on the contrary, the first condition of existence for all earlier industrial classes. Constant revolutionising of production, uninterrupted disturbance of all social conditions, everlasting uncertainty and agitation distinguish the bourgeois epoch from all earlier ones. All fixed, fast-frozen relations, with their train of ancient and venerable prejudices and opinions, are swept away, all new-formed ones become antiquated before they can ossify. All that is solid melts into air, all that is holy is profaned, and men and women are at last compelled to face with sober senses, their real conditions of life, and their relations with their kind.[5]

More specifically, according to Marx in the passage which follows, this 'constant revolutionising' has three main effects: economic and cultural globalization; subjection of the countryside to the towns; and political centralization in the form of new state-led or state-created nations. What is this but – as Berman describes it in the subtitle of his fine book – 'the experience of modernity'?

The culture of capital is the systemic instantiation of a Mephistophelean spirit of negation. And what is the *Communist Manifesto* from the standpoint of such a negation – a *Manifesto* without belief in the world-historical agency of the working classes, and with an acknowledgement of the powers of states and capitals to contain what had appeared to Marx as ultimately unmanageable crises; what is the *Communist Manifesto* in this context – in which the 'sorcerer' of modern society has regained a certain crucial measure of control over its powers – but, as Berman puts it, 'the archetype of a century of modernist manifestoes and movements to come . . . the first great modernist work of art'?[6] When, in his Preface to the 1893 Italian edition of the *Manifesto*, Engels wrote of Dante as 'both the last poet of the Middle Ages and the first poet of modern times', in order to conjure the prospect of the 'new Dante, who will mark the hour of birth of this new proletarian era', he was appealing to national sentiment in Italy. Yet it is hard to read this passage without imputing a reference (if only unconscious) to Marx and to the *Manifesto* itself. However, if the era that was approaching was not in fact a proletarian one, but rather one of capitalism on a global scale, what does Marx become, if not the poet of the transition to capitalism; a prefiguration, in epic mode, of Baudelaire and Flaubert? The *Manifesto* appears as a work of modernist historiography: the experience of mid nineteenth-century European capitalism, writ large.

As Berman argues, the *Manifesto*'s prose is driven by, and expresses in dissident form, a relentless temporal logic of negation, which derives, historically, from the logic of capital itself. Once the histori-cally-specific political demands, and corresponding social content, of such a manifesto are set aside or judged to be superceded, it would seem, it cannot but appear (as it appears to Berman) in its pure modernist form, as an *identification with*, and *will to*, this abstract temporal logic itself. As I have argued elsewhere, in its purest form, modernism simply *is* the cultural affirmation of the abstract temporal logic of negation.[7] Think, for example, of the first great Russian Futurist Manifesto of 1912, the Hylaea group's wonderfully entitled *Slap in the Face of Public Taste*, with the second of its 'orders' regarding poets' rights: the right to 'feel an insurmountable hatred for the language existing before their time'. Or of the yearning, at once theoretically abstract and phenomenologically concrete, expressed in the great concluding sentence of the first *Manifesto of Surrealism* (1924): 'Existence is elsewhere'.[8]

The 'melting vision' of Berman's modernist Marx extends beyond the specific futurities of qualitative historical novelty in the name of which such manifestoes are written (be they communist, futurist, or surrealist), to a generalised existential modernism that dissolves political subjectivity into the movement of time itself. Berman's Marx is, in this respect, rather surprisingly, something of a poststructuralist Marx. This is a modernism which celebrates in *ecstatic* fashion

> the glory of modern energy and dynamism, the ravages of modern disintegration and nihilism, the strange intimacy between them; the sense of being caught in a vortex where all facts and values are whirled, exploded, decomposed, recombined; a basic uncertainty about what is basic, what is valuable, even what is real; a flaring up of the most radical hopes in the midst of their radical negations.[9]

'Time is everything, man is nothing; at the most, he is time's carcase. Quality no longer matters.'[10] Or at least, that's how it looks from the standpoint of the 'fact' of modern industry. But is this standpoint all that's left after the demise of the proletariat as the agent of history? Is there really no time left in the *Manifesto*, for us, today, other than the time of capital, culturally generalised into that of an abstract, badly infinite modernity? No time other than that of the new as the 'ever-same', as Benjamin put it; the new as 'an invariant: the desire for the new', in Adorno's words?[11] Is there no time other than the time of 'uninterrupted disturbance of all social conditions, everlasting uncertainty and agitation', which is nonetheless, mysteriously, somehow restricted in its play to the compass of a single social form (capitalism)? No time but that of the expanded reproduction of capital, the relentless self-expansion of the value-form? Is there no place left in the text of the *Manifesto*, for us, today, for another time, a qualitatively different time, a different kind of futurity, a *historical futurity*, closer to the text's original intent?

It is hard to pursue such questions without running into a barrier: the theoretical failure of Marxism to address the question of 'history' as a problem about the character of historical time. The Marxist tradition has tended either to reject the field of the philosophy of history as such, in the name of a temporally naive notion of historiography as a science (in which the future appears only as an extrapolation of past and present within a naturalised chronological time – never as a dimension of social being in its own right); or to adopt the temporal structure of Hegelianism (the eternal present as the standpoint of absolute knowing). More often, it has tried to do both at once. Marxism lacks a philosophically adequate conception of historical time.[12] Yet, in the text of the *Manifesto*, historical time, a *qualitative* historical time, looms large; not merely in the sense of the historian, the sense of the past ('The history of all hitherto existing society is the history of class struggles'), but in the existential sense of a universalised *demand* on the future, dynamised by the present, claiming that future for itself: 'In place of the old bourgeois society, with its classes and class antagonisms, we shall have an association, in which the free development of each is the condition for the free development of all.' *We shall have* . . . a non-capitalist future. This is a demand not unlike that about which Kant writes in the *Critique of Judgment*: the 'strange' demand made by the reflective judgment of singularity which requires agreement from all.[13] It would be a mistake to take this 'we shall have' for a prediction, in any straightforward sense of the term. The *Manifesto* displays, in a practical form, a sophistication about historical time which is lacking from Marx's methodological writings about history.

There is a powerful existential dimension to the *Communist Manifesto*, a particular quality of *futurity*, which, as Berman recognises, belies the sociological schematism and historical stagism of its account of classes and modes of production. Berman's reading focuses on this dimension. Indeed, it celebrates it. Yet it also *de*historicises it – takes the history out of it – in a very particular way. It dehistoricises its futurity, its identification with qualitative *historical* novelty, by reducing it to the abstract temporal logic of negation of a generalised modernity. In fact, paradoxically, it dehistoricises it (the quality of its futurity) in the very act of purporting to explain it, historically, as the cultural affect of a particular form of social time: the time of the expanded reproduction of capital, the revolutionary temporality of the bourgeoisie. The impulse towards a different future, a *non-capitalist* future, is thus evacuated from the text, not merely by Berman's notorious neglect of its historical argumentation (the class struggle), but at the level of its temporal-existential form as well. Berman's reading partakes in the dehistoricising movement of the purely existentialist, heroic modernism which it purports to explain. Yet what meaning can Marx's 'we shall have' possess – a 'we shall have' of qualitative historical novelty – today, when the horizon of socialist revolution has disappeared? What meaning can it have except, as

Berman implies, that of an abstractly energising hope, circulating within the closed walls of the disintegrative turbulence of capitalist societies themselves? Or to put the same question another way: from where else might the existential force of the *Manifesto* derive?

One way to approach this question is through an analysis of the temporality of the text as a historical and cultural form.[14]

2. MONTAGE AND MEDIATION IN THE MANIFESTO FORM

The first thing to note is that the *Communist Manifesto* is the syncretic product of a number of pre-existing, historically discrete literary forms, each of which represents a separate compositional element, the history of which may be traced through the *Manifesto*'s relations to earlier texts and manuscipt materials by Marx and Engels themselves. To begin with, for example, one might attend to the text's origins in the catechism form of Engels' *Principles of Communism* (October 1847), which was a revised version of his own earlier *Draft of a Communist Confession of Faith*, from June of the same year – the written-up version of the draft programme discussed at the First Congress of the Communist League. Comparison of the three documents reveals successive transformations of the catechism form as it is progressively subordinated to, and integrated into, a narrative form. Thus, the first version (June 1847) begins:

> Question 1: *Are you a Communist?*
> Answer: Yes.
> Question 2: *What is the aim of the Communists?*
> Answer: To organize society in such a way that every member of it can develop and use all his [/her] capacities and powers in complete freedom and without thereby infringing the basic conditions of society.
> Question 3: *How do you wish to achieve this aim?*
> Answer: By elimination of private property and its replacement by common property . . .[15]

This is a suitable form for a secret society – as the League of the Just had been, out of which the Communist League emerged – or a religious sect. It is a formal, repetitive, ritualised dialogue form.

In Engels' second version, four months later, this has become:

> Question 1: *What is Communism?*
> Answer: Communism is the doctrine of the conditions for the emancipation of the proletariat.

Question 2: *What is the proletariat?*
Answer: The proletariat is that class of society which . . .[16]

The mode of address has been generalised and objectivised. The content of the dialogue is no longer focused on the existential dimension of being and acting, on becoming a communist – a confession of faith – but on the principles of the doctrine itself. We have moved from the cellar into the schoolroom.

In the final version, the *Manifesto* itself, mainly written by Marx in January 1848, after a brief period of collaboration with Engels the previous month, there is a dramatic shift of register into the famous Gothic narrative mode:

> A spectre is haunting Europe – the spectre of Communism. All the powers of old Europe have entered into a holy alliance to exorcise this spectre: Pope and Czar, Metternich and Guizot, French radicals and German police spies . . .

Or, if you prefer to take section one as the proper beginning, into a sweeping historical panorama:

> The history of all hitherto existing societies is the history of class struggles. Freeman and slave, patrican and plebeian, lord and serf, guild-master and journeyman, in a word, oppressor and oppressed, stood in constant opposition to one another, carried on an uninterrupted, now hidden, now open, a fight that each time ended, either in a revolutionary re-constitution of society at large, or in the common ruin of the contending classes.

Only at the very end of section two, nearly two thirds of the way through the text as a whole, do we find the programmatic list of measures that the communists plan to undertake (this is another embedded form: the political programme). By comparison, the *Draft of a Communist Confession of Faith* placed the demands of the movement up front, although it stated them only in the most general terms. Moreover, here, in the *Manifesto*, these demands are subordinated to a wider narrative, within which they are but a transitional moment, extending into a qualitatively different future, which climaxes with an account of what it is that 'we shall have' in place of the old bourgeois society: 'an association, in which the free development of each is the condition for the free development of all.' The temporal locus of the text is no longer the eternal present of secret society or schoolroom, but the contradictory historical present of capitalist societies, packed tight with the productive energies of human history and the accumulated memories of struggles between classes, bursting with the anticipation of a specific future (communism).

Yet the existential dimension of the earlier versions persists, not merely in the phenomenological force of the descriptions of the revolutionary temporality of capitalist societies (highlighted by Berman) and the degradation of labour within them (which he ignores), but in the intermittent irruption into the narrative of the 'we' and the 'you': the registration in direct speech of the displaced survival of the catechism, through which the contradictions of the historical process are given voice in rhetorical form. There is a subtle interweaving within the text of the *Manifesto* of what Benveniste distinguishes with his technical use of the terms 'narrative' and 'discourse': where *discourse* is a linguistic form marked by the temporal proximity of its objects to the present of its utterance, while *narrative* cultivates temporal distance and objectivity, through the preferential use of the third person, along with the aorist, imperfect and pluperfect tenses, avoiding the present, perfect and future.[17] This is in many ways a problematic distinction, theoretically, but it is useful here nonetheless, to register the shifts between verb tenses and modes of address within the *Manifesto*, through which the enormous weight of its narrative content (history as the history of modes of production and the conflicts between their constitutive social classes) is brought to bear on the point of the present of reading.

Section two of the *Manifesto* begins in the schoolmasterly, question-and-answer mode of Engels' *Principles of Communism* – 'In what relation do the Communists stand to the proletarians as a whole?' – but as the answer develops, voices proliferate. Objections interject ('Do you mean the property of the petty artisan and of the small peasant, a form of property that preceded the bourgeois form? . . . Or do you mean modern bourgeois property?), multiply ('But does wage labour create any property for the labourer?'), and are rebuffed ('Not a bit. It creates capital.', etc). The text becomes the site of an argument in the fullest sense of the word, as the reader is pulled back and forth between different standpoints within the overall narrative flow.

Allied to this is the complex universality and singularity of the text's 'we'. Not only is the dialogical 'you' – 'You are horrified at our intending to do away with private property' - multiple and flexible, projecting the reader into the position of various objectors, but Marx also clearly exploits the fourth of the poets' rights ordered by the first of the Russian Futurist manifestoes (referred to above): namely, the right 'to stand on the rock of the word "we" amidst the sea of boos and outrage'.[18] This rock is only rarely inhabited these days; people fear the colonialising impulses it arouses. Yet Marx's 'we' is at once differential and cumulative. It is the authorial 'we' of the writer; the more inclusive 'we' of author and readers (the 'we' of 'as we have seen, above'); the specific and strongly distinguishing 'we' of 'we communists'; and finally, climactically, it is the universal 'we' of the 'we shall have', which is also the 'we' of *what* we shall have: namely, 'an association in which the free development of each [each 'I'] is the condition for the free development of all' – the 'we' of an absolute (one might say, a 'philosophical') universality via which the reader passes, almost without noticing, into the standpoint of a post-capitalist historical view; a 'we' through which we readers, in the present, are offered an oppositional political identity within the present, through identification with the *individuated* universality of a 'we' of the future: 'an association in which . . . each . . . for . . . all'.

Finally, one might mention the length of the text, the duration of reading and conceiving. The *Manifesto*'s combination of brevity (a mere fourteen thousand words), with breadth (human societies past and future), characteristic of the manifesto as a form, produces a vibrant imagism at the heart of the narrative, as vast swathes of historical experience are condensed into single images: 'all that is solid melts into air'. The brevity of the text seals it up into an autonomous totality which figures history as a whole, producing an eschatological effect similar to that described by Walter Benjamin in his account of the production of 'now-time' out of the ruptural force of the dialectical image: the image at 'the now of recognisability', as he called it in his *Arcades Project*.[19]

It is surprising that Benjamin left us without a reading of the *Communist Manifesto*, without doubt the most 'Benjaminian' of Marx's texts, and, one might argue, the high point of the German Romantic influence on Marx. (The essence of Romanticism, for Benjamin, lay in its messianism.)[20] Yet Benjamin did leave us an account of capitalist modernity as cultural meltdown – 'a vast process in which literary forms are being melted down'[21] – in his writings of the 1920s and 30s. And he connected this meltdown, explicitly, to new experiences of time, associated with the interacting forces of commodification, technology and urbanism (one might add, migration); forces which gave rise to new media and forms of representation (photography, film, newspapers, advertisments) in relation to which the history of the manifesto form itself must be located. If Dadaism was an attempt to match the effects of film within the (technically obsolete) medium of painting,[22] so the *Manifesto* may be understood as an attempt to invent a literary form of political communication appropriate to a period of mass politics on an international scale. (Ease of translation is an important feature of the directness of its style.) 'One of the foremost tasks of art has always been the creation of a demand which could be fully satisfied only later'[23] – in this case, by television.

The sense of an autonomous totality, produced by the sweeeping historical overview of the first two sections of the *Manifesto* (sections three and four are in many ways programmatic appendages), has all the radically temporalising qualities associated by Benjamin with the timelessness of the dialectical image. We find a similar historiographical timelessness, or absolutization of narrative unity via a deregulation of the play of the opposition of 'narrative' to 'discourse', in Rancière's reading of Michelet as the historian of 'the absolute nominal phrase', which abolishes temporal markers in order to absolutize the meaning of the present.[24] The temporality of the *Manifesto* cannot be reduced to that of the absolute nominal phrase; it is far more internally complex than that. Yet a not dissimilar effect is produced by its first two sections as a whole, by their imagistic force. They function much like a history painting, a triptych, in which images of past, present, and future coalesce as tensely interacting forms. In fact, one could argue that this peculiar effect of radical futurity via temporal suspension is a feature of the absolutism of the manifesto form in general, in which, as Tristan Tzara put it, one must 'organize prose into a form that is absolutely and irrefutably obvious'.[25] A manifesto being, on Tzara's definition: 'a communication made to the whole world, whose only pretension is the discovery of an instant cure for political, astronomical, artistic, parliamentary, agronomical and literary syphilis ... it is always right.'[26] A manifesto is primarily a performance. (Tzara, incidentally, declared himself to be as against manifestos, 'in principle', as he was 'against principles'.)[27] The *Communist Manifesto* is distinguished by the way it offsets the arbitrariness of the literary absolutism inherent in the manifesto form (demonstrated so brilliantly by Tzara) with historical argumentation woven throughout both its narrative and discursive modes. Ultimately, however, the force of this argument is dependent upon the structure of experience constructed by the manifesto form.

Marx drew on a multiplicity of received forms to forge the 'absolute obviousness' of the *Communist Manifesto*: the catechism, the historical narrative, the gothic tale, the political programme – to which one might add the critique (the critique of political economy, condensed into the description of capitalism) and the literary review (of previous socialist and communist literature, in section three). Six different literary forms, at least, fused together within the framework of a seventh: the manifesto. The *Communist Manifesto* is a *montage*. It stages 'a rebirth of the epic out of the technique of montage'.[28] More specifically, it constructs a complex existential mediation of historical time through a syncretic combination of historically discrete literary forms, each of which retains an aspect of autonomy within the whole. It embodies a historical futurity of qualitative newness, independent of its penultimate narrative act (proletarian revolution), in the historical dimension of its cultural form. Add to this, the contextual dimension of its reception – the way in which meaning is produced as an articulation or reorganisation of existing structures of experience – and one begins to get a sense of the extraordinary density of historical relations which underlie and animate the apparent simplicity of its appeal. None of this is registered in Berman's modernist reading; brilliant as it is in its (ironically) limited way.

There is a complex plurality of times at play in the *Manifesto* in addition to the revolutionary temporality of capital; forms of temporality which survive the demotion in the historical role of its main character (the proletariat, purported agent of the new era); forms of futurity which construct the prospect of the qualitative historical novelty of a post-capitalist society out of the experience of the contradictions of the existing social form. Berman's Marx, on the other hand, is a one-dimensional modernist, in thrall to the disintegrative effects of time itself. Berman's reading of the *Manifesto* aims to 'give modernist art and thought a new solidity and invest its creations with an unsuspected resonance and depth.'[29] Yet it is the pure temporal modernism of the desire for the new, the new as an invariant, alone, which he uncovers; thereby robbing the *Manifesto* of its distinctive historical resonance and depth. For the *Manifesto* surely belongs to another modernism, to what Jeff Wall has called 'the dream of a modernism with social content', an 'openly socially critical modernist art',[30] in which formal innovation is a reflective but nonetheless *constructive* play with the culturally mediated aspects of social forms; a modernism for which form is the medium for the expression of the contradictions of historically specific social relations. This dream continues to inspire a diverse array of cultural projects. It serves well as a description of Walter Benjamin's work. The idea that cultural forms are sites for the articulation of social contradictions is central to such a dream. I would therefore like to end with some brief remarks about the absence from Berman's reading of the *Manifesto* of the contradictory social content underlying the revolutionary temporality of capital; an absence which, read symptomatically, draws our attention to certain crucial weaknesses within the *Manifesto* itself.

3. UTOPIANISM AND 'SOBER SENSE'

It is a remarkable feature of Berman's reading of the *Manifesto* that while it restricts itself to the horizon of capital (positing capital as the source of its utopian energy), it is nonetheless parasitic on a utopian vision that is integrally connected to Marx's discourse on communism, a discourse which Berman neglects. This is the sleight of hand that transfigures Marx's appreciation of the enormous, but relative, historical advance of capitalism into an *absolutization* of its productivity, independent of its status as a historical (and therefore, of necessity, eventually a *passing*) social form. Berman transfers the 'absolutism' of the *Manifesto*'s theoretical and literary form wholly onto capital, yet, from the standpoint of the text's narrative structure, the (socially contradictory) productivity of capitalism appears as a historical advance only from the point of view of a *post*-capitalist future; a point of view that Berman's Marx can no longer sustain. In this respect (with regard to the temporal logic of the text), Berman's reading suffers from a fatal incoherence: it invests capital with a utopian charge which cannot, even theoretically, be redeemed. Hence its reduction of utopianism to energetics: 'the glory of modern energy and dynamism, the ravages of modern disintegration and nihilism', and 'the strange intimacy between them'. What Berman leaves out is any account of the social sources of the dynamism of capital, the revolutionary temporality of which he celebrates.

The reason this was possible lies within the *Manifesto* itself: in a series of systematic slippages and contradictions in its treatment of the relations between its four main ideas: the *bourgeoisie*, the *proletariat*, *communism* and *capital*. Space prohibits a proper discussion of these relations here. Suffice to say, the *Manifesto*: (1) conflates the bourgeoisie with capital; while (2) placing the proletariat outside of capital (neglecting its existence as variable capital); thereby (3) enabling a conflation of the proletariat with communism; while (4) reducing capitalism to the logic of capital (neglecting its articulations with other, historically received social forms). As a result, its inherently 'discursive' futurity is curtailed; subordinated to the proletariat's 'narrative' role. The dynamism that the *Manifesto* attributes to the bourgeoisie ('i.e. capital', as the English translation has it at one point) must actually be considered an effect of the dialectic of social classes, as structured, not only by the conditions of capital accumulation, but by the *totality* of social relations obtaining at any particular time. (Think of the importance of immigration to the history of capitalism, for example; not simply in the paradigm-case of the USA, but as a whole.) The power of capital to annihilate received social forms has turned out to be considerably less absolute (indeed, considerably less desirable from the standpoint of the accumulation of capital) than Marx supposed. This is one of the main things that the *Manifesto* draws our attention to today, via the failure of its imagined negation: the continuing vitality within the most advanced capitalist societies of supposedly 'pre-capitalist' social forms.

It is extraordinary that Berman should choose to absolutise the disintegrative, purely abstract temporal modernism of the *Manifesto*'s 'melting' vision – the elimination of every social bond other than 'naked self-interest' – at the very moment when a whole complex of non-economic (or at least, not immediately economic) social relations has come to the fore, politically, in advanced capitalist societies; including all those that the *Manifesto* would have capitalism dissolve (religion, occupational status, family, nation, age, sex), along with others (such as race and ethnicity) which it fails to mention. This is of enormous significance, not only because of what it tells us about the importance to capitalism of what the value-form would destroy (or at best, ignore) – what Balibar calls 'the binding agents of a historical collectivity of individuals', which are subject to a contradictory reintegration into the circuits of capital[31] – but also because of what it has to tell us about the constitutive role of fantasy in social and political processes. For despite Berman's selection of 'sober sense' as one of the most important features of the *Manifesto*'s celebration of capitalism – the compulsion of men and women to face 'their real conditions of life and their relations with their kind' – sober sense, in this specific sense of a theoretically adequate 'demystified' sense, is actually and understandably rather thin on the ground. It is more likely to be via a consideration of the ineliminability of fantasy and imagination from the constitution of social and political identities that the relations between *finitude*, *futurity*, and *social form* are to be understood.

The social forms that Marx would have capitalism destroy live on within it, transformed, as both points of identification and functioning relations, suffused with fantasy in ways which cannot be fully comprehended apart from their 'non-capitalistic dimensions'. For a future beyond capitalism has been figured from its very beginnings, not merely by pre-capitalist social forms (romantic anti-capitalism), but in the concept of *political* community itself. Writing of the experience of history made possible by the technology of the photograph, Benjamin remarks that the beholder feels an irresistible urge to search . . . for the tiny spark of contingency, of the Here and Now, with which reality has so to speak seared the subject, to find the inconspicuous spot where in the immediacy of that long forgotten moment the future subsists so eloquently that we, looking back, may rediscover it.[32]

Reading the *Communist Manifesto* today, one can find a number of such spots, not in those parts which are closest to us, but in those 'sparks of contingency' which now seem farthest away.

NOTES

1. Eric Hobsbawm, *The Age of Revolution*, London, 1962; *The Age of Capital*, London, 1975.
2. Marshall Berman, *All That Is Solid Melts into Air: The Experience of Modernity*, Verso, London, 1982, p.92.
3. Hegel, *Science of Logic*, trans. W.H.Johnson and L.G. Struthers, George Allen and Unwin, London, 1929, Vol.1, p.164.
4. This essay is a truncated version of a paper presented to the conference 'The Criticism of the Future' organized by the School of English at the University of Kent, Canterbury, England, 11 July 1997, from which a broader philosophical argument has been removed. An extended version, reflecting more widely upon the question of 'what is living and what is dead' in Marx's text, will appear in John Fletcher et al, *Return of the Gothic*, forthcoming.

    Quotations from the *Manifesto* are taken from the English translation in Karl Marx and Frederick Engels, *Collected Works*, Volume 6, Progress Publishers, Moscow, 1976, pp. 477-519. This translation also appears in a pocket-book edition by the same publisher (1952ff), along with translations of various of Marx's and Engels' Prefaces.
5. Translation altered to amend 'man' to 'men and women', 'people' or 'human' as appropriate, in the spirit of the critique of abstract humanism in *The German Ideology* (1845).
6. Berman, *All That Is Solid*, pp.89, 102.
7. Peter Osborne, *The Politics of Time: Modernity and Avant-Garde*, Verso, London and New York, 1995, pp.13-14, 23.
8. Anna Lawton (ed.), *Russian Futurism Through its Manifestos, 1912-1928*, trans. Anna Lawton and Herbert Eagle, Cornell University Press, Ithaca and London, 1988, pp.51-2; 'Manifesto of Surrealism' in André Breton, *Manifestos of Surrealism*, trans. Richard Seaver and Helen R. Lane, University of Michigan Press, Ann Arbor, 1972, p.47.
9. Berman, *All That Is Solid*, p.121.
10. Karl Marx, 'The Poverty of Philosophy' (1947), in Marx/Engels, *Collected Works* 6, p.127.
11. Walter Benjamin, 'Central Park', trans. Lloyd Spencer, *New German Critique* 34 (Winter 1985), p.46 ; Theodor W. Adorno, *Aesthetic Theory*, trans. C. Lenhardt, Routledge, London and New York, 1984, p.41.
12. See Osborne, *The Politics of Time*, pp.3, 23-32.
13. Immanuel Kant, *Critique of Judgment* (1790), trans. Werner S. Pluhar, Hackett, Indianapolis/Cambridge, 1987, p.58. Hannah Arendt insisted that it was here, in

the *Critique of Judgment*, that Kant's political philosophy was to be found. See her *Lectures on Kant's Political Philosophy*, University of Chicago Press, Chicago, 1982.

14. What follows is not intended as a comprehensive analysis. It merely outlines some of the main features to which such an approach could be expected to attend.

15. Engels, 'Draft of a Communist Confession of Faith', in Marx/Engels, *Collected Works*, 6, p.96.

16. Engels, 'Principles of Communism', in *ibid.*, p.341.

17. Emile Benveniste, *Problems in General Linguistics*, trans. Mary Elizabeth Meek, University of Miami Press, Coral Gables, 1971, pp.195–215.

18. *Russian Futurism*, p.52.

19. Walter Benjamin '[Re The Theory of Knowledge, Theory of Progress]', in Gary Smith (ed.), *Benjamin: Philosophy, Aesthetic, History*, Chicago University Press, Chicago, 1989, pp. 50ff.

20. Walter Benjamin, 'The Concept of Criticism in German Romanticism'(1920), in his *Selected Writings. Volume 1, 1913–1926*, Harvard University Press, Cambridge MA and London, 1996, pp. 185–6, note 3. Benjamin quotes Friedrich Schlegel: 'The revolutionary desire to realize the kingdom of God on earth is the elastic point of progressive civilization and the inception of modern history.' See also Philippe Lacou-Labarthe and Jean-Luc Nancy, *The Literary Absolute: The Theory of Literature in German Romanticism*, trans. Philip Bernard and Cheryl Lester, SUNY, 1988.

21. Benjamin, 'The Author as Producer', in his *Understanding Brecht*, trans. Anna Bostock, New Left Books, London, 1977, p.89.

22. Benjamin, 'The Work of Art in the Age of Mechanical Reproduction', in his *Illuminations*, Fontana, London, 1973, p.239.

23. *Ibid.*

24. Jacques Rancière, *The Names of History: On the Poetics of Knowledge*, trans. Hassan Melehy, Minnesota University Press, Minneapolis, 1994.

25. Tristan Tzara, 'Dada Manifesto' (1918), in his *Seven Dada Manifestos and Lampisteries*, trans. Barbara Wright, Calder Publications, London, 1977, p.3.

26. Tzara, 'Dada Manifesto on Feeble Love and Bitter Love', in *ibid*, p.33.

27. Tzara, 'Dada Manifesto', in *ibid*, p.3.

28. Howard Caygill, *Walter Benjamin: The Colour of Experience*, Routledge, London and New York, 1998, p.71. Caygill uses the phrase to summarise Benjamin's reading of Döblin's novel, *Berlin Alexanderplatz*.

29. *All That Is Solid*, p.122.

30. Jeff Wall, *Dan Graham's Kammerspiel*, Art Metropole, Toronto, p.100.

31. Etienne Balibar, in Etienne Balibar and Immanuel Wallerstein, *Race, Nation, Class: Ambiguous Identities*, trans. Chris Turner,Verso, London and New York, 1991, p.8.

32. Walter Benjamin, 'A Small History of Photography', in his *One-Way Street and Other Writings*, trans. Edmund Jephcott and Kingsley Shorter, New Left Books, London, 1979, p.243.

SEEING IS BELIEVING: MARX'S *MANIFESTO*, DERRIDA'S APPARITION

Paul Thomas

WHAT'S IN A WORD?

To begin at the beginning: Why *Manifesto* of the Communist Party? Why not 'programme', 'platform', or 'declaration of principles'? Why not 'decree' or 'proclamation'? The noun 'manifesto' has the currency it enjoys today, and not just in English, largely because of Marx's own choice of the word. Even though he did not invent it (he is likely to have adopted it from an important source, Sylvain Maréchal's 1796 *Manifeste des Egaux*),[1] it is Marx who bears much or even most of the responsibility for putting the word on our lexicological map.

Not just in English: this gives us an important clue. *Manifestation* in French means 'demonstration' shading over into 'protest'. *Manifestant* is the French (or German), *manifestante* the Spanish or Italian, for 'demonstrator'. 'Manifestant' was sometimes used in English after the 1860s, but was duly supplanted (by the 1880s, according to the OED) by the word 'demonstrator' or 'protester'. The German verb *manifestieren* means ' to declare'; the Italian nouns *manifestazióne* and *manifestino* mean 'performance' and 'leaflet, pamphlet or broadside' respectively.

Thus far 'manifesto' seems to mean that which makes manifest, or demonstrates – demonstrates in the additional sense in which a scientific truth is demonstrated, by being made public or visible. A manifesto, that is to say, can have nothing arcane or recondite about it. It has to be accessible. One could of course say the same about decrees or edicts. Yet a manifesto cannot be equated with a proclamation or *ukase* because it is not necessarily issued from a pre-given position of power. To the contrary, demonstrations or manifestations are generally protests, public protests, against what those in positions of power get up to, or away with. They involve that we make our voices heard, and that we be willing to put ourselves, our bodily safety, on the line. *Manifestus* in Latin literally means 'struck by the hand' (*fendere* means 'to strike') but came to have the meaning of 'evident, clear or plain'. But this is *only part* of its meaning in English too, as a glance at historical dictionaries will reveal. My Webster's gives us for the verb 'to manifest' the following, to be sure: 'to reveal, make appear, show plainly, make public, disclose to the eye or understanding'. (The word 'make' is important and stands out here, for reasons I shall get to presently). Webster's goes on to give us 'to reveal, show, exhibit, display, declare, or discover'. (In keeping with this, the only non-obselete usage of 'manifest' as a noun in English means a list of a ship's cargo, an invoice that is to be shown or exhibited at the customhouse). Accordingly, the OED adds to Webster's inventory of meanings of the verb 'to manifest' these others: 'to be evidence of, prove or attest; to expound or unfold; to display, to give evidence of possessing, to reveal the presence of, to evince'. Yet, intriguingly, these apparently anodyne listings are not the synonyms of 'manifest' they might appear to be at first glance. To see this we must turn again to Webster's characterization of 'manifest', this time as an adjective: 'What is *clear* can be seen in all its bearings; what is *plain* can be seen by any man without study or reflection; what is *obvious* lies directly in the way, and must be seen by every one; what is *evident* is seen forcibly, and leaves no hesitation in the mind; what is *manifest* is evident in a very high degree, striking upon the mind at once with overpowering conviction'. This hits the nail on the head. If anything is to be manifest, it has to be *made* manifest (as in the Biblical English of the King James Bible). And *making* manifest is precisely what Marx is up to in the *Communist Manifesto*, as we shall see, in a variety of different, though interdependent, senses. Making manifest, so understood, is not just a form of words, or what the French call a *façon de parler*. It is a kind of action – as Marx, I shall argue, was perfectly well aware.

WHAT'S IN AN OPENING LINE?

First we must undertake a detour, for there is another understanding of 'manifestation,' not touched on above, that has enjoyed some recent intellectual currency for all the wrong reasons. This is its understanding as 'apparition'. In some ways regrettably, it has become impossible to write about Marx's *Manifesto* during the 1990s without invoking Jacques Derrida's *Specters of Marx*, which is itself an invocation of Marx. But not the Marx I am writing about. Derrida, to be brief, wants the 'spectre haunting Europe' in the *Manifesto's* (probably mistranslated) opening line to be haunting Marx too – as an instance of the uncanny or of *das Unheimliche*, much as Freud had understood the term. The reasons why Derrida wants to make this move, indeed the reasons why *das Unheimliche* has become so suddenly fashionable for the first time, can only briefly occupy us here. Derrida wants the spectre haunting Europe to be haunting Marx too for reasons having much more to do with 'spectrality' as such than with Marx. Derrida gives 'spectrality' a great deal of work to do; he believes that a world purged or cleansed of 'spectrality' – much as he assigns this understanding of 'spectrality' to Marx – would be a world of pure presence, immediacy, materiality, objectivity, facticity, a reified world of things that lack a past dimension. (Such a world would correspond to Fukuyama's notorious 'end of history', which Derrida nicely, and correctly, terms 'apocalyptic'). Without 'spectrality', Derrida claims, philosophy would be displaced by a bland Anglo-American anti-speculative positivism and empiricism. Whether or not 'spectrality', so understood, is the legitimate counterpart to the very globalizing tendencies Derrida is surely right to detest depends on whether more is made to hang on the hook of the concept of 'spectrality' than it can reasonably be expected to bear. Overload seems distinctly likely: but over and above this question, a fairly obvious interjection – one which seems not to have occurred to Derrida – imposes itself. This is that twentieth-century 'spectrality' can be imposed by technological means. The Walter Benjamin that Derrida invokes calls upon us to preserve and sustain a 'weak messianic' power in dark patches of our history, but we should remember that this same Walter Benjamin also wrote 'The Work of Art in the Age of Mechanical Reproduction', for reproduction these days can, and commonly does, include the reproduction of 'spectrality' itself.[2]

Derrida, for reasons outlined above, reads Marx's *Gespenst* as what the French term a *revenant*, that which comes or comes again from beyond the grave to haunt and horrify the living. While this interpretation – and all translation is interpretation, as Derrida is only too well aware – enables Derrida to inscribe Marx within a 'hauntology' by which Derrida himself is evidently ensorcelled, there are problems with it.

The first is that Marx's spectre or *Gespenst* may not be a *revenant* in the above sense at all. It is noteworthy that the most recent, and most accomplished, translation into English of the *Manifesto* (that done by

Terrell Carver for Cambridge University Press in 1996) renders Marx's *Ein Gespenst geht um in Europa* in much the same way as had the original English-language rendition in George Julian Harney's *The Red Republican* in 1850: 'a spectre stalks the land of Europe'.[3] 'Stalks' as a verb of motion is a much more likely translation of the German verb *umgehen in* than is 'haunts', and was so in Marx's day as in our own.[4] In view of the entire, immense superstructure Derrida erects on the basis of a much less orthodox translation of Marx's celebrated opening line (which he claims – disingenuously? – he had forgotten), we must outline a second problem. Who is supposed to be afraid of Marx's spectre? Marx himself immediately specifies the 'holy alliance', the real-life Holy Alliance of the 'Congress System', 'of Pope and Tsar, Metternich and Guizot, French radicals and German police'. While these may have recoiled in various degrees of horror, feigned or otherwise, at the spectre they themselves had invented and invoked, it is more to the point that they were bent on seeing to it, with every power at their disposal, that others should quake in their boots at the onset of this apparition. The Holy Alliance, after all, was not made up of holy innocents; not to mince words, they were an instance of full-fledged reaction, with blood on their hands. If 'all that is holy is profaned,'[5] why should the self-proclaimed Holy Alliance, of all people, be exempt? The 'spectre of communism' was one they conjured up to make people afraid of it.

ON SORCERY AND WITCHHUNTS

To what end, after all, was the Holy Alliance allied in the first place? For the sake of a 'witchhunt'. Carver's translation should once again give us pause. We all know that witchhunts always find what they are looking for. Witches may never have existed – they too were 'apparitions' – but witchhunts invariably found them all the same. Witchhunts accuse others, those their perpetrators call witches, of conjuring up evil spirits; but, in a neat ideological inversion, witchhunts themselves conjure up witches *as* evil spirits. They willfully mischaractertize the objects of their concern to the point of inventing them out of thin air, or of calling them into being.

We also know that witchhunts and communists go together, that these indeed have gone together ever since (and, as we shall see, even before) we could speak of 'communism' at all. 'Where is the opposition that has not been smeared as communistic by its enemies in government?', asks the *Manifesto* – a question that sounds like a minute-bell through twentieth-century, let alone nineteenth-century, history. Witchhunts had needed witchcraft to the extent of inventing it, of calling their adversaries, witches, into being. So too anti-communist witchhunts, their heirs and successors, need their own spectral communists, to the point of finding these where none exist, producing real victims who are likely to be guilty of nothing at all. Examples, sad to say, abound.

Marx, whatever Derrida may think, is *unafraid* of the spectre the Holy Alliance and its lackeys had conjured up. His object in the *Manifesto* is in large part to dispel such fears. 'It is high time for communists to lay before the world their perspectives, their goals, their principles, and to counterpose to the horror stories of communism a manifesto of the party itself'. Most translations of the *Manifesto* into English give us 'nursery tales' for Carver's 'horror stories,' which can occlude the fact that in 1848 – especially in 1848 ! – there was no hard-and-fast distinction between nursery tales and horror stories (think of Hans Christian Andersen and the brothers Grimm) and with it the fact that those who recounted the latter did so with the wish of instilling fear among their listeners (and, less often, themselves too). But fear is the last emotion Marx wished to instill – which means that if the spectre stalking the land is spirit not made flesh, this is to be under-stood as meaning spirit not *yet* made flesh. It is unsubstantiated, perhaps, but this is to say that it awaits its substantiation, a substan-tation that only Marx and his readers can give it.

To put the same point another way, Marx's spectre does not hark back to anything that came before it. It doesn't come from beyond the grave to plague or torment us. It is not a reminder of some past or primordial existence. It is meant to point forwards, projectively and prospectively, not backwards and retroactively. And this is to say that there is, quite simply, nothing uncanny or *unheimlich* about it at all, whatever Derrida and others may think. Quite to the contrary, Marx's spectre sets us the task of finding it a home or making it a home in the world. It is not dreadful save to those who have prior cause to dread its advent. To the rest of us it is a tocsin, a call to action. As Frederic Jameson has pointed out, the *Hamlet* Marx's spectre suggested to Derrida was itself 'not a ghost story'; 'it did not merely tell about some grisly hold of the past on the present . . . but rather showed the apparition of the past in the act of provoking future action and calling for retribution by the living'. To extend Jameson's point, the 'spectrality' of the future differs in kind from that of the past (or of the *revenant*). While it too may not be at one with the present, this is the case only to the extent that 'its blurred lineaments . . . announce or foretell themselves'. Because Marx's *Manifesto* is in this sense proleptic in its argumentation, the spectrality Derrida misprises is in fact a 'form of the most radical politicization . . . far from being locked into the repetitions of neurosis and obsession (like the *unheimlich*), it is energetically future-oriented and active'. And in this way, as Jameson proceeds to indicate, 'the spectrality of the future . . . answers to the haunting spectrality of the past, which is historicity itself'.[7]

ON THE SPECTRAL AND THE PREMONITORY

The deeper question begged by all this is, of course, whether an emergent social phenomenon's lack of visibility is 'a sign of its inescapable spectrality' (as Derrida seems to think, but which seems preposterous) or, instead, in Malcolm Bull's words 'a historically significant indication of the nature and location of positive values in contemporary society'[8]. *Inescapable* spectrality is emphatically not the register of the *Manifesto*. To appropriate an intriguing observation from Bull (who is, I think, right to perceive a pattern here), beliefs of the kind that are calls to action have often been 'everywhere condemned and nowhere to be found'. Fervent denunciations of the evils of atheism, for instance, predated, preceded and (in a sense) provoked the appearance of real, self-professed, flesh-and-blood atheists on the historical stage. These duly manifested themselves in the flesh once their adversaries had prepared the way, invoked them and (as it were) told them what they'd have to do. Moreover, 'just as the invention of atheism had taken place without anybody actually advocating the position', so too 'the invention and repudiation of anarchism occurred without the intervention of any anarchists. No-one espoused an explicitly anarchist position until William Godwin, and no-one used "anarchist" in a positive sense until Proudhon. However, that did not prevent anarchists from being roundly abused' at every turn. Similarly, later in the nineteenth century, 'there was no-one claiming to be a nihilist, just a chorus of outraged moralists arguing that nihism was an outrage'. The temper of the times is often a complex business. Atheism, anarchism, nihilism – these form what Bull calls a 'series of spectral negations' each of which 'is not so much unrealizable as temporarily disembodied'.[9] Those who duly came to embody the positions in question are not spectres or *revenants* but people who felt capable of acting out positively a role that others were bent on condemning, out of hand, as unthinkable and outrageous.

Marx, when he wrote the *Manifesto*, was clearly one of these people. But in saying this I must make my sense clear. I have no wish to reduce Marx's communism to Bull's patterning; if ever a political document proved premonitory and outlived the circumstances of its conception, the *Manifesto* is that document. Even so, Bull's patterning can cast significant light on what Marx was up to in the *Manifesto* (and elsewhere), and can (as has become necessary) give the lie to Derrida into the bargain. The spectre circulating, then in Europe and later elsewhere, may have been in a certain sense wraithlike – but not, surely not, in the sense of being a *revenant* or reminder. It was then something originary and unprecedented. It seemed wraithlike and threatening because the Holy Alliance and its minions, in their outrage and condemnation, could not give it form, could not even see or identify it clearly, but their rhetoric created a space in which Marx could etch his notoriously bold outlines. Why else could Marx have insisted so brazenly that people were 'compelled to face with sober senses'[10] something that, to others (who lacked, and needed to lack, the perception) presented to the world as sheer delirium or nightmare? The disembodiment of Marx's spectre (*pace* Derrida) is purely provisional; it awaits the embodiment that the *Manifesto* – that the *Manifesto*'s very language – proceeded, with no small flourish, to give it. In its pages Marx is openly, publicly, ostentatiously, brazenly declaring himself and his collaborators to be communists; in so doing he is naming communism itself, identifying it as a doctrine, movement and method of social analysis. He is pulling it together, fusing and synthesizing tendencies which, but for his efforts, might have remained fissiparous or even contradictory. He is seizing the time, giving substance to something that appeared to the cowed and craven to be frightening as mere form. Marx's writing the *Manifesto of the Communist Party* was an act of unexampled and audacious theoretical originality.

In advancing so ambitious a claim I am only too uncomfortably aware that the temper of our *fin-de-siècle* times, as I write, seems to be decidedly arrayed against Marxism in general and thus against its distillate, the *Manifesto*, in particular. The considerable intellectual *éclat* of Derrida's *Specters of Marx* (which bucks a trend and ostentatiously refrains from disparaging Marx or his *Manifesto*) can have no other explanation. Even the extant secondary literature on the *Manifesto* (if this generalization is permissible), which is also generally admiring, effectively damns it with faint praise all the same – by parading an admiration for its eloquence or forcefulness without explaining either of these characteristics. And this in turn can be a way of extracting it from the body of Marx's thought and action, of consigning the *Manifesto*, not to oblivion (for who in truth could remain indifferent to its forcefulness?) but to the mid-nineteenth century, as though this were a bygone, long-forgotten era. To do so is to make of the *Manifesto* a mere *pièce de circonstance*, which is exactly what it is not. Every word it says about capital and wage-labour explains why the nineteenth century has not yet really been surpassed, (except by the calendar) .

Here I am only too happy to buck the same trend as Derrida bucked in 1994, albeit for different reasons. My sense is that what Marx accomplished in the *Manifesto* is almost immeasurable. (Without retracting what I've said against Derrida, I must add in fairness that he too, in what has to be his most *engagé* book to date, senses its immeasurability). But the dimensions of Marx's accomplishment cannot be gauged or even approached if we isolate the *Manifesto*, as though it were a set-piece, from the body of Marx's thought and action as a whole. Far from wishing to underestimate or misprize one of *Marx's* most *engagé* writings under the impress of current events, I propose to raise the stakes of my argument by proposing that even a hundred and fifty years after its composition, we have not even begun to think through the enormity of what Marx achieved as a theorist when he wrote it.

Marx, to get this argument into perspective, may have been guilty of a certain hubris when he wrote in *The German Ideology* that 'where speculation ends, in real life . . . real, positive science begins'.[11] My point is that Marx's claim had a real content to it, and that having advanced it he did not rest content, 'blissfully satisfied with his own construction'.[12] He proceeded to act it out, to put it into practice, and (*pace* Derrida) to give it bodily form. Marx's insight was simply –simply! – that theory, to be effective, can no longer rest content with producing empty, abstract nostrums of the kind that would put the world to rights by virtue of their very elaboration, or their intellectual elegance. If people fail to act on the basis of their beliefs – as Marx proceeded to act on the basis of his – they might as well be whistling in the dark in propounding or expounding such beliefs, or indulging themselves in what Marx had already, archly (but not at all unfairly), called 'theoretical bubble-blowing'.[13]

What is most unforgiveable and ironic, Marxologically at any rate, about Derrida's *Specters of Marx* is that he sees a connection between *The Manifesto of the Communist Party* and *The German Ideology*, a connection that really is there to be made, but he draws it out in a way that could not be more misleading – or more fatal to his own argument. He reads back his misprized notion of spectre as *revenant* from the *Manifesto* to *The German Ideology*. So unwarranted a misreading results in confusion considerably worse confounded. The longest section of the manuscript Marx and Engels left 'to the gnawing criticism of the mice' deals with Max Stirner. Derrida thinks that because Stirner's *Spuk*, Marx's spectre and their common ancestor, Hegel's *Geist* , are all *revenants*, the figure of the *revenant* is the 'common stake (inciting) the polemic'.[14] The trouble is that Marx, for his part, set out to ridicule and deflate what he sees as Stirner's quintessentially Young-Hegelian, i.e. *too*-Hegelian obsession with spooks, spectres, apparitions and the like, categories which Stirner according to Marx takes far too seriously! For Stirner, 'history becomes a mere history of pseudo-ideas, a history about spirits and spectres, while the real empirical history that is the basis of this ghostly history is only utilized to provide bodies for these spectres . . . (Stirner) writes an undisguised ghost story (*Geistergeschichter*)'.[15] Stirner takes not the world, but only his 'delirious fantasy' about the world as his subject. Derrida thinks Stirner 'poached' the spectres of Marx, spectres that were never there to be poached in the first place; Marx for his part thinks Stirner poaches 'snipe existing only in the mind'.[16] His point is one that Derrida would have done well to take on board: that attempts to achieve concreteness by the conjuring away or exorcism of spectres, ghosts, apparitions, *und so weiter*, attempts that are effected, that is to say, on the basis of deficient principle, will result only in *re*-enchantment, the construction of an even more imaginary entity than one started out with – an insight that, as Marshall Berman has memorably pointed out, Marx extends in the pages of the *Manifesto* itself, where the bourgeoisie are explicitly portrayed not as ghostbusters but as sorcerers' apprentices, unable by their very nature to control the forces that they are obliged to conjure up.[17]

The question raised by all of the above is, of course, that of how concreteness *is* to be achieved amidst the welter of illusions that Marx is concerned to puncture, not just in the *Manifesto* but in *The German Ideology* (and *The Eighteenth Brumaire*) too.[18] A full answer would entail exceeding my brief, which is to write about the *Manifesto* after a century and a half, and my needlessly repeating arguments already made elsewhere.[19] Yet it is germane to the enterprise at hand to indicate that the *Manifesto*, if it is looked at 'with sober senses', contains and even embodies what are more than hints at what an answer involves.

That knowledge of history can enjoy a premonitory status is a leitmotif of the *Manifesto*. As Jerrold Siegel remarks, '[c]entral to the historical vision that Marx offered [in the *Manifesto*] was the theme of revelation: modern life revealed basic features of history that had previously remained mysterious or hidden'.[20]

This is a claim not just about history but about knowledge of history, knowledge that is necessarily theoretical in scope. Yet this is theory of the kind that overreaches and exceeds the 'given' boundaries of theorizing or of empty, arid speculation of the Hegelian or Young-Hegelian kind – as Georg Lukács recognized.[21] It is the proletariat's theoretical sophistication, and not the sheer weight of its numbers in a world where 'Communists direct their attention chiefly to Germany'[22] (where the proletariat was comparatively meagre in number) that is finally to count or be crucial. The importance of this point invites and yet resists overstatement. Marx, Sheldon Wolin has pointed out, 'founded a new conception of politics, revolutionary in intent, proletarian in concern, and internationalist in scope and organization'.[23] This new conception of what politics could, and should become involved a new conception of theory with which we *still* need to come to terms. The point here is not that Marx was alone in devoting his life to a revolutionary cause he regarded as an urgent agenda. The merest glance at the wonderland of nineteenth-century revolutionary theorizing would show that Marx did not lack for company, or even companionship, in this quest. Yet there is something singular about Marx's project that lodges in the mind. In 1857 we find him writing to Engels: 'I am working madly through the nights so that, before the deluge, I shall at least have the outlines clear'.[24] This has to stand as one of the most extraordinary statements about theorizing ever made. It's not Louis XIV's notorious, but oddly complacent, 'après moi le déluge' so much as 'because of what I can *do* – the deluge', a deluge that is not, like Louis XIV's, going to happen anyway but a deluge that isn't about to happen if Marx's principled argument finds insufficient takers. Small wonder, perhaps that Prometheus was the most inspiring 'saint' on Marx's calendar. But it is a matter, surely, not just of Prometheus, the bringer of fire, but also of Archimedes: Marx views theorizing as a lever with which to move the world. And whatever we may think of the movement he effected, it *did* move the world.

But how, in the end, are we to assess his accomplishment? It is customary, or at least admissible to portray Marx as having stood at the point of intersection of three intellectual tendencies, which were also political tendencies: the plebeian revolutionary radicalism that had surfaced in the course of the French Revolution, under the influence of Rousseau's insistence that social rank and moral worth during the *ancien régime* were inversely related; the cognate Hegelian insistence that mankind redeem the world of philosophical speculation, instead of wallowing in it self-indulgently, by recognizing itself in a world it had consciously made; and the then-new 'science' of political economy that had surfaced most markedly in Scotland and England and had had more than a glancing effect on the French and German Enlightenments. All well and good. Yet Marxian theory should on no account be reduced to merely occupying the point where these meridians intersected for the first and only time. Marxian theory transcended their intersection in a way that anyone doing intellectual labour should find inspirational. At the very least it raised the possibility that the much-vaunted 'unity of theory and practice' can indeed become a reality, and can embody what Ernst Bloch so memorably termed 'futurity' (*das Zukunftige*).

The Marxian enterprise, I am suggesting by way of conclusion, was in the fullest sense of the term a *political* enterprise. The *Manifesto* in particular gave expression to a wish that the scope of politics, and of theory, be extended, given more meaning and greater resonance than politics or theory had ever had heretofore. Only such an expansion, we should still remember, can render the 'revolutionary unity of theory and practice' anything other than an empty phrase or *Redeweise*. Such a unity of the theoretical and the practical, the *Manifesto* could also remind us, cannot be an arbitrary juxtaposition, but only a genuine convergence or confluence of forces that could otherwise remain as antagonistic in perpetuity as they still are today.

NOTES

1. Most readily encountered, perhaps, in Raymond Postgate, *Revolution from 1789 to 1906: Documents Selected and Edited with Notes and Introductions*, Gloucester, Mass., Peter Smith, 1969, pp. 54–6.
2. I am thinking of the film *Forrest Gump*, a disgraceful and sinister travesty of history that (far from innocently) converts what had been a playful conceit in Woody Allen's *Zelig* into a systematic fabulation. But the technological spectral has longer, and deeper roots. See David King, *The Commissar Vanishes. The Falsification of Photographs and Art in Stalin's Russia*, New York, Henry Holt, 1997, *passim*; Peter Kenez, 'Soviet Cinema in the Age of Stalin', in Richard Taylor and Derek Spring, eds., *Stalinism and Soviet Cinema*, New York and London, Routledge, 1993, pp. 54–68; and Paul Thomas, review of the same volume, *Film Quarterly*, Vol. 50, No. 1, Fall 1996, pp. 63–4.
3. Marx, *Later Political Writings*, edited and translated by Terrell Carver, Cambridge

University Press, 1996, p. 1. Helen McFarlane, the un-named original translator of the *Manifesto*, which appeared unsigned as *German Communism: Manifesto of the German Communist Party* on the title page of George Julian Harney's *The Red Republican*, 9 November, 1850, renders the opening line as 'a frightful hobgoblin stalks throughout Europe'. (The title page is reproduced in Dirk J. Struik, *Birth of the Communist Manifesto*, New York, International Publishers, 1971, p. 146).

4. *Umgehen in*, according to *Cassell's German Dictionary*, means to go round, to revolve, to circulate, to circumvent, to make a circuit or detour, to approach in a roundabout way, to associate, to have to do with, to be occupied with, to have dealings with, to handle, manage or have in mind. Only then does Cassell's render *umgehen in* as 'to haunt' (or to walk around, elude or evade). My point is that none of these meanings, not even 'to haunt' itself, has any necessary connection with the *revenant* as such, and that *umgehen in* can almost always be rendered by verbs of motion or (re)location. 'Haunt' can in any case mean frequent (*haüfig besuchen*); infect, overrun, afflict or punish (*heimsuchen*); plague, vex, torment or annoy (*plagen*); or pursue, follow, trail, persecute or prosecute (*verfolgen*). That all these renderings of 'to haunt' precede *umgehen in* in Cassell's proves nothing, but suggests a kind of multivalence that Derrrida's *revenant* , if anything, tends to foreclose. My contention is that Marx, for his part, was and must have been aware of the various meanings and senses of the German verb he saw fit to employ, all of which tell us something about the effect on the reader he wanted it to have.

5. I prefer the more orthodox 'holy' to Carver's 'sacred' (see Marx, *Later Political Writings*, p. 4) for reasons that are evident in my text.

6. *Later Political Writings*, p. 1.

7. Frederic Jameson, 'Marx's Purloined Letter', *New Left Review*, 209, Jan.–Feb. 1995, pp. 103–4.

8. Malcolm Bull, 'The Ecstasy of Philistinism,' *New Left Review*, 219, Sept–Oct 1996, pp. 22–41, esp. pp.26–7.

9. Bull, *passim*.

10. For 'compelled to face with sober senses', Carver gives us 'finally forced to take a down-to-earth view'; (See *Later Political Writings*, p, 4); the difference seems trifling.

11. Marx and Engels, *The German Ideology*, translated and edited by Sala Ryazanskaya, Moscow, Progress Publishers, 1964, pp. 38–9. Marx may for that matter have been guilty of a certain scientism too, though my doubts about this are a matter of record. See Paul Thomas, 'Marx and Science', *Political Studies*, vol. XXIV, March 1976, pp. 1–24.

12. *The German Ideology*, p. 197.

13. See Paul Thomas, *Karl Marx and the Anarchists*, London and New York, Routledge, 1985, pp. 125–74.

14. Jacques Derrida, *Specters of Marx*, translated by Peggy Kamuf, New York and London, Routledge, 1994, p. 132; *The German Ideology*, p. 470.

15. *The German Ideology*, p. 135.

16. Derrida, *Specters of Marx*, p. 140: *The German Ideology*, p. 470.

17. See Marshall Berman, *All That Is Solid Melts Into Air. The Experience of Modernity*, Harmondsworth, Penguin Books, 1988, esp. pp. 87--129, for a dazzling interpretation which can be faulted only by the observation that the presumed quote from the *Manifesto* in Berman's title isn't there in the German-language original. I am grateful to Seyla Benhabib for being the first to point this out to me. Carver

renders it, again correctly, as 'Everything feudal and fixed goes up in smoke'. See *Later Political Writings*, p. 4.

18. See Paul Thomas, *Alien Politics: Marxist State Theory Retrieved*, New York and London, Routledge, 1994, pp 87–109.
19. Thomas, *Karl Marx and the Anarchists* and *Alien Politics, passim.*
20. Jerrold Siegel, *Marx's Fate*, Princeton, Princeton University Press, 1978, p. 195.
21. Georg Lukács, *History and Class Consciousness*, translated by Rodney Livingstone, Cambridge, Mass., MIT Press, 1971. The book was written almost a half-century before Lukács would authorize its full translation.
22. *Later Political Writings*, p. 30.
23. Sheldon Wolin, quoted in *Karl Marx and the Anarchists*, p. 13.
24. *Marx-Engels Werke* (MEW), Berlin, Dietz, vol. XXIX, 1966, p. 225

THE MAKING OF THE MANIFESTO

Rob Beamish

INTRODUCTION

The anonymous, 23 page, *Manifest der Kommunistischen Partei* was rushed off the presses in London in the latter part of February 1848 by the central committee of the Communist League but still arrived in Berlin, Cologne, Königsberg and other parts of Prussia too late to play a major role in the revolutionary activities unfolding later the next month.[1] Nevertheless, compact, cogent, and compelling in its imagery and rhetoric, the *Communist Manifesto* (as its title became after the 1872 Leipzig edition), was destined to be the founding document of a longer-term revolution whose ultimate fate is, contrary to today's right-wing orthodoxy, by no means resolved.

Surprisingly, Marx's and Engels' published accounts of the *Manifesto* tend to obscure what they achieved in the pamphlet, above all because they ignore the important controversies and conflicts that led up to it. Thus, for example, in the preface to the 1872 German edition, Marx and Engels presented the contentious and, at times, confrontational history leading up to the writing of the *Manifesto* in the following manner.

> The Communist League, an international association of workers, which could of course be only a secret one, under the conditions obtaining at the time, commissioned us, the undersigned, at the Congress held in London in November, 1847, to write for publication a detailed theoretical and practical programme of the Party. Such was the origin of the following *Manifesto*, the manuscript of which travelled to London to be printed a few weeks before the February Revolution.[2]

While Marx's recollection included in *Herr Vogt*, and Engels' longer 1885 account, are more informative, they too are still silent on a number of important issues related to the history of the Communist League and, more important, the historical, political, and intellectual context within which the *Manifesto* was developed and written.[3] In the Preface to the 1888 edition (which echoes his preface statement to the

1883 edition), Engels wrote the following:

> The *Manifesto* being our joint production, I consider myself bound to state that the fundamental proposition which forms its nucleus belongs to Marx. That proposition is: That in every historical epoch, the prevailing mode of economic production and exchange, and the social organisation necessarily following from it, form the basis upon which is built up, and from which alone can be explained the political and intellectual history of that epoch; that consequently the whole history of mankind (since the dissolution of primitive tribal society, holding land in common ownership) has been a history of class struggles, contests between exploiting and exploited, ruling and oppressed classes; that the history of these class struggles forms a series of evolutions in which, nowadays, a stage has been reached where the exploited and oppressed class – the proletariat – cannot attain its emancipation from the sway of the exploiting and ruling class – the bourgeoisie – without, at the same time, and once and for all emancipating society at large from all exploitation, oppression, class distinction and class struggles.[4]

To a certain extent Engels' statement is true (although it tends somewhat to exaggerate the role that he himself played in actually writing the *Manifesto*), but it presents at least two problems. First, Engels' statement reflects Marx's 1859 Preface to *A Contribution to the Critique of Political Economy* more than it does the text of the *Manifesto*, although there are certainly phrases and sections of the *Manifesto* that sound strikingly like the Preface (both highly compressed texts).

Second, and more important, it directs the reader's attention to selected themes and issues in the *Manifesto* while ignoring others. The *Manifesto* is one of the high-water points in Marx's life because four crucial currents converged in its production: (a) it was written on the basis of a fundamental resolution to the major epistemological and theoretical issues Marx had been struggling with since 1836; (b) it represents the victory of Marx's intellectual vision in the political arena – his triumph as the intellectual and inspirational leader of the Communist League (and hence also of his critique of other forms of socialism – Part III of the *Manifesto*); (c) Marx's astute use of rhetoric and imagery enhances the important subjective side of Marx's revolutionary perspective (class struggle involves class consciousness and the *Manifesto* was to provide workers with a deeper, conscious understanding of their reality, of their role in history, and to inspire them to take appropriate action given Marx's analysis of the situation); (d) Marx's relationship with Engels – Marx owed a major debt to Engels in reaching the intellectual stage he was at when he wrote the *Manifesto*, but there were also differences and the relationship between the *Manifesto* and Engels' earlier 'Basic Principles of Communism' needs to be better understood than it has tended to be in the past.

Fortunately, by turning to Marx's and Engels' correspondence, their writing projects from 1841 through to February 1848, and some later scholarly work, we can construct a more illuminating account that not only shows the theoretical, political, and strategic debates, conflicts and, eventually, animosities out of which the *Manifesto* emerged, but also permits one to appreciate the full extent to which the form and content of the *Manifesto* are the result of intense intellectual and political battles fought by Marx, Engels, and their supporters as they tried to direct and lead the fledgling communist movement of the 1840s. The *Manifesto* was ultimately a collective effort of people who were trying to understand the prevailing social conditions so they could change them; to see this more precisely allows us to demystify and 'de-reify' it as a source of eternal truths, and return it to its proper place in the annals of the struggle for socialism as one of many documents – a key one to be sure – constructed within, and thus influenced by, a particular set of historical circumstances.

HISTORICAL BACKGROUND

It was France, in general, and Paris in particular from which communist and socialist ideas were transmitted into Germany.[5] In addition, because industrial workers constituted only a small portion of the population – and, as ex-artisans, they tended to long more for a nostalgic past than a socialist or communist future – the critique of capitalist social relations appealed more to members of the intellectual elite in Germany than to the industrial workers.[6] As a result, the spread of ideas tended to take place through written exchanges in books, periodicals, newspapers, and circulars, and debate within associations and discussion groups, rather than emanating from the shop floor.[7]

For these reasons, it is not surprising that the *Manifesto* was commissioned and produced by an association – the Communist League – that had descended from the 'League of the Outlawed (*Bund der Geächteten*),' comprised mainly of German artisans who had settled in Paris following an abortive uprising in Frankfurt in 1833.[8] Inside the conspiratorial atmosphere existing in Paris during the late 1830s, a group with a more proletarian orientation broke away from the League of the Outlawed in 1836 to form the 'League of the Just (*Bund der Gerechten*)' which sought to 'free Germany from the yoke of abhorrent oppression, end the enslavement of humanity, and realize the fundamental rights of man.'⁹ Although the new League's members shared certain basic ideas, they embraced a wide variety of socialist or communist beliefs and positions – Moses Hess, Wilhelm Weitling, Charles Fourier, Joseph-Pierre Proudhon, Auguste Blanqui, Etienne Cabet, Robert Owen, Ludwig Feuerbach, and the Left-Hegelians all had their adherents and advocates – and there was considerable debate, tension and confrontation among members as the League tried to work out a unified outlook and programme.¹⁰ In 1838, for example, the League commissioned Weitling's *Mankind As It Is and As It Ought To Be*, which served as the League's first coherent theoretical statement and acted in the early years as 'a programme and a confession of faith, more or less as a "Communist Manifesto".'¹¹ But the influence of the French communists such as Blanqui and his *Société des Saisons* (1837–39) also exerted a strong, competing influence, while the French Utopian Socialists also continued to press their position. In the aftermath of a failed Blanquist uprising on May 12, 1839, many of the League's members were expelled from France – mostly to London – and any gains that had been made in the development of a uniform outlook were brought to a temporary close.

Arriving in London, the majority of those who had belonged to the League of the Just in Paris now joined, along with numerous other German workers and artisans, the 'German Workers' Educational Society,' founded on February 7, 1840, while simultaneously reconstituting the League inside the Society in a semi-clandestine fashion. Carl Schapper, Heinrich Bauer, and Joseph Moll assumed the leadership of this 'London branch' of the League, with Schapper looking after organization in London, Moll renewing contacts with members in France, and Bauer establishing contacts with the Swiss members who had coalesced around the leadership of Weitling. The next few years were marked by intense debates over the Fourier-inspired ideas of Cabet, and the adoption and later rejection of Weitling's and Hermann Kriege's beliefs that 'the greatest deeds are accomplished by the emotions that move the masses.' Equally significant were growing contacts with British trade unions, the Owenites, and the Chartists.

Within the British left at that time there were two movements of particular note. One was the general appeal of the 'London Working Men's Association' for increased international solidarity, which led William Lovett to found 'The Democratic Friends of all Nations' under the slogan 'All Men are Brethren.' But while Lovett was trying to draw the workers together through an appeal for international harmony, George Julian Harney, secretary to the republican and worker-oriented 'Democratic Association,' established a more radical group in 1846 – 'The Fraternal Democrats' – which called 'to all oppressed classes of every land . . . to unite themselves for the triumph of their common cause.' '"Divide and rule" is the motto of the oppressor,' Harney's group proclaimed; '"Unite yourselves for victory" should be ours.'[12] Harney's Fraternal Democrats brought the left wing of the Chartists together with the revolutionary-oriented emigres from the continent (including the League of the Just) although it remained a very loose association of like-minded individuals and did not consolidate itself into a formal group.

In view of its increased contact with Harney's and Lovett's groups, the German Workers' Educational Society also adopted the slogan '*Alle Menschen sind Brüder*' and placed central importance on the goal of emancipating the international proletariat.[13] Equally important, thanks to the increasingly international orientation of the German Workers' Educational Society, the Central Committee of the London-based branch of the League of the Just, operative within the Society, was able to eclipse the importance of the groups in Paris, Switzerland, and Germany and assume the main leadership role for the League as a whole.

Thus, between 1834 and 1846, the German communist movement had consolidated itself as an international organization, with its leadership in London, acting through the openly constituted German Educational Worker's Association and the smaller, semi-clandestine and more radical, League of the Just, and in association with the Democratic Friends of all Nations and Fraternal Democrats. Although the movement had originally been strongly influenced by the French revolutionary perspectives advocated by Blanqui and Barbès, as well as the imagery of Weitling, this had been tempered by contact with the British trade unions, the Owenites and the Chartists. By 1846, while the movement was still in search of a unified political and theoretical position on which it could base its activities, it had made great strides in consolidating itself and making common cause with the rest of the international proletariat.[14] It was at this point that the movement actively sought Marx's inclusion in its membership.

MARX'S DEVELOPMENT FROM 1836–1846

If the League of the Just underwent significant changes from 1834 to 1846, they pale in comparison to the transformation that Marx's ideas underwent in the same period.[15] Switching from the University of

Bonn to the University of Berlin in 1836, Marx took Eduard Gans' course in jurisprudence, which led him to seriously address Gans' liberal Hegelian world view and its implications. The result was the first major turn in Marx's intellectual life – an immersion in Hegel's philosophy and active involvement with the so-called Left-Hegelians, whose ideas were taken in a historical-materialist direction by Ludwig Feuerbach in *The Essence of Christianity* (and then more fully in his *Provisional Theses for the Reform of Philosophy*), and in another direction by Bruno Bauer and other members of the 'Doctors' Club' who focused on the phenomenological development of self-consciousness – a direction which ultimately led to the 'true' socialism that Marx would reject and criticize vehemently in the mid-1840s.[16]

After receiving his doctoral degree from the University of Jena in April 1841, Marx worked with Bauer in Bonn to develop the *Atheistic Archives*, failed to get an anticipated university position, and was forced to return to Trier in December due to his father-in-law's grave illness.[17] While in Trier, Marx began what would become a two-year association with Arnold Ruge when he submitted an article entitled 'Comments on the Latest Prussian Censorship Instruction' for publication in Ruge's *Deutsche Jahrbücher*.[18]

In April 1842, Marx's intellectual orientation came to its second turning-point when he moved to Cologne and became involved with the city's liberal opposition movement and the *Rheinische Zeitung*. As the newspaper's editor, Marx found himself '. . . in the embarrassing position of having to discuss what is known as material interests' as well as being occupied 'with economic questions.'[19] In addition, as his journalistic involvement with concrete issues grew, Marx became increasingly disenchanted with the Left-Hegelians' abstract ruminations about communism and atheism and formally broke from them in his article 'Herwegh's and Ruge's Relation to "The Free".'[20] Before the year was over Marx also found himself dealing with the 'echo of French socialism and communism, slightly tinged by philosophy' expressed by some contributors to the paper, forcing him to read, among other writings, Proudhon's *Qu'est ce que la propriété?*, Théodore Dézamy's *Calomnies et politique de M. Cabet*, as well as Pierre Leroux and Considèrent in his effort to thoroughly assess the communists' position.[21]

By the end of 1842, the Prussian government had become increasingly apprehensive about the *Rheinische Zeitung* and, on January 21, 1843, scheduled the paper's closure for March 31 although Marx, ready to start up a new project with Ruge – the *Deutsch-Französische*

Jahrbücher – resigned as editor on March 18.[22] Three further developments in Marx's life now followed closely upon one another. First, convinced that Germany would not permit the freedom of expression he required, Marx moved to Paris, where he came to know most of the leaders in the French workers' movement, established contact with the Paris branch of the League of the Just, immersed himself in the French socialists' and communists' animated debates, and, most important, saw at first hand the living and working conditions of the German immigrant workers in Paris as well as the spirit of solidarity that characterised their associations and meetings.[23]

Second, in early March 1843, Marx read Feuerbach's newly published 'Provisional Theses on the Reform of Philosophy' and found in them a key to the genuine transcendence of Hegel's philosophy. Between March and August 1843, Marx used Feuerbach's work as his departure point for a thoroughgoing critique of paragraphs 261–313 of Hegel's *Philosophy of Right*.[24] Third, his work with Ruge on the *Deutsch-Französische Jahrbücher* brought him into contact with theoretical work – Engels' *Outlines of a Critique of Political Economy*, and Hess's work on the essence of money – that would lead him to draw together the insights he had derived from Feuerbach's critique of Hegelian philosophy, the material experiences of the French working class, and the material-economic questions he had first confronted at the *Rheinische Zeitung*.[25]

In the 'Introduction,' to his 'Critique of Hegel's *Philosophy of Right*,' Marx adopted the language of class struggle and identified the proletariat as the key agent in the creation of significant social change.[26] 'Where then,' Marx wrote in a text that was still aimed at a progressive, educated, philosophically-oriented German readership, 'is the *positive* possibility of a German emancipation?'

> *Answer.* In the formation [*Bildung*] of a class with *radical chains*, a class of bourgeois society which is no class of bourgeois society, an estate which is the dissolution of all estates, a sphere which possesses a universal character by its universal suffering and claims no *particular* right because no *particular wrong* but *wrong generally* is perpetrated against it; which can no longer invoke an *historical* but only a *human* title; which does not stand in any one-sided opposition [*Gegensatz*] to the consequences but in an all-round opposition to the premises of the essence of the German state [*Staatswesens*]; a sphere, finally, which cannot emancipate itself without emancipating itself from all other spheres of society thereby emancipating all the other spheres of society, which, in a word, is the *total sacrifice* [*völlig Verlust*] of mankind, thus which can gain for itself only through the *full recovery of mankind*. This dissolution of society as a particular estate is the *proletariat*.[27]

Having reached this preliminary level of synthesis and identifying the crucial role of the proletariat in the project of human emancipation, Marx immersed himself in the study of political economy.[28] Between April and August 1844, he assembled a draft of the results of that work – the so-called Paris Manuscripts – including a preface which indicated the scope of the undertaking he envisaged. In a plan formulated in similar terms in 1858, Marx proposed to move from his critique of political economy to produce separate critiques of the state, law, ethics, and civil life as well as a concluding pamphlet that would show their interconnection to political economy.[29]

While the Paris Manuscripts are a rich source of insight into Marx's ideas and their development, what is most significant in this particular context is the degree to which Marx, in a very short period of time, determined that a critical understanding of the political economy of capitalist society was vitally important for the prospects of socialism. Indeed, by February 1, 1845, Marx was so confident about the impor-tance of his Feuerbachian-Hegelian inspired critique of political economy and his ability to produce it that he signed a contract with Carl F. J. Leske to publish a two volume study – *Kritik der Politik und National-Ökonomie*.[30]

Two further events of note must be added to this picture of Marx's intellectual development at this time. First, although Marx and Engels had had a rather cool encounter in November 1842, when they met again in Paris between August 28 and September 6, 1844, they found themselves in full agreement on a host of issues and positions.[31] Second, on January 25, 1845, Marx was expelled from Paris and moved to Brussels. Not long after arriving in Brussels, stimulated perhaps by Max Stirner's *Ego and His Own* (in which Marx and Engels are portrayed as communist disciples of Feuerbach), perhaps by word of Bauer's forthcoming reply to the *Holy Family* – 'Characteristics of Ludwig Feuerbach' – and certainly by his own continued reflections on how to best present his critique of political economy to the public, Marx returned to a critical reflection upon Feuerbach's materialism. In March 1845, just before Engels also arrived in Brussels, Marx drafted his eleven 'Theses on Feuerbach' which served as the basis for the full elaboration of their emerging historical and materialist position which Marx and Engels spent from September 1845 to April 1846 devel-oping into a two volume study, *The German Ideology*.[32]

MARX AND THE LEAGUE OF THE JUST

Marx's arrival in Brussels placed him in the centre of a strong socialist community – Moses Hess and Engels were his neighbours, while Hermann Kriege (a disciple of Weitling), Wilhelm Wolff, George Weerth and other socialists lived nearby. Electing to take advantage of the city's location in the middle of the Paris-London-Cologne triangle, its free atmosphere, and the presence of so many socialists with European contacts, Marx, Engels and a close friend, Philippe Gigot, founded a 'Communist Correspondence Committee' which would put European communists in touch with one another.[33] While encountering some difficulty at the outset, Correspondence Committees were established in several European centres and began to exchange circulars. It was in this way that Marx, in the spring of 1846, first established contact with Schapper, Moll, and Bauer and the League of the Just in London.[34]

The relationship did not begin smoothly, however. At a March 1846 meeting of the Brussels Committee, Marx, in the presence of Weitling, launched into a stinging critique of the latter's 'Craft Workers' Communism' and of the German 'true socialists.' According to Paul Annenkov, '[Marx's] sarcastic speech boiled down to this:'

> to rouse the population without giving them any firm, well-thought-out reasons for their activity would be simply to deceive them. ... To call to the workers without any strictly scientific ideas or constructive doctrine, especially in Germany, was equivalent to vain dishonest play at preaching which assumes an inspired prophet on the one side and on the other only gaping asses.[35]

In a similar fashion, Marx and the Brussels Correspondence Committee prepared and distributed a lithograph circular that denounced the communism of his socialist neighbour Kriege and his planned Phalanstery in America.[36]

On June 6,1846, in response to a letter in which Marx had invited the League of the Just to establish a Communist Correspondence Committee in London, he received a reply praising the idea of enhancing communication among communists and also indicating that, like Marx, the London communists had rejected ideas of revolution through conspiracy or, 'à la Weitling,' through spiritual inspiration. On the other hand, the Londoners felt that Marx's vehement denunciations of both Weitling and Kriege were counter-productive; the goal of the League of the Just and the London Correspondence Committee, which they would found, was to encourage and facilitate the exchange of ideas, not destroy it.[37]

Eleven days later Schapper, Moll and Bauer wrote to Marx giving more details of their association and indicating where there was, and where there might not be, agreement with him. But the crux of their letter was the following:

> We believe that all these different orientations [to communism articulated above] must be expressed and that only through a communist congress, where all the orientations are represented in a cold-blooded and brotherly discussion, can unity be brought to our propaganda. . . . If people from all the communist positions were sent, if intellectuals and workers from all lands met together, then there is no doubt that a lot of barriers, which still stand in the way, would fall. In this congress all of the different orientations and types of communism would be discussed peacefully and without bitterness and the truth would certainly come through and win the day.[38]

A letter from Harney to Marx three days later indicated that the Brussels Committee's correspondence with the London Committee had clarified the major misunderstandings that had existed and that they '[had] received the adhesion of the London friends:' Harney then added, 'of course after this I cannot hesitate to afford you every assistance in my power.'[39] Toward the end of January 1847 the tie was strengthened when Moll went to Brussels on behalf of the League of the Just to encourage Marx to join the League.[40] Marx was attracted to the idea that he could play a significant role in a workers' organization but he made his membership conditional upon the removal from the League's statutes of anything that encouraged a 'superstitious attitude' to authority, and on the League's commitment to publishing a manifesto of its position. Moll agreed with the principles behind Marx's conditions, although he noted that there could be some resistance to Marx's ideas within the League and it would be his task to convince members at the congress to adopt them.[41]

Transforming the League of the Just into a more formal association which would advance the interests of the international workers' movement was the logical outcome of the League's activities from its inception. That final step began when the League convened its first international congress in London from June 2nd to 9th, 1847. Engels attended as the representative of the Paris Communist Correspondence Committee and Wilhelm Wolff, in view of Marx's financial problems, represented the Brussels Committee.

Until Andréas's 1968 discovery of several key documents, it was thought that this first congress had accomplished little more than a name change to the Communist League, the adoption of the new slogan *'Proletarier aller Länder vereinigt Euch*! (Workers of all Countries, Unite!)' and agreement that the London Committee would draft a new programme and set of rules after the congress.[42] But we now know from the League's first two circulars and their associated documents that drafts for a new set of rules and a programme statement – in the form of a 'Communist Confession of Faith (*Glaubenbekenntnis*)' – were completed before the congress ended.[43] These were then circulated for consideration so that they could be revised and adopted at a second congress scheduled for November 29, 1847.

Before these documents became available, most discussions of the history of the *Manifesto* had used Engels' November 23–24 1847 letter to Marx in Brussels for insight into the drafting of the text. This has meant that certain differences and tensions still existing in the League were overlooked, thereby diminishing Engels' and Marx's accomplishments in shaping the League's orientation, minimizing Marx's achievement in receiving the task of writing the *Manifesto* and underestimating the leadership role he assumed in the Communist League on the eve of the 1848 Revolution.

Just prior to the second congress of the Communist League (on 23/24 November), Engels sent Marx the following from Paris.

> Give a little thought to the Confession of Faith [*Glaubenbekenntnis*]. I think we would do best to abandon the catechetical form and call the thing Communist *Manifesto*. Since a certain amount of history has to be narrated in it, the form hitherto adopted is quite unsuitable. I shall be bringing with me the one from here, which I did; it is in simple narrative form, but wretchedly worded, in a tearing hurry.[44]

Earlier accounts have confused 'the Confession of Faith' with Engels' October 1847 'Basic Principles of Communism (*Grundsätze des Kommunismus*),' which is a different document – the one put together 'in a tearing hurry' that he was taking with him to the second congress.[45] The distinction is important for several reasons. First, by reading the original June 1847 'Confession of Faith,' one can see how successful Engels had already been in influencing the content of the League's programme statement, while also recognizing that he had not been totally successful in shaping some of its key aspects.[46] Second, a lot was at stake since the League's request that the various communities and circles should debate and propose revisions to the 'Confession of Faith' was not an idle suggestion, nor was it treated that way.[47] Prior to Engels' return to Paris in mid-October Moses Hess, in particular, drafted and submitted for authorization to the Paris circle a significantly revised 'Confession' which was undoubtedly much more consistent with his Utopian-infused vision of communism than the materialist position Engels had advocated at the first congress.[48] One can appreciate that Engels' desire to discard the catechetical form and change the name to something that would be more easily identified with his and Marx's position, rather than Hess's and the Fourierist positions within the League, was a matter of the most basic principles that would guide the League.[49] This last point is worth following a bit further.

In 1844, Hess had published in the Paris *Vorwärts* a 'Communist Confession in Questions and Answers [*Kommunistisches Bekenntnis in Fragen und Antworten*].'[50] While the draft 'Communist Confession of Faith' of June 1847 does not directly duplicate Hess's 'Confession,' there is little doubt that Hess's document played a central role in the drafting of the 1847 'Confession of Faith.' For example, the answer to one of the 1847 draft's most important questions – 'What is the aim of the communists?' – is completely consistent with that of Hess and other Utopian Socialists and quite far removed from the position of Marx and Engels. The answer – '[t]o organize society in such a way that each of its members can develop and utilize all his potentialities and powers in full freedom without jeopardizing the foundations of this society' – directly captures the essence of the main theme in Hess's 'Confession' – especially questions 20 to 40.[51] By constituting the answer to this key question, Hess's 'Confession' – which was Fourierist in tone and claimed that the loss of freedom and the separation of humankind from its natural capacities through the presence of a cash-based social system (recalling Hess's 'Essence of Money') was the central problem of existing social arrangements – strategically influenced the rest of the agenda in the League's initial programme statement.

As a result of the influence of Hess's document, the goal of the communists in the 1847 draft 'Confession' was the abolition of private property, 'replacing it by the community of goods.'[52] But while Hess's 'Confession' appears to have played a dominant influence in the 1847 draft 'Confession,' its domination was tempered by Engels' successes. For example, Hess's document includes questions and answers about marriage. These may initially appear to be a rather unconventional inclusion in a draft programme until one remembers the centrality of sexual relationships in many of Fourier's utopian-socialist writings. The theme was included in the June 1847 'Confession,' as well as the later *Manifesto*, probably because of the influence of Hess's 'Confession' but also because the goals of socialism had been, in the minds of many, closely associated with Fourier's writings and thus with the idea of the creation of a 'community of women.'

Hess's argument in his 'Confession' followed Fourier – it is the existing property relations that prevent men and women from expressing their sexual relationships naturally; real marriage will only exist when genuine freedom exists in all social relationships. But the implications of this theme as it was tied to the 'community of goods' by Hess, was not consistent with the values and vision of the membership of the Communist League – quite the opposite.[53] As a result, in response to the question, 'Will the community of women not be proclaimed at the same time as the community of goods?' the 1847 draft 'Confession' noted, 'Not at all.' 'We shall interfere with the private relationship between husband and wife, and the family in general , only in so far as the new order of society would be hampered by the preservation of the existing forms.'[54] And while there does not appear to be a copy of Hess's proposed revisions to the 'Confession,' one can be sure that he would have wanted to reduce or eliminate the discussion of the proletariat and replace it with a statement about humankind's natural powers and their expression through freedom of action; one can also understand how such revisions would have moved Engels to decide that some significant changes were needed to the 1847 draft 'Confession.'[55]

Upon his return to Paris Engels outmanoeuvred Hess by going through Hess's draft in detail. One can imagine the response from an audience of workers as the committed materialist Engels, went through Hess's proposal. 'I dealt with this point by point,' Engels wrote to Marx,

> and was not yet half way through when the lads declared themselves *satisfaits*. *Completely unopposed*, I got them to entrust me with the task of drafting a new one [i.e. Engels' 'Basic Principles of Communism'] which would be discussed next Friday by the district and will be sent to London *behind the backs of the communities* [Engels' emphases].'[56]

At about the same time Engels had been battling with Hess the Central Authority of the Brussels' Circle received a letter from the League's Central Committee in London emphasizing how important it was for Marx to attend the next congress.[57] On November 27, therefore, Marx began his journey to London via Ostend, where he met Engels and the Belgian communist Victor Tedesco, to take an active role in the second

Congress of the Communist League.[58]

PRODUCING THE MANIFESTO

During the second congress – November 29 to December 10, 1847 – one can be certain that the League's new rules and the content of its programme statement were thoroughly debated. Marx's and Engels' success in carrying the congress is clearly evident in the League's newly-stated aim. The June draft 'Rules of the Communist League' had declared that 'the League aims at the emancipation of humanity by spreading the theory of the community of property and its speediest possible practical introduction.' The Rules adopted at the end of November show a fundamentally revised aim: 'The aim of the League is the overthrow of the bourgeoisie, the rule of the proletariat, the abolition of the old bourgeois society which rests on the antagonism of classes, and the foundation of a new society without classes and without private property.'[59] But although agreement had been reached, there was not enough time for the League to prepare a final version of its programme statement. This task was assigned to Marx.

Marx arrived back in Brussels by mid-December but did not turn his attention immediately to drafting the *Manifesto*. Instead, he spent the rest of the month delivering lectures on wage-labour to the German Workers' Educational Association.[60] Engels arrived in Brussels on December 17 but was in Paris four days later – where he stayed until the end of January – leaving Marx to write the *Manifesto* alone.[61]

On January 26, 1848, the following communication from Schapper, Bauer and Moll – 'In the name of and by order of the Central Committee' – arrived in Brussels.

> The Central Committee charges its regional committee in Brussels to communicate with Citizen Marx, and to tell him that if the Manifesto of the Communist Party, the writing of which he undertook to do at the recent congress, does not reach London by February 1st of the current year, further measures will have to be taken against him. In the event of Citizen Marx not fulfilling his task, the Central Committee requests the immediate return of the documents placed at Citizen Marx's disposal.[62]

Marx, exercising his significant talents of synthesis, polemic, and rhetoric, pressed forward with his draft of the text. The *Manifesto's* opening salvo (which is improved rhetorically in the 1888 English translation) *'Ein Gespenst geht um in Europa – das Gespenst des Kommunismus'* was apparently derived from Wilhelm Schulz's article on Communism contained in an 1846 *Staatslexikon*.[63] Schulz wrote, '*Seit wenigen Jahren ist in Deutschland vom Kommunismus die Rede, und schon is er zum drohenden Gespenst geworden, vor dem de Einen sich fürchten, und womit die Andern Furcht einzujagen suchen* (For a few years in Germany there is talk of Communism, and already it has become a threatening spectre for those who fear it and with which others seek to create fear).'[64] This set the stage for the Communist League's programme statement in a far more dramatic fashion than any of the earlier 'confessions of faith' had ever managed. It also allowed Marx to move directly into his first dominant theme – '[t]he history of all hitherto existing societies is the history of class struggles' – and introduce the dramatic history that Engels had suggested and attempted to incorporate to a certain extent in his 'Basic Principles of Communism'. In Parts I and II of the pamphlet, as Andréas shows in considerable detail and Ryazanoff indicates in a different manner, Marx drew from ideas generally contained in his earlier writings although he relied particularly heavily upon their formulation in *The Poverty of Philosophy*, *The German Ideology*, *The Holy Family*, the notes to *Wage-Labour and Capital*, as well as Engels' texts 'The Status Quo in Germany,' *The Condition of the Working Class in England*, and 'The Basic Principles of Communism.'[65]

Parts III and IV of the *Manifesto* indicate the extent to which the pamphlet was not simply a rallying cry for the workers of the world or a positive statement of the Communist League's position but also one that had emerged from a thorough debate about different socialist strategies and theories. Having established its position, the programme statement directly challenged those who might challenge its leadership of the international workers' movement. In these parts of the *Manifesto*, Marx drew upon the 'documents placed at Citizen Marx's disposal' by the Central Committee, being particularly careful to answer questions posed in a November 1846 circular, while also amplifying upon the critique of other schools and systems of socialism presented in a February 1847 circular, and in a September 1847 trial number of the *Communist Journal*.[66]

The first edition of the *Manifesto* was an anonymous pamphlet of 23 pages that went through four printings, with the first printing serving as the basis for the text that appeared in serial form in the *Deutsche Londoner Zeitung* from March 3 to July 28, 1848.[67] The second edition was a 30-page anonymous pamphlet, most likely published in April or May 1848 and this, along with an 1866 edition, served as the basis for all future editions of the *Manifesto*. It is interesting to note that although the preamble to the *Manifesto* stated that it would soon appear in English, French, German, Italian, Flemish and Danish, with the exception of a Swedish translation in 1849, no translation was published in 1848–49.[68] Eventually published in more than 35 languages, in some 544 editions that appeared between 1848 and 1918 alone, and dispersed throughout the world, the *Manifesto* has carried the Communist League's message well beyond the wildest dreams of its most optimistic adherents.

CONCLUSION

What the inside story of the making of the *Communist Manifesto* shows is that while the document was drafted in its final form by Karl Marx, and the final credit for its organization and rhetorical style is due to him, the content and message of the *Manifesto* were really the product of an extended, intense, but open debate among committed communist-internationalists as they sought to define their programme and understand the world they wanted to change. Moreover, the *Manifesto* was a document that was produced within the context of a political struggle by people who were directly embroiled in it. It is not a canon of eternal truths; it is a product of open debate and a search for solutions to the major problems confronting the working class of 1847–48. The situation of the socialist movement today is not entirely different from the one it faced in 1847. Once again, it will not be by abstract analysis alone, but by the synthesis of theory with the thinking and practice of people engaged in efforts to enhance the world, that effective new orientations will be given to contemporary struggles.

NOTES

1. While the first printing of the *Manifesto* was completed in London by mid to late February 1848, it was not until March 20 that a thousand copies from London arrived in Paris and these did not systematically make their way into Germany for at least another 10 days; see *Karl Marx: Chronik seines Lebens in Einzeldaten*, compiled by the Marx-Engels-Lenin Institute Moscow, Berlin: Makol Verlag, n.d., pp. 48–49; *Karl Marx/Friedrich Engels: Historisch kritische Gesamtausgabe* (hereafter *MEGA*), Pt. I, Vol. 6, edited by D. Ryazanoff and V. Adoratski, Berlin: Marx-Engels Verlag, p. 683.
2. *Communist Manifesto: Socialist Landmark*, an appreciation, together with the original text and prefaces, written for the Labour Party by Harold Laski, London: George Allen and Unwin Ltd., 1948, p. 101. See also the preface to the 1888 edition (*ibid.*, p. 112).

3. See, in particular, Karl Marx, *Herr Vogt*, in *Marx/Engels Collected Works* (hereafter *MECW*), Vol. 17, New York: International Publishers, pp. 78–81; Friedrich Engels, 'On the History of the Communist League,' *Karl Marx/Friedrich Engels: Selected Works* (hereafter *MESW*), Vol. 2, Moscow: Progress Publishers, 1970, pp. 173–83.
4. *Communist Manifesto: Socialist Landmark, op. cit.*, p. 116. See virtually the same paragraph in Engels' preface to the German edition of 1883 (p. 105).
5. Kägi (*Genesis des historischen Materialismus*, Vienna, 1965, p. 157ff), documents the high level of activity in Paris at the time making it the undisputed centre of socialist thought.
6. See David McLellan, *Karl Marx: His Life and Thought*, London: Macmillan Press, 1973, pp. 1–16; Wolfgang Mönke, 'Introduction,' *Moses Hess Philosophische und sozialistische Schriften 1837–1850*, Vaduz/Liechtenstein: Topos Verlag, 1980, pp. xii–xvii; Ernst Schraepler, 'Der Bund der Gerechten: Seine Tätigkeit in London 1840–1847,' *Archiv für Sozialgeschichte*, II, 1962, p. 5.
7. As a result, three of the early, indigenous sources of German socialist thought that exercised significant influence were Moses Hess's *The Sacred History of Mankind* (1837), Wilhelm Weitling's *Mankind As It Is and As It Ought To Be* (1839), and Lorenz von Stein's *The Socialism and Communism of Present Day France* (1842).
8. The material presented in this section is largely drawn from E. Schraepler, 'Der Bund der Gerechten,' *op. cit.*. See also D. McLellan, *Karl Marx, op. cit.*; F. Bender, 'Introduction,' *The Communist Manifesto*, edited by F. Bender, New York: W.W. Norton & Co., 1988, p. 10; Friedrich Engels, 'Zur Geschichte des Bundes der Kommunisten,' *Karl Marx/Friedrich Engels Werke* (hereafter *MEW*), Vol. 21, edited by the Institute for Marxism-Leninism and the Central Committee of the Socialist Unity Party, Berlin: Dietz Verlag, p. 206.
9. See E. Schraepler, 'Der Bund der Gerechten,' *op. cit.*, p. 6.
10. See, for example, the letter from Carl Schapper, Joseph Moll and Heinrich Bauer to Marx, 17 VII 1846, in the new *Karl Marx/Friedrich Engels Gesamtausgabe* (hereafter *MEGA2*), Pt. III, Vol. 2, edited by the Institute for Marxism-Leninism and the Central Committees of the Communist Party of the Soviet Union and the Socialist Unity Party of Germany, Berlin: Dietz Verlag, pp. 250–55.
11. E. Schraepler, 'Der Bund der Gerechten,' *op. cit.*, p. 613.
12. The quotation is from *ibid.*, p. 19; on the League's position with Weitling, see Carl Schapper *et al.* to Marx, 6 VI 1846, *MEGA2*, Pt. III, Vol. 2, p. 220.
13. See Max Nettlau, 'Londoner deutsche kommunistische Diskussionen, 1845,' *Archiv für die Geschichte des Sozialismus und der Arbeiterbewegung*, x, 1925, pp. 360–381.
14. See, for example, the Communist Correspondence Committee in London to the Communist Correspondence Committee in Brussels, 11 XI 1846, *MEGA2*, Pt. III, Vol. 2, pp. 317–20.
15. Because this period of Marx's life has been so well documented, I will restrict myself to highlighting only the most important issues that relate to the history of the *Manifesto*. Among numerous potential sources, see, for example, Karl Marx, 'Preface' *A Contribution to the Critique of Political Economy*, in *MECW*, Vol. 29, pp. 261–3; David McLellan, *Marx Before Marxism*, Harmondsworth: Penguin Books Ltd., 1972; Helmut Reichelt, 'Introduction,' *Texte zur materialistischen Geschichtsauffassung*, Frankfurt/M: Verlag Ullstein, 1975, pp. 9–85; D. McLellan, *Karl Marx, op. cit.*, pp. 16–40; Franz Mehring, *Karl Marx*, translated by E.

Fitzgerald, London: George Allen & Unwin, 1936; Bob Jessop and Charlie
Malcolm-Brown (Editors), *Karl Marx's Social and Political Thought*, Vol. 1 (Marx's
Life and Theoretical Development), New York: Routledge, Chapman and Hall,
1990.

16. On Marx's immersion in Hegel, see Karl to Heinrich Marx, 10–11 XI 1837,
    MECW, Vol. 1, pp. 12–15, 18–20.
17. Some of the work Marx accomplished in Bonn can be seen in *MEGA2*, Pt. IV,
    Vol. 1, pp. 293–376.
18. See Marx to Ruge, 10 II 1842, *MEW*, Vol. 27, p. 395. In view of the style Marx
    later employed in the *Manifesto*, it is worth noting McLellan's (*Karl Marx, op. cit.*,
    p. 44) comments that the article is a '... masterpiece of polemical exegesis,
    demonstrating the great pamphleteering talent in the style of Boerne that [Marx]
    was to exhibit throughout his life. All his articles of the Young Hegelian period
    ... were written in an extremely vivid style: his radical and uncompromising
    approach, his love of polarisation, his method of dealing with opponents' views
    by *reductio ad absurdum*, all led him to write very antithetically. Slogan, climax,
    anaphora, parallelism, antithesis and chiasmus (especially the latter two) were all
    employed by Marx.'
19. Karl Marx, 'Preface' *A Contribution to the Critique of Political Economy*, in
    MECW, Vol. 29, pp. 261–2. The articles to which Marx was referring were
    'Proceedings of the Sixth Rhine Province Assembly,' 'Polemical Articles Against
    the *Allgemeine Zeitung*,' 'Justification of the Correspondent from Mosel;' see
    MECW, Vol. 1, pp. 132–81, 359–60, 332–58.
20. See *Karl Marx: Chronik, op. cit.*, p. 14; *MEGA*, Pt. I, Vol. 1, p. 309; Marx to
    Ruge, 30 XI 1842, *The Letters of Karl Marx*, selected and edited by Saul Padover,
    Englewood Cliffs New Jersey: Prentice-Hall, 1979, pp. 19–21.
21. See *Karl Marx: Chronik, op. cit.*, p. 13; *MEGA*, Pt. I, Vol. 1, pp. 263, 314, 573–4.
22. See *Karl Marx: Chronik, op. cit.*, p. 17. See also Marx to Ruge, 25 I 1843,
    concerning the closing of the paper; Marx to Ruge, 13 III 1843, concerning the
    Jahrbücher as well as Marx's invitation to Feuerbach to take part in the project
    (*The Letters of Karl Marx, op. cit.*, pp. 21–3, 23–4, 32–4.
23. See Marx to Feuerbach, 11 VIII 1844, *ibid.*, pp. 34–7.
24. Karl Marx, 'Contribution to the Critique of Hegel's Philosophy of Law,' *MECW*,
    Vol. 3, pp. 3–129.
25. On the influence Hess's 'On the Essence of Money' may have had on Marx, see
    W. Mönke, *Moses Hess: Philosophische und sozialistische Schriften, 1837–50, op.
    cit.*, p. lxix; see the draft text pp. 329–359.
26. The 1843 'Critique' is a pivotal document in Marx's intellectual development in
    the way he brought his reading of Feuerbach's *Provisional Theses* to bear on (a) his
    concrete experiences among the French socialists and the emigre working class in
    Paris and (b) his readings on the historical development of France, Germany and
    England; see *MEGA2*, Pt. IV, Vol. 2, pp. 9–281.
27. Karl Marx, 'Contribution to the Critique of Hegel's Philosophy of Law:
    Introduction,' *MECW*, Vol. 3, p. 186 – I have revised the translation to more
    accurately reflect the German (*MEGA*, Pt. I, Vol. 1, pp. 619–20). See also Marx's
    comments in 'Critical Notes on the Article by a Prussian,' (*MECW*, Vol. 3, p.
    202) – especially 'A philosophical people can find its corresponding practice only
    in socialism, hence it is only in the *proletariat* that it can find the dynamic element
    of its emancipation.'

28. The majority of the notes Marx made during this period were first reproduced in *MEGA*, Pt. I, Vol. 3, pp. 437–583 and more fully in *MEGA2*, Pt. IV, Vol. 2, 1981, pp. 279–579.

29. See *MECW*, Vol. 3, p. 231. For Marx's 1858 plan, see Karl Marx, *Grundrisse*, translated by M. Nicolaus, Harmondsworth: Pelican Books, 1973, p. 108.

30. See *MEGA*, Pt. I, Vol. 3, p. 30; Marx to Engels October 1844, January 22 and March 7, 1845 (*MECW*, Vol. 38, pp. 6, 16, 23) as well as Engels' advanced notices of the work published in *The New Moral World* (*MEW*, 2, pp. 514–19). Most accounts of this contract indicate Marx signed it with Carl W. Leske but Mönke (*Moses Hess: Philosophische und sozialistische Schriften, 1837–50, op. cit.*, note 172a, p. 506) corrects the misunderstanding that led to this error.

31. See *Karl Marx: Chronik, op. cit.*, p. 14.

32. See Bruno Bauer, 'Charakteristik Ludwig Feuerbachs,' *Wigandsvierteljahrschrift*, III, 1845 cited in *Karl Marx: Chronik, op. cit.*, p. 29; Max Stirner, *The Ego and His Own*, translated by S. Byington, edited by J. Martin, New York: Libertarian Book Club, 1963; Marx to Leske, 1 VIII 1846, where he noted that his critique of political economy had to be preceded by 'a polemical piece against German philosophy and *German socialism* up till the present' (*MECW*, Vol. 38, p. 50); see also *Karl Marx: Chronik, op. cit.*, p. 28; Marx to Joseph Weydemeyer, 14–16 V 1846, *MECW*, Vol. 38, pp. 41–2. For the 'Theses' and *The German Ideology* see *MECW*, Vol. 5, pp. 3–5, 6–8; 19–539.

33. *Karl Marx: Chronik, op. cit.*, pp. 31–2; Marx to Proudhon, 5 V 1846, *MECW*, Vol. 38, pp. 38–40; see Proudhon's 17 V 1846 reply *MEGA2*, Pt. III, Vol. 2, pp. 205–7; see also Marx *et al.*, to Gustav Köttgen, 15 VI 1846, *ibid.*, pp 12–16. For Engels' first communications with the Correspondence Committee during his stay in Paris (19 VIII 1846, 16 IX 1846, 23 X 1846), see *MECW*, Vol. 38, pp. 56–60, 60–7, 81–6.

34. See *Karl Marx: Chronik, op. cit.*, p. 31; Engels to Marx, November-December 1846, *MECW*, Vol. 38, pp. 91–2.

35. Paul Annenkov, 'From the Essay "A Wonderful 10 Years",' *Reminiscences of Marx and Engels*, Moscow: Foreign Languages Publishing House, n.d., p. 271. See also *Karl Marx: Chronik, op. cit.*, pp. 31–2; Hess to Marx, 20 V 1846, 29 V 1846, *MEGA2*, Pt. III, Vol. 2, pp. 208–9, 211.

36. See *MECW*, Vol. 6, pp. 35–51. In *Herr Vogt* Marx indicated that 'we published a series of pamphlets, partly printed, partly lithographed, in which we mercilessly criticized the hotchpotch of Franco-English socialism or communism and German philosophy which formed the secret doctrine of the League at that time. In its place, we proposed the scientific study of the economic structure of bourgeois society as the only tenable theoretical foundation. Furthermore, we argued in a popular form that it was not a matter of putting some utopian system into effect but of conscious participation in the historic process revolutionizing society before our very eyes' (*MECW*, Vol. 17, p. 80).

37. See The Communist Correspondence Committee in London to Karl Marx, 6 VI 1846, *MEGA2* Pt. III, Vol. 2, pp. 219–23.

38. Carl Schapper, Joseph Moll, Henry Bauer to Karl Marx, 17 VII 1846, *MEGA2*, Pt. III, Vol. 3, pp. 252–53.

39. George Julian Harney to the Brussels Correspondence Committee, 20 VII 1846, *ibid.*, p. 263.

40. See *Karl Marx: Chronik, op. cit.*, p. 37.

41. See D. McLellan, *Karl Marx, op. cit.*, pp. 171–2; F. Mehring, *Karl Marx, op. cit.*, pp. 138–9; K. Marx, *Herr Vogt*, in *MECW*, Vol. 17, p. 81.

42. See B. Andréas, *Gründungsdokumente des Bundes der Kommunisten (Juni bis September 1847)*, Hamburg: Hauswedell & Co., 1969. Mehring's classic biography is very superficial on this part of Marx's life; see *Karl Marx, op. cit.*, pp. 136–47. Surprisingly both Bender ('Introduction,' *The Communist Manifesto, op. cit.*, pp. 12–13) and McLellan (*Karl Marx, op. cit.*, pp. 172–83) tend to overlook these documents in their discussions of this point in Marx's life.

43. See 'Rules of the Communist League (June 1847),' 'A Circular of the First Congress of the Communist League to the League Members. June 9, 1847,' 'The Central Authority to the League,' *MECW*, Vol. 6, pp. 585–588, 589–600, 601–15.

44. Engels to Marx, 23–24 XI 1847, *MECW*, Vol. 38, p. 149.

45. See, for example, Arnold Winkler, *Die Entstehung des 'Kommunistischen Manifestes': Eine Untersuchung, Kritik und Klärung*, Vienna: Manzsche Verlag, 1936, pp. 240–44; H. Laski, 'Introduction,' *Communist Manifesto, op. cit.*, pp. 24–5; F. Mehring, *Karl Marx, op. cit.*, pp. 147–8; F. Bender, 'Historical and Theoretical Backgrounds of the *Communist Manifesto*,' *The Communist Manifesto, op. cit.*, pp. 12–14.

46. Similar insight can be gained by comparing the draft rules from June 1847 to the final rules of December 1847; cf. *MECW*, Vol. 6, pp. 585–88, 633–38.

47. The second circular reviews the debates as they took place in Sweden, Germany, Holland, America, France, Switzerland, and Belgium; see 'The Central Authority to the League,' *MECW*, Vol. 6, pp. 603–13.

48. See *Karl Marx: Chronik, op. cit.*, p. 40. For a discussion of the relationship between Hess and Marx and Engels at this time, see W. Mönke, *Moses Hess Philosophische und sozialistische Schriften, op. cit.*, pp. xcvi–c; see also Engels to the Communist Correspondence Committee in Brussels, 16 IX 1846, *MECW*, Vol. 38, pp. 64–5.

49. It is not known exactly why Engels suggested the term manifesto. It may well be that he borrowed the term from Victor Considérant's 1843 'Principles of Socialism: Manifesto of the Democracy of the Nineteenth Century' which was reissued in 1847. This would have made some sense since there is a high degree of overlap between the two positions in terms of the image of capitalist society and the role of the proletariat. It is, however, incorrect to claim as Varlaam Tcherkesoff (*Pages of Socialist History*, New York: C.B. Cooper, 1902, pp. 55–66) has that Marx and Engels simply copied Considérant's ideas; see Rondel Davidson, 'Reform versus Revolution: Victor Considérant and the *Communist Manifesto*,' *Social Science Quarterly*, 58 (1), 1977, pp. 74–85.

50. The 'Confession' was also republished in 1846/47 in a two volume collection *Rheinische Jahrbücher zur gesellschaftlichen Reform*; see '*Kommunistisches Bekenntniss in Fragen und Antworten*,' in W. Mönke, *Moses Hess Philosophische und sozialistische Schriften, op. cit.*, pp. 359–68; see also pp. lxxxii–lxxxiii.

51. See F. Engels, 'Draft of the Communist Confession of Faith,' *Birth of the Communist Manifesto, op. cit.*, pp. 163; Moses Hess, 'Kommunistisches Bekenntnis in Fragen und Antworten,' *Moses Hess: Philosophische und sozialistische Schriften, op. cit.*, pp. 362–4.

52. The 'community of goods' was based in part on the productive powers of the society but also 'on the fact that in the consciousness of every human being there

exist certain tenets as indisputable principles, tenets which, being the result of whole historical development, are not in need of proof.' These tenets were then identified – 'each human being is in search of happiness' and 'the happiness of the individual is inseparably linked to the happiness of all, etc.' (see *Birth of the Communist Manifesto, op. cit.*, pp. 163).

53. For Fourier's position on sexual relationships, see, for example, Mark Poster (Editor), *Harmonian Man: Selected Writings of Charles Fourier,* Garden City New York: Doubleday & Co., 1971, pp. 75–89, 115–119, 202–237, 238–280.

54. F. Engels, 'Draft of the Communist Confession of Faith,' *Birth of the Communist Manifesto, op. cit.*, pp. 168. The text then acknowledges that 'the family relationship has been modified in the course of history by the property relationships and periods of development' and that consequently the ending of private property will 'therefore also substantially affect this family relationship.'

55. See especially questions 1–13, Moses Hess, 'Kommunistisches Bekenntnis in Fragen und Antworten,' *Moses Hess: Philosophische und sozialistische Schriften, op. cit.*, pp. 359–61.

56. See Engels to Marx, 25–26 X 1847, *MECW*, Vol. 38, pp. 138–9.

57. See The Central Authority of the Communist League to the Brussels Circle, 18 X 1847, *MEGA2*, Pt. III, Vol. 2, p. 368. The letter indicated the League would do everything possible to assist Marx with his costs.

58. See Engels to Marx, 14–15 XI 1847, *MECW*, Vol. 38, pp. 142–5; *Karl Marx: Chronik, op. cit.*, p. 41.

59. See *MECW*, Vol. 6, pp. 585, 633.

60. See *Karl Marx: Chronik, op. cit.*, p. 42; *MEGA*, Pt. I, Vol. 6, pp. 473, 680. It is on the rough notes for these lectures that Marx wrote out a draft outline for Section III of the *Manifesto*; see *MEGA*, Pt. I, Vol. 6, p. 650. The notes Marx used in his lectures are printed in *MECW*, Vol. 6, pp. 415–37; the notes were revised and published as *Wage-Labour and Capital* in the *Neue Rheinische Zeitung* in 1849; see *MESW*, Vol. 1, pp. 142–74. Marx remained engaged with other workers' groups, such as the Brussels Democratic Association, trying to bring them into the new Communist League; see *MEGA*, Pt. I, Vol. 6, p. 636.

61. See Engels to Marx, 14 I 1848, *MECW*, Vol. 38, p. 153. Contrary to the Preface statements of 1872 and 1888 (see *The Communist Manifesto: Socialist Landmark, op. cit.*, pp. 101, 112) when one takes into account the timing of Engels' visit to Brussels and return to Paris as well as the correspondence discussed below, it is clear that Engels did not directly participate in the writing of the text that went to London as the *Manifesto*. This should not diminish, however, Engels' significant contribution at the two congresses – especially the first one – the impact of his draft The Basic Principles of Communism, and the correspondence and discussions he had with Marx during this period; see also *MEGA*, Pt. I, Vol. 6, pp. 682–3.

62. Cited in *The Communist Manifesto of Karl Marx and Friedrich Engels*, edited, with an introduction, explanatory notes and appendices by D. Ryazanoff, New York: Russell & Russell Inc., 1963, pp. 21–2. It seems unlikely that Marx met the February 1st deadline but he must have delivered the manuscript to London by early to mid-February. The minutes of the London 'Workingmen's Educational Society' indicate February 29, 1848 approval of the transfer of funds covering the costs of the *Manifesto's* publication. Working backwards from that date, the pamphlet was probably printed the preceding week (February 22–29) or as early

as February 14–21. Since the page proofs were set in the office of the Worker's Educational Society (191 Drury Lane, High Holborn) with the gothic character set the Society had purchased in the summer of 1847, and then delivered to the printer, J. E. Burghard, at his shop at 46 Liverpool Street, Bishopsgate by Friedrich Lessner, it seems that Marx must have submitted the manuscript to London in early to mid-February; see B. Andréas, *Le Manifeste Communiste de Marx et Engels, op. cit.*, pp. 9–10; Friedrich Lessner, 'Erinnerungen eines Arbeiters an Karl Marx,' *Karl Marx als Denker, Mensch und Revolutionär*, edited by D. Ryazanoff, Berlin: Verlag für Literatur und Politik, 1928, p. 115.

63. *MEGA*, Pt. I, Vol. 6, p. 525. The German word *Gespenst* is ambiguous; it can mean ghost, apparition, phantom, nightmare, or spectre. Indeed, Helen Macfarlane, in the first English translation of the *Manifesto* (it appeared in Harney's weekly *The Red Republican* in 1850) translated the opening sentence as 'A frightful hobgoblin stalks throughout Europe' (see *MEGA2*, Pt. I, Vol. 10, pp. 605). The selection of the word spectre clearly captures the intended image of terror felt by the bourgeoisie while also linking nicely to the concept of a 'holy alliance' that opposes the movement.

64. See B. Andréas, *Le Manifeste Communiste de Marx et Engels, op. cit.*, pp. 3–4. There is an obvious link between Schulz's sentence and Marx's opening salvo. Those who maintain that Marx took the line from Lorenz Stein's *Socialism and Communism in Present Day France* have to argue either that Marx did not understand Stein's intention when he wrote 'an ominously threatening nightmare [*Gespenst*], in whose actuality no one wants to believe . . .' or that he intended to turn the phrase back on Stein, but that seems an unlikely stretch; see *ibid.*, p. 3; cf. Arnold Winkler, *Die Entstehung des 'Kommunistischen Manifestes,' op. cit.*, pp. 128ff.

65. See B. Andréas, *Le Manifeste Communiste de Marx et Engels, op. cit.*, pp. 2–3; D. Ryazanoff, *The Communist Manifesto of Karl Marx and Friedrich Engels, op. cit.*, pp. 69–254.

66. See *ibid.*, pp. 286–318.

67. Marx and Engels were first declared the authors of the *Manifesto* when its third section was published in numbers V and VI (May-October, 1850) of the *Neue Rheinische Zeitung*; see *MEGA2*, Pt. I, Vol. 10, p. 445; B. Andréas, *Le Manifeste Communiste de Marx et Engels, op. cit.*, p. 27; see also note 61 above.

68. See B. Andréas, *Le Manifeste Communiste de Marx et Engels, op. cit.*, pp. 14–24.

THE COMMUNIST MANIFESTO

Karl Marx and Friedrich Engels

A spectre is haunting Europe – the spectre of communism. All the powers of old Europe have entered into a holy alliance to exorcise this spectre: Pope and tsar, Metternich and Guizot, French Radicals and German police-spies.

Where is the party in opposition that has not been decried as communistic by its opponents in power? Where is the opposition that has not hurled back the branding reproach of communism, against the more advanced opposition parties, as well as against its reactionary adversaries?

Two things result from this fact:

I. Communism is already acknowledged by all European powers to be itself a power.

II. It is high time that Communists should openly, in the face of the whole world, publish their views, their aims, their tendencies, and meet this nursery tale of the spectre of communism with a manifesto of the party itself.

To this end, Communists of various nationalities have assembled in London, and sketched the following manifesto, to be published in the English, French, German, Italian, Flemish and Danish languages.

I. BOURGEOIS AND PROLETARIANS

The history of all hitherto existing society is the history of class struggles.

Freeman and slave, patrician and plebeian, lord and serf, guild-master and journeyman, in a word, oppressor and oppressed stood in constant opposition to one another, carried on an uninterrupted, now hidden, now open fight, a fight that each time ended, either in a revolutionary reconstitution of society at large, or in the common ruin of the contending classes.

In the earlier epochs of history, we find almost everywhere a complicated arrangement of society into various orders, a manifold gradation of social rank. In ancient Rome we have patricians, knights, plebeians, slaves; in the Middle Ages, feudal lords, vassals, guild-masters, journeymen, apprentices, serfs; in almost all of these classes, again, subordinate gradations.

The modern bourgeois society that has sprouted from the ruins of feudal society has not done away with class antagonisms. It has but established new classes, new conditions of oppression, new forms of struggle in place of the old ones.

Our epoch, the epoch of the bourgeoisie, possesses, however, this distinctive feature: It has simplified the class antagonisms. Society as a whole is more and more splitting up into two great hostile camps, into two great classes directly facing each other – bourgeoisie and proletariat.

From the serfs of the Middle Ages sprang the chartered burghers of the earliest towns. From these burgesses the first elements of the bourgeoisie were developed.

The discovery of America, the rounding of the Cape, opened up fresh ground for the rising bourgeoisie. The East-Indian and Chinese markets, the colonisation of America, trade with the colonies, the increase in the means of exchange and in commodities generally, gave to commerce, to navigation, to industry, an impulse never before known, and thereby, to the revolutionary element in the tottering feudal society, a rapid development.

The feudal system of industry, in which industrial production was monopolised by closed guilds, now no longer sufficed for the growing wants of the new markets. The manufacturing system took its place. The guild-masters were pushed aside by the manufacturing middle class; division of labour between the different corporate guilds vanished in the face of division of labour in each single workshop.

Meantime the markets kept ever growing, the demand ever rising. Even manufacture no longer sufficed. Thereupon, steam and machinery revolutionised industrial production. The place of manufacture was taken by the giant, modern industry, the place of the industrial middle class by industrial millionaires, the leaders of whole industrial armies, the modern bourgeois.

Modern industry has established the world market, for which the discovery of America paved the way. This market has given an immense development to commerce, to navigation, to communication by land. This development has, in its turn, reacted on the extension of industry; and in proportion as industry, commerce, navigation, railways extended, in the same proportion the bourgeoisie developed, increased its capital, and pushed into the background every class handed down from the Middle Ages.

We see, therefore, how the modern bourgeoisie is itself the product of a long course of development, of a series of revolutions in the modes of production and of exchange.

Each step in the development of the bourgeoisie was accompanied by a corresponding political advance of that class. An oppressed class under the sway of the feudal nobility, an armed and self-governing association in the medieval commune; here independent urban republic (as in Italy and Germany), there taxable 'third estate' of the monarchy (as in France); afterwards, in the period of manufacture proper, serving either the semi-feudal or the absolute monarchy as a counterpoise against the nobility, and, in fact, corner-stone of the great monarchies in general – the bourgeoisie has at last, since the establishment of modern industry and of the world market, conquered for itself, in the modern representative state, exclusive political sway. The executive of the modern state is but a committee for managing the common affairs of the whole bourgeoisie.

The bourgeoisie, historically, has played a most revolutionary part.

The bourgeoisie, wherever it has got the upper hand, has put an end to all feudal, patriarchal, idyllic relations. It has pitilessly torn asunder the motley feudal ties that bound man to his 'natural superiors,' and has left no other nexus between man and man than naked self-interest, than callous 'cash payment.' It has drowned the most heavenly ecstasies of religious fervour, of chivalrous enthusiasm, of philistine sentimentalism, in the icy water of egotistical calculation. It has resolved personal worth into exchange value, and in place of the numberless indefeasible chartered freedoms, has set up that single, unconscionable freedom – Free Trade. In one word, for exploitation, veiled by religious and political illusions, it has substituted naked, shameless, direct, brutal exploitation.

The bourgeoisie has stripped of its halo every occupation hitherto honoured and looked up to with reverent awe. It has converted the physician, the lawyer, the priest, the poet, the man of science, into its paid wage labourers.

The bourgeoisie has torn away from the family its sentimental veil, and has reduced the family relation to a mere money relation.

The bourgeoisie has disclosed how it came to pass that the brutal display of vigour in the Middle Ages, which reactionaries so much admire, found its fitting complement in the most slothful indolence. It has been the first to show what man's activity can bring about. It has accomplished wonders far surpassing Egyptian pyramids, Roman aqueducts, and Gothic cathedrals; it has conducted expeditions that put in the shade all former exoduses of nations and crusades.

The bourgeoisie cannot exist without constantly revolutionising the instruments of production, and thereby the relations of production, and with them the whole relations of society. Conservation of the old modes of production in unaltered form, was, on the contrary, the first condition of existence for all earlier industrial classes. Constant revolutionising of production, uninterrupted disturbance of all social conditions, everlasting uncertainty and agitation distinguish the bourgeois epoch from all earlier ones. All fixed, fast frozen relations, with their train of ancient and venerable prejudices and opinions, are swept away, all new-formed ones become antiquated before they can ossify. All that is solid melts into air, all that is holy is profaned, and man is at last compelled to face with sober senses his real conditions of life and his relations with his kind.

The need of a constantly expanding market for its products chases the bourgeoisie over the whole surface of the globe. It must nestle everywhere, settle everywhere, establish connections everywhere.

The bourgeoisie has through its exploitation of the world market given a cosmopolitan character to production and consumption in every country. To the great chagrin of reactionaries, it has drawn from under the feet of industry the national ground on which it stood. All old-established national industries have been destroyed or are daily being destroyed. They are dislodged by new industries, whose introduction becomes a life and death question for all civilised nations, by industries that no longer work up indigenous raw material, but raw material drawn from the remotest zones; industries whose products are consumed, not only at home, but in every quarter of the globe. In place of the old wants, satisfied by the production of the country, we find new wants, requiring for their satisfaction the products of distant lands and climes. In place of the old local and national seclusion and self-sufficiency, we have intercourse in every direction, universal interdependence of nations. And as in material, so also in intellectual production. The intellectual creations of individual nations become common property. National one-sidedness and narrow-mindedness become more and more impossible, and from the numerous national and local literatures there arises a world literature.

The bourgeoisie, by the rapid improvement of all instruments of production, by the immensely facilitated means of communication, draws all, even the most barbarian, nations into civilisation. The cheap prices of its commodities are the heavy artillery with which it batters down all Chinese walls, with which it forces the barbarians' intensely obstinate hatred of foreigners to capitulate. It compels all nations, on pain of extinction, to adopt the bourgeois mode of production; it compels them to introduce what it calls civilisation into their midst, i.e., to become bourgeois themselves. In one word, it creates a world after its own image.

The bourgeois has subjected the country to the rule of the towns. It has created enormous cities, has greatly increased the urban population as compared with the rural, and has thus rescued a considerable part of the population from the idiocy of rural life. Just as it has made the country dependent on the towns, so it has made barbarian and semi-barbarian countries dependent on the civilised ones, nations of peasants on nations of bourgeois, the East on the West.

The bourgeoisie keeps more and more doing away with the scattered state of the population, of the means of production, and of property. It has agglomerated population, centralised means of production, and has concentrated property in a few hands. The necessary consequence of this was political centralisation. Independent, or but loosely connected provinces, with separate interests, laws, governments and system of taxation, became lumped together into one nation, with one government, one code of laws, one national class interest, one frontier and one customs tariff.

The bourgeoisie, during its rule of scarce one hundred years, has created more massive and more colossal productive forces than have all preceding generations together. Subjection of nature's forces to man, machinery, application of chemistry to industry and agriculture, steam navigation, railways, electric telegraphs, clearing of whole continents for cultivation, canalisation of rivers, whole populations conjured out of the ground – what earlier century had even a presentiment that such productive forces slumbered in the lap of social labour?

We see then: the means of production and of exchange, on whose foundation the bourgeoisie built itself up, were generated in feudal society. At a certain stage in the development of these means of production and of exchange, the conditions under which feudal society produced and exchanged, the feudal organisation of agriculture and manufacturing industry, in one word, the feudal relations of property became no longer compatible with the already developed productive forces; they became so many fetters. They had to be burst asunder; they were burst asunder.

Into their place stepped free competition, accompanied by a social and political constitution adapted to it, and by the economic and political sway of the bourgeois class.

A similar movement is going on before our own eyes. Modern bourgeois society with its relations of production, of exchange and of property, a society that has conjured up such gigantic means of production and of exchange, is like the sorcerer who is no longer able to control the powers of the nether world whom he has called up by his spells. For many a decade past the history of industry and commerce is but the history of the revolt of modern productive forces against modern conditions of production, against the porperty relations that are the conditions for the existence of the bourgeoisie and of its rule. It is enough to mention the commercial crises that by their periodical return put the existence of the entire bourgeois society on its trial, each time more threateningly. In these crises a great part not only of the existing products, but also of the previously created productive forces, are periodically destroyed. In these crises there breaks out an epidemic that, in all earlier epochs, would have seemed an absurdity – the epidemic of over-production. Society suddenly finds itself put back into a state of momentary barbarism; it appears as if a famine, a universal war of devastation had cut off the supply of every means of subsistence; industry and commerce seem to be destroyed. And why? Because there is too much civilisation, too much means of subsistence, too much industry, too much commerce. The productive forces at the disposal of society no longer tend to further the development of the conditions of bourgeois property; on the contrary, they have become too powerful for these conditions, by which they are fettered, and so soon as they overcome these fetters, they bring disorder into the whole of bourgeois society, endanger the existence of bourgeois property. The conditions of bourgeois society are too narrow to comprise the wealth created by them. And how does the bourgeoisie get over these crises? On the one hand, by enforced destruction of a mass of productive forces; on the other, by the conquest of new markets, and by the more thorough exploitation of the old ones. That is to say, by paving the way for more extensive and more destructive crises, and by diminishing the means whereby crises are prevented.

The weapons with which the bourgeoisie felled feudalism to the ground are now turned against the bourgeoisie itself.

But not only has the bourgeoisie forged the weapons that bring death to itself; it has also called into existence the men who are to wield those weapons – the modern working class – the proletarians.

In proportion as the bourgeoisie, i.e., capital, is developed, in the same proportion is the proletariat, the modern working class, developed – a class of labourers, who live only so long as they find work, and who find work only so long as their labour increases capital. These labourers, who must sell themselves piecemeal, are a commodity, like every other article of commerce, and are consequently exposed to all the vicissitudes of competition, to all the fluctuations of the market.

Owing to the extensive use of machinery and to division of labour, the work of the proletarians has lost all individual character, and, consequently, all charm for the workman. He becomes an appendage of the machine, and it is only the most simple, most monotonous, and most easily acquired knack, that is required of him. Hence, the cost of production of a workman is restricted, almost entirely, to the means of subsistence that he requires for his maintenance, and for the propagation of his race. But the price of a commodity, and therefore also of labour, is equal to its cost of production. In proportion, therefore, as the repulsiveness of the work increases, the wage decreases. Nay more, in proportion as the use of machinery and division of labour increases, in the same proportion the burden of toil also increases, whether by prolongation of the working hours, by increase of the work exacted in a given time, or by increased speed of the machinery, etc.

Modern industry has converted the little workshop of the patriarchal master into the great factory of the industrial capitalist. Masses of labourers, crowded into the factory, are organised like soldiers. As privates of the industrial army they are placed under the command of a perfect hierarchy of officers and sergeants. Not only are they slaves of the bourgeois class, and of the bourgeois state; they are daily and hourly enslaved by the machine, by the overlooker, and, above all, by the individual bourgeois manufacturer himself. The more openly this despotism proclaims gain to be its end and aim, the more petty, the more hateful and the more embittering it is.

The less the skill and exertion of strength implied in manual labour, in other words, the more modern industry becomes developed, the more is the labour of men superseded by that of women. Differences of age and sex have no longer any distinctive social validity for the working class. All are instruments of labour, more or less expensive to use, according to their age and sex.

No sooner is the exploitation of the labourer by the manufacturer, so far at an end, that the receives his wages in cash, than he is set upon by the other portions of the bourgeoisie, the landlord, the shopkeeper, the pawnbroker, etc.

The lower strata of the middle class – the small tradespeople, shopkeepers, and retired tradesmen generally, the handicraftsmen and peasants – all these sink gradually into the proletariat, partly because their diminutive capital does not suffice for the scale on which modern industry is carried on, and is swamped in the competition with the large capitalists, partly because their specialised skill is rendered worthless by new methods of production. Thus the proletariat is recruited from all classes of the population.

The proletariat goes through various stages of development. With its birth begins its struggle with the bourgeoisie. At first the contest is carried on by individual labourers, then by the work people of a factory, then by the operatives of one trade, in one locality, against the individual bourgeois who directly exploits them. They direct their attacks not against the bourgeois conditions of production, but against the instruments of production themselves; they destroy imported wares that compete with their labour, they smash to pieces machinery, they set factories ablaze, they seek to restore by force the vanished status of the workman of the Middle Ages.

At this stage the labourers still form an incoherent mass scattered over the whole country, and broken up by their mutual competition. If anywhere they unite to form more compact bodies, this is not yet the consequence of their own active union, but of the union of the bourgeoisie, which class, in order to attain its own political ends, is compelled to set the whole proletariat in motion, and is moreover yet, for a time, able to do so. At this stage, therefore, the proletarians do not fight their enemies, but the enemies of their enemies, the remnants of absolute monarchy, the landowners, the non-industrial bourgeois, the petty bourgeoisie. Thus the whole historical movement is concentrated in the hands of the bourgeoisie; every victory so obtained is a victory for the bourgeoisie.

But with the development of industry the proletariat not only increases in number; it becomes concentrated in greater masses, its strength grows, and it feels that strength more. The various interests and conditions of life within the ranks of the proletariat are more and more equalised, in proportion as machinery obliterates all distinctions of labour, and nearly everywhere reduces wages to the same low level. The growing competition among the bourgeois, and the resulting commercial crises, make the wages of the workers ever more fluctuating. The unceasing improvement of machinery, ever more rapidly developing, makes their livelihood more and more precarious; the collisions between individual workmen and individual bourgeois take more and more the character of collisions between two classes. Thereupon the workers begin to form combinations (trades unions) against the bourgeois; they club together in order to keep up the rate of wages; they found permanent associations in order to make provision beforehand for these occasional revolts. Here and there the contest breaks out into riots.

Now and then the workers are victorious, but only for a time. The real fruit of their battles lies, not in the immediate result, but in the ever expanding union of the workers. This union is helped on by the improved means of communication that are created by modern industry, and that place the workers of different localities in contact with one another. It was just this contact that was needed to centralise the numerous local struggles, all of the same character, into one national struggle between classes. But every class struggle is a political struggle. And that union, to attain which the burghers of the Middle Ages, with their miserable highways, required centuries, the modern proletarians, thanks to railways, achieve in a few years.

This organisation of the proletarians into a class, and consequently into a political party, is continually being upset again by the competition between the workers themselves. But it ever rises up again, stronger, firmer, mightier. It compels legislative recognition of particular interests of the workers, by taking advantage of the divisions among the bourgeoisie itself. thus the ten-hours' bill in England was carried.

Altogether, collisions between the classes of the old society further in many ways the course of development of the proletariat. The bourgeoisie finds itself involved in a constant battle. At first with the aristocracy; later on, with those portions of the bourgeoisie itself, whose interests have become antagonistic to the progress of industry; at all times with the bourgeoisie of foreign countries. In all these battles it sees itself compelled to appeal to the proletariat, to ask for its help, and thus, to drag it into the political arena. The bourgeoisie itself, therefore, supplies the proletariat with its own elements of political and general education, in other words, it furnishes the proletariat with weapons for fighting the bourgeoisie.

Further, as we have already seen, entire sections of the ruling classes are, by the advance of industry, precipitated into the proletariat, or are at least threatened in their conditions of existence. These also supply the proletariat with fresh elements of enlightenment and progress.

Finally, in times when the class struggle nears the decisive hour, the process of dissolution going on within the ruling class, in fact within the whole range of old society, assumes such a violent, glaring character, that a small section of the ruling class cuts itself adrift, and joins the revolutionary class, the class that holds the future in its hands. Just as, therefore, at an earlier period, a section of the nobility went over to the bourgeoisie, so now a portion of the bourgeoisie goes over the proletariat, and in particular, a portion of the bourgeois ideologists, who have raised themselves to the level of comprehending theoretically the historical movement as a whole.

Of all the classes that stand face to face with the bourgeoisie today, the proletariat alone is a really revolutionary class. The other classes decay and finally disappear in the face of modern industry; the proletariat is its special and essential product.

The lower middle class, the small manufacturer, the shopkeeper, the artisan, the peasant, all these fight against the bourgeoisie, to save from extinction their existence as fractions of the middle class. They are therefore not revolutionary, but conservative. Nay more, they are reactionary, for they try to roll back the wheel of history. If by chance they are revolutionary, they are so only in view of their impending transfer into the proletariat; they thus defend not their present, but their future interests; they desert their own standpoint to place themselves at that of the proletariat.

The 'dangerous class,' the social scum, that passively rotting mass thrown off by the lowest layers of old society, may, here and there, be swept into the movement by a proletarian revolution; its conditions of life, however, prepare it far more for the part of a bribed tool of reactionary intrigue.

In the conditions of the proletariat, those of old society at large are already virtually swamped. The proletarian is without property; his relation to his wife and children has no longer anything in common with the bourgeois family relations; modern industrial labour, modern subjection to capital, the same in England as in France, in America as in Germany, has stripped him of every trace of national character. Law, morality, religion, are to him so many bourgeois prejudices, behind which lurk in ambush just as many bourgeois interests.

All the preceding classes that got the upper hand, sought to fortify their already acquired status by subjecting society at large to their conditions of appropriation. The proletarians cannot become masters of the productive forces of society, except by abolishing their own previous mode of appropriation, and thereby also every other previous mode of appropriation. They have nothing of their own to secure and to fortify; their mission is to destroy all previous securities for, and insurances of, individual property.

All previous historical movements were movements of minorities, or in the interest of minorities. The proletarian movement is the self-conscious, independent movement of the immense majority, in the interest of the immense majority. The proletariat, the lowest stratum of our present society, cannot stir, cannot raise itself up, without the whole superincumbent strata of official society being sprung into the air.

Though not in substance, yet in form, the struggle of the proletariat with the bourgeoisie is at first a national struggle. The proletariat of each country must, of course, first of all settle matters with its own bourgeoisie.

In depicting the most general phases of the development of the proletariat, we traced the more or less veiled civil war, raging within existing society, up to the point where that war breaks out into open revolution, and where the violent overthrow of the bourgeoisie lays the foundation for the sway of the proletariat.

Hitherto, every form of society has been based, as we have already seen, on the antagonism of oppressing and oppressed classes. But in order to oppress a class, certain conditions must be assured to it under which it can, at least, continue its slavish existence. The serf, in the period of serfdom, raised himself to membership in the commune, just as the petty bourgeois, under the yoke of feudal absolutism, managed to develop into a bourgeois. The modern labourer, on the contrary, instead of rising with the progress of industry, sinks deeper and deeper below the conditions of existence of his own class. He becomes a pauper, and pauperism develops more rapidly than population and wealth. And here it becomes evident, that the bourgeoisie is unfit any longer to be the ruling class in society, and to impose its conditions of existence upon society as an over-riding law. It is unfit to rule because it is incompetent to assure an existence to its slave within his slavery, because it cannot help letting him sink into such a state, that it has to feed him, instead of being fed by him. Society can no longer live under this bourgeoisie, in other words, its existence is no longer compatible with society.

The essential condition for the existence and for the sway of the bourgeois class, is the formation and augmentation of capital; the condition for capital is wage labour. Wage labour rests exclusively on competition between the labourers. The advance of industry, whose involuntary promoter is the bourgeoisie, replaces the isolation of the labourers, due to competition, by their revolutionary combination, due to association. The development of modern industry, therefore, cuts from under its feet the very foundation on which the bourgeoisie produces and appropriates products. What the bourgeoisie therefore produces, above all, are its own grave-diggers. Its fall and the victory of the proletariat are equally inevitable.

II PROLETARIANS AND COMMUNISTS

In what relation do the Communists stand to the proletarians as a whole?

The Communists do not form a separate party opposed to other working class parties.

They have no interests separate and apart from those of the proletariat as a whole.

They do not set up any sectarian principles of their own by which to shape and mould the proletarian movement.

The Communists are distinguished from the other working class parties by this only: 1. In the national struggles of the proletarians of the different countries, they point out and bring to the front the common interests of the entire proletariat, independently of all nationality. 2. In the various stages of development which the struggle of the working class against the bourgeoisie has to pass through, they always and everywhere represent the interests of the movement as a whole.

The immediate aim of the Communists is the same as that of all the other proletarian parties: Formation of the proletariat into a class, overthrow of the bourgeois supremacy, conquest of political power by the proletariat.

The theoretical conclusions of the Communists are in no way based on ideas or principles that have been invented, or discovered, by this or that would-be universal reformer.

They merely express, in general terms, actual relations springing from an existing class struggle, from a historical movement going on under our very eyes. The abolition of existing property relations is not at all a distinctive feature of communism.

All property relations in the past have continually been subject to historical change consequent upon the change in historical conditions.

The French Revolution, for example, abolished feudal property in favour of bourgeois property.

The distinguishing feature of communism is not the abolition of property generally, but the abolition of bourgeois property. But modern bourgeois private property is the final and most complete expression of the system of producing and appropriating products that is based on class antagonisms, on the exploitation of the many by the few.

In this sense, the theory of the Communists may be summed up in the single sentence: Abolition of private property.

We Communists have been reproached with the desire of abolishing the right of personally acquiring property as the fruit of a man's own labour, which property is alleged to be the groundwork of all personal freedom, activity and independence.

Hard-won, self-acquired, self-earned property! Do you mean the property of the petty artisan and of the small peasant, a form of property that preceded the bourgeois form? There is no need to abolish that; the development of industry has to a great extent already destroyed it, and is still destroying it daily.

Or do you mean modern bourgeois private property?

But does wage labour create any property for the labourer? Not a bit. It creates capital, i.e., that kind of property which exploits wage labour, and which cannot increase except upon condition of begetting a new supply of wage labour for fresh exploitation. Property, in its present form, is based on the antagonism of capital and wage labour. Let us examine both sides of this antagonism.

To be a capitalist, is to have not only a purely personal, but a social, *status* in production. Capital is a collective product, and only by the united action of many members, nay, in the last resort, only by the united action of all members of society, can it be set in motion.

Capital is therefore not a personal, it is a social power.

When, therefore, capital is converted into common property, into the property of all members of society, personal property is not thereby transformed into social property. It is only the social character of the property that is changed. It loses its class character.

Let us now take wage labour.

The average price of wage labour is the minimum wage, i.e., that quantum of the means of subsistence which is absolutely requisite to keep the labourer in bare existence as a labourer. What, therefore, the wage labourer appropriates by means of his labour, merely suffices to prolong and reproduce a bare existence. We by no means intend to abolish this personal appropriation of the products of labour, an appropriation that is made for the maintenance and reproduction of human life,a and that leaves no surplus wherewith to command the labour of others. All that we want to do away with is the miserable character of this appropriation, under which the labourer lives merely to increase capital, and is allowed to live only in so far as the interest of the ruling class requires it.

In bourgeois society, living labour is but a means to increase accumulated labour. In communist society, accumulated labour is but a means to widen, to enrich, to promote the existence of the labourer.

In bourgeois society, therefore, the past dominates the present; in communist society, the present dominates the past. In bourgeois society capital is independent and has individuality, while the living person is dependent and has no individuality.

And the abolition of this state of things is called by the bourgeois, abolition of individuality and freedom! And rightly so. The abolition of bourgeois individuality, bourgeois independence, and bourgeois freedom is undoubtedly aimed at.

By freedom is meant, under the present bourgeois conditions of production, free trade, free selling and buying. But if selling and buying disappears, free selling and buying disappears also. This talk about free selling and buying, and all the other 'brave words' of our bourgeoisie about freedom in general, have a meaning, if any, only in contrast with restricted selling and buying, with the fettered traders of the Middle Ages, but have no meaning when opposed to the communist abolition of buying and selling, of the bourgeois conditions of production, and of the bourgeoisie itself.

You are horrified at our intending to do away with private property. But in your existing society, private property is already done away with for nine-tenths of the population; its existence for the few is solely due to its non-existence in the hands of those nine-tenths. You reproach us, therefore, with intending to do away with a form of property, the necessary condition for whose existence is the non-existence of any property for the immense majority of society.

In one word, you reproach us with intending to do away with your property. Precisely so; that is just what we intend.

From the moment when labour can no longer be converted into capital, money, or rent, into a social power capable of being monopolised, i.e., from the moment when individual property can no longer be transformed into bourgeois property, into capital, from that moment, you say, individuality vanishes.

You must, therefore, confess that by 'individual' you mean no other person than the bourgeois, than the middle-class owner of property. This person must, indeed, be swept out of the way, and made impossible.

Communism deprives no man of the power to appropriate the products of society; all that it does is to deprive him of the power to subjugate the labour of others by means of such appropriation.

It has been objected, that upon the abolition of private property all work will cease, and universal laziness will overtake us.

According to this, bourgeois society ought long ago to have gone to the dogs through sheer idleness; for those of its members who work, acquire nothing, and those who acquire anything, do not work. The whole of this objection is but another expression of the tautology: There can no longer be any wage labour when there is no longer any capital.

All objections urged against the communistic mode of producing and appropriating material products, have, in the same way, been urged against the communistic modes of producing and appropriating intellectual products. Just as to the bourgeois, the disappearance of class property is the disappearance of production itself, so the disappearance of class culture is to him identical with the disappearance of all culture.

That culture, the loss of which he laments, is, for the enormous majority, a mere training to act as a machine.

But don't wrangle with us so long as you apply, to our intended abolition of bourgeois property, the standard of your bourgeois notions of freedom, culture, law, etc. Your very ideas are but the outgrowth of the conditions of your bourgeois production and bourgeois property, just as your jurisprudence is but the will of your class made into a law for all, a will whose essential character and direction are determined by the economical conditions of existence of your class.

The selfish misconception that induces you to transform into eternal laws of nature and of reason, the social forms springing from your present mode of production and form of property – historical relations that rise and disappear in the progress of production – this misconception you share with every ruling class that has preceded you. What you see clearly in the case of ancient property, what you admit in the case of feudal property, you are of course forbidden to admit in the case of your own bourgeois form of property.

Abolition of the family! Even the most radical flare up at this infamous proposal of the Communists.

On what foundation is the present family, the bourgeois family, based? On capital, on private gain. In its completely developed form this family exists only among the bourgeoisie. But this state of things finds its complement in the practical absence of the family among the proletarians, and in public prostitution.

The bourgeois family will vanish as a matter of course when its complement vanishes, and both will vanish with the vanishing of capital.

Do you charge us with wanting to stop the exploitation of children by their parents? To this crime we plead guilty..

But, you will say, we destroy the most hallowed of relations, when we replace home education by social.

And your education! Is not that also social, and determined by the social conditions under which you educate, by the intervention direct or indirect, of society, by means of schools, etc.? The Communists have not invented the intervention of society in education; they do but seek to alter the character of that intervention, and to rescue education from the influence of the ruling class.

The bourgeois claptrap about the family and education, about the hallowed correlation of parent and child, becomes all the more disgusting, the more, by the action of modern industry, all family ties among the proletarians are torn asunder, and their children transformed into simple articles of commerce and instruments of labour.

But you Communists would introduce community of women, screams the whole bourgeoisie in chorus.

The bourgeois sees in his wife a mere instrument of production. He hears that the instruments of production are to be exploited in common, and, naturally, can come to no other conclusion than that the lot of being common to all will likewise fall to the women.

He has not even a suspicion that the real point aimed at is to do away with the status of women as mere instruments of production.

For the rest, nothing is more ridiculous than the virtuous indignation of our bourgeois at the community of women which, they pretend, is to be openly and officially established by the Communists. The Communists have no need to introduce community of women; it has existed almost from time immemorial.

Our bourgeois, not content with having the wives and daughters of their proletarians at their disposal, not to speak of common prostitutes, take the greatest pleasure in seducing each other's wives.

Bourgeois marriage is in reality a system of wives in common and thus, at the most, what the Communists might possibly be reproached with is that they desire to introduce, in substitution for a hypocritically concealed, an openly legalised community of women. For the rest, it is self-evident, that the abolition of the present system of production must bring with it the abolition of the community of women springing from that system, i.e. of prostitution both public and private.

The Communists are further reproached with desiring to abolish countries and nationality.

The workingmen have no country. We cannot take from them what they have not got. Since the proletariat must first of all acquire political supremacy, must rise to be the leading class of the nation, must constitute itself *the* nation, it is, so far, itself national, though not in the bourgeois sense of the word.

National differences and antagonisms between peoples are daily more and more vanishing, owing to the development of the bourgeoisie, to freedom of commerce, to the world market, to uniformity in the mode of production and in the conditions of life corresponding thereto.

The supremacy of the proletariat will cause them to vanish still faster. United action of the leading civilised countries at least, is one of the first conditions for the emancipation of the proletariat.

In proportion as the exploitation of one individual by another is put an end to, the exploitation of one nation by another will also be put an end to. In proportion as the antagonism between classes within the nation vanishes, the hostility of one nation to another will come to an end.

The charges against communism made from a religious, a philosophical and, generally, from an ideological standpoint, are not deserving of serious examination.

Does it require deep intuition to comprehend that man's ideas, views,and conceptions, in one word, man's consciousness, changes with every change in the conditions of his material existence, in his social relations and in his social life?

What else does the history of ideas prove, than that intellectual production changes its character in proportion as material production is changed? The ruling ideas of each age have ever been the ideas of its ruling class.

When people speak of ideas that revolutionise society, they do but express the fact, that within the old society, the elements of a new one have been created, and that the dissolution of the old ideas keeps even pace with the dissolution of the old conditions of existence.

When the ancient world was in its last throes, the ancient religions were overcome by Christianity. When Christian ideas succumbed in the eighteenth century to rationalist ideas, feudal society fought its death battle with the then revolutionary bourgeoisie. The ideas of religious liberty and freedom of conscience, merely gave expression to the way of free competition within the domain of knowledge.

'Undoubtedly,' it will be said, 'religious, moral, philosophical and juridical ideas have been modified in the course of historical development. But religion, morality, philosophy, political science, and law, constantly survived this change.'

'There are, besides, eternal truths, such as Freedom, Justice, etc., that are common to all states of society. But communism abolishes eternal truths, it abolishes all religion, and all morality, instead of constituting them on a new basis; it therefore acts in contradiction to all past historical experience.'

What does this accusation reduce itself to? The history of all past society has consisted in the development of class antagonisms, antagonisms that assumed different forms at different epochs.

But whatever form they may have taken, one fact is common to all past ages, viz., the exploitation of one part of society by the other. No wonder, then, that the social consciousness of past ages, despite all the multiplicity and variety it displays, moves within certain common forms, or general ideas, which cannot completely vanish except with the total disappearance of class antagonisms.

The communist revolution is the most radical rupture with traditional property relations; no wonder that its development involves the most radical rupture with traditional ideas.

But let us have done with the bourgeois objections to communism.

We have seen above, that the first step in the revolution by the working class, is to raise the proletariat to the position of ruling class, to win the battle of democracy.

The proletariat will use its political supremacy to wrest, by degrees, all capital from the bourgeoisie, to centralise all instruments of production in the hands of the state, i.e., of the proletariat organised as the ruling class; and to increase the total of productive forces as rapidly as possible.

Of course, in the beginning, this cannot be effected except by means of despotic inroads on the rights of property, and on the conditions of bourgeois production; by means of measures, therefore, which appear economically insufficient and untenable, but which, in the course of the movement, outstrip themselves, necessitate further inroads upon the old social order, and are unavoidable as a means of entirely revolutionising the mode of production.

These measures will of course be different in different countries.

Nevertheless in the most advanced countries, the following will be pretty generally applicable.

1. Abolition of property in land and application of all rents of land to public purposes.

2. A heavy progressive or graduated income tax.

3. Abolition of all right of inheritance.

4. Confiscation of the property of all emigrants and rebels.

5. Centralisation of credit in the hands of the state, by means of a

national bank with state capital and an exclusive monopoly.

6. Centralisation of the means of communication and transport in the hands of the state.

7. Extension of factories and instruments of production owned by the state; the bringing into cultivation of waste lands, and the improvement of the soil generally in accordance with a common plan.

8. Equal obligation of all to work. Establishment of industrial armies, especially for agriculture.

9. Combination of agriculture with manufacturing industries; gradual abolition of the distinction between town and country, by a more equable distribution of the population over the country.

10. Free education for all children in public schools. Abolition of children's factory labour in its present form. Combination of education with industrial production, etc.

When, in the course of development, class distinctions have disappeared, and all production has been concentrated in the hands of a vast association of the whole nation, the public power will lose its political character. Political power, properly so called, is merely the organised power of one class for oppressing another. If the proletariat during its contest with the bourgeoisie is compelled, by the force of circumstances, to organise itself as a class; if, by means of a revolution, it makes itself the ruling class, and, as such, sweeps away by force the old conditions of production, then it will, along with these conditions, have swept away the conditions for the existence of class antagonisms and of classes generally, and will thereby have abolished its own supremacy as a class.

In place of the old bourgeois society, with its classes and class antagonisms, we shall have an association, in which the free development of each is the condition for the free development of all.

III. SOCIALIST AND COMMUNIST LITERATURE

1. Reactionary Socialism

a. Feudal Socialism

Owing to their historical position, it became the vocation of the aristocracies of France and England to write pamphlets against modern bourgeois society. In the French Revolution of July 1830, and in the English reform agitation, these aristocracies again succumbed to the hateful upstart. Thenceforth, a serious political struggle was altogether out of the question. A literary battle alone remained possible. But even in the domain of literature the old cries of the restoration period had become impossible.

In order to arouse sympathy, the aristocracy was obliged to lose sight, apparently, of its own interests, and to formulate its indictment against the bourgeoisie in the interest of the exploited working class alone. Thus the aristocracy took their revenge by singing lampoons on their new master, and whispering in his ears sinister prophecies of coming catastrophe.

In this way arose feudal socialism: half lamentation, half lampoon; half echo of the past, half menace of the future; at times, by its bitter, witty and incisive criticism, striking the bourgeoisie to the very heart's core, but always ludicrous in its effect, through total incapacity to comprehend the march of modern history.

The aristocracy, in order to rally the people to them, waved the proletarian alms-bag in front for a banner. But the people, so often as it joined them, saw on the hindquarters the old feudal coats of arms, and deserted with loud and irreverent laughter.

One section of the French Legitimists and 'Young England,' exhibited this spectacle.

In pointing out that their mode of exploitation was different to that of the bourgeoisie, the feudalists forget that they exploited under circumstances and conditions that were quite different, and that are now antiquated. In showing that, under their rule, the modern proletariat never existed, they forget that the modern bourgeoisie is the necessary offspring of their own form of society.

For the rest, so little do they conceal the reactionary character of their criticism, that their chief accusation against the bourgeoisie amounts to this, that under the bourgeois regime a class is being developed, which is destined to cut up root and branch the old order of society.

What, they upbraid the bourgeoisie with is not so much that it creates a proletariat, as that is creates a *revolutionary* proletariat.

In political practice, therefore, they join in all coercive measures against the working class; and in ordinary life, despite their high falutin' phrases, they stoop to pick up the golden apples dropped from the tree of industry, and to barter truth, love, and honour for traffic in wool, beetroot-sugar, and potato spirits.

As the parson has ever gone hand in hand with the landlord, so has clerical socialism with feudal socialism.

Nothing is easier than to give Christian asceticism a socialist tinge. Has not Christianity declaimed against private property, against marriage, against the state? Has it not preached in the place of these, charity and poverty, celibacy and mortification of the flesh, monastic life and Mother Church? Christian socialism is but the holy water with which the priest consecrates the heart-burnings of the aristocrat.

b. Petty-Bourgeois Socialism

The feudal aristocracy was not the only class that was ruined by the bourgeoisie, not the only class whose conditions of existence pined and perished in the atmosphere of modern bourgeois society. The mediaeval burgesses and the small peasant proprietors were the precursors of the modern bourgeoisie. In those countries which are but little developed, industrially and commercially, these two classes will vegetate side by side with the rising bourgeoisie.

In countries where modern civilisation has become fully developed, a new class of petty bourgeois has been formed, fluctuating between proletariat and bourgeoisie, and ever renewing itself as a supplementary part of bourgeois society. The individual members of this class, however, are being constantly hurled down into the proletariat by the action of competition, and, as modern industry develops, they even see the moment approaching when they will completely disappear as an independent section of modern society, to be replaced, in manufactures, agriculture and commerce, by overlookers, bailiffs and shopmen.

In countries, like France, where the peasants constitute far more than half of the population, it was natural that writers who sided with the proletariat against the bourgeoisie, should use their criticism of the bourgeois regime, the standard of the peasant and petty bourgeois, and from the standpoint of these intermediate classes should take up the cudgels for the working class. Thus arose petty-bourgeois socialism. Sismondi was the head of this school, not only in France but also in England.

This school of socialism dissected with great acuteness the contradictions in the conditions of modern production. It laid bare the hypocritical apologies of economists. It proved, incontrovertibly, the disastrous effects of machinery and division of labour; the concentration of capital and land in a few hands; overproduction and crises; it pointed out the inevitable ruin of the petty bourgeois and peasant, the misery of the proletariat, the anarchy in production, the crying inequalities in the distribution of wealth, the industrial war of extermination between nations, the dissolution of old moral bonds, of the old family relations, of the old nationalities.

In its positive aims, however, this form of socialism aspires either to restoring the old means of production and of exchange, and with them the old property relations, and the old society, or to cramping the modern means of production and of exchange within the framework of the old property relations that have been, and were bound to be, exploded by those means. In either case, it is both reactionary and utopian.

Its last words are: Corporate guilds for manufacture; patriarchal relations in agriculture.

Ultimately, when stubborn historical facts had dispersed all intoxicating effect of self-deception, this form of socialism ended in a miserable fit of the blues.

c. German or 'True' Socialism

The socialist and communist literature of France, a literature that originated under the pressure of a bourgeoisie in power, and that was the expression of the struggle against this power, was introduced into Germany at a time when the bourgeoisie, in that country, had just begun its contest with feudal absolutism.

German philosophers, would-be philosophers, and men of letters eagerly seized on this literature, only forgetting that when these writings immigrated from France into Germany, French social conditions had not immigrated along with them. In contact with German social conditions, this French literature lost all its immediate practical significance, and assumed a purely literary aspect. Thus, to the German philosophers of the eighteenth century, the demands of the first French Revolution were nothing more than the demands of 'Practical Reason' in general, and the utterance of the will of the revolutionary French bourgeoisie signified in their eyes the laws of pure will, of will as it was bound to be, of true human will generally.

The work of the German *literati* consisted solely in bringing the new French ideas into harmony with their ancient philosophical conscience, or rather, in annexing the French ideas without deserting their own philosophic point of view.

This annexation took place in the same way in which a foreign language is appropriated, namely by translation.

It is well known how the monks wrote silly lives of Catholic saints *over* the manuscripts on which the classical works of ancient heathendom had been written. The German *literati* reversed this process with the profane French literature. They wrote their philosophical nonsense beneath the French original. For instance, beneath the French criticism of the economic functions of money, they wrote 'alienation of humanity,' and beneath the French criticism of the bourgeois state, they wrote, 'dethronement of the category of the general,' and so forth.

The introduction of these philosophical phrases at the back of the French historical criticisms they dubbed 'Philosophy of Action,' 'True Socialism,' 'German Science of Socialism,' 'Philosophical Foundation of Socialism,' and so on.

The French socialist and communist literature was thus completely emasculated. And, since it ceased in the hands of the German to express the struggle of one class with the other, he felt conscious of having overcome 'French one-sidedness' and of representing, not true requirements, but the requirements of truth; not the interests of the proletariat, but the interests of human nature, of man in general, who belongs to no class, has no reality, who exists only in the misty realm of philosophical phantasy.

This German socialism, which took its school-boy task so seriously and solemnly, and extolled its poor stock-in-trade in such mountebank fashion, meanwhile gradually lost its pedantic innocence.

The fight of the German and especially of the Prussian bourgeoisie against feudal aristocracy and absolute monarchy, in other words, the liberal movement, became more earnest.

By this, the long-wished-for opportunity was offered to 'True' Socialism of confronting the political movement with the socialist demands, of hurling the traditional anathemas against liberalism, against representative government, against bourgeois competition, bourgeois freedom of the press, bourgeois legislation, bourgeois liberty and equality, and of preaching to the masses that they had nothing to gain, and everything to lose, by this bourgeois movement. German socialism forgot, in the nick of time, that the French criticism, whose silly echo it was, presuposed the existence of modern bourgeois society, with its corresponding economic conditions of existence, and the political constitution adapted thereto, the very things whose attainment was the object of the pending struggle in Germany.

To the absolute governments, with their following of parsons, professors, country squires and officials, it served as a welcome scarecrow against the threatening bourgeoisie. It was a sweet finish after the bitter pills of floggings and bullets, with which these same governments, just at that time, dosed the German working class risings.

While this 'True' Socialism thus served the governments as a weapon for fighting the German bourgeoisie, it, at the same time, directly represented a reactionary interest, the interest of the German philistines. In Germany the petty-bourgeois class, a relic of the sixteenth century, and since then constantly cropping up again under various forms, is the real social basis of the existing state of things.

To preserve this class is to preserve the existing state of things in Germany. The industrial and political supremacy of the bourgeoisie threatens it with certain destruction – on the one hand, from the concentration of capital; on the other, from the rise of a revolutionary proletariat. 'True' Socialism appeared to kill these two birds with one stone. It spread like an epidemic.

The robe of speculative cobwebs, embroidered with flowers of rhetoric, steeped in the dew of sickly sentiment, this transcendental robe in which the German Socialists wrapped their sorry 'eternal truths,' all skin and bone, served to wonderfully increase the sale of their goods amongst such a public.

And on its part, German socialism recognised, more and more, its own calling as the bombastic representative of the petty-bourgeois philistine.

It proclaimed the German nation to be the model nation, and the German petty philistine to be the typical man. To every villainous meanness of this model man it gave a hidden, higher, socialistic inter-pretation, the exact contrary of its real character. It went to the extreme length of directly opposing the 'brutally destructive' tendency of communism, and of proclaiming its supreme and impartial contempt of all class struggles. With very few exceptions, all the so-called socialist and communist publications that now (1847) circulate in Germany belong to the domain of this foul and enervating literature.

2. Conservative or Bourgeois Socialism

A part of the bourgeoisie is desirous of redressing social grievances, in order to secure the continued existence of bourgeois society.

To this section belong economists, philanthropists, humanitarians, improvers of the condition of the working class, organisers of charity, members of societies for the prevention of cruelty to animals, temperance fanatics, hole-and-corner reformers of every imaginable kind. This form of socialism has, moreover, been worked out into complete systems.

We may cite Proudhon's *Philosophie de la Misère* [*Philosophy of Poverty*] as an example of this form.

The socialistic bourgeois want all the advantages of modern social conditions without the struggles and dangers necessarily resulting therefrom. They desire the existing state of society minus its revolutionary and disintegrating elements. They wish for a bourgeoisie without a proletariat. The bourgeoisie naturally conceives the world in which it is supreme to be the best; and bourgeois socialism develops this comfortable conception into various more or less complete systems. In requiring the proletariat to carry out such a system, and thereby to march straightway into the social New Jerusalem, it but requires in reality, that the proletariat should remain within the bounds of existing society, but should cast away all its hateful ideas concerning the bourgeoisie.

A second and more practical, but less systematic, form of this socialism sought to depreciate every revolutionary movement in the eyes of the working class, by showing that no mere political reform, but only a change in the material conditions of existence, in economical relations, could be of any advantage to them. By changes in the material conditions of existence, this form of socialism, however, by no means understands abolition of the bourgeois relations of production, an abolition that can be effected only by a revolution, but administrative reforms, based on the continued existence of these relations; reforms therefore, that in no respect affect the relations between capital and labour, but, at the best, lessen the cost, and simplify the administrative work of bourgeois government.

Bourgeois socialism attains adequate expression, when, and only when, it becomes a mere figure of speech.

Free trade: for the benefit of the working class. Protective duties: for the benefit of the working class. Prison reform: for the benefit of the working class. This is the last word and the only seriously meant word of bourgeois socialism.

It is summed up in the phrase: the bourgeois is a bourgeois – for the benefit of the working class.

3. Critical-Utopian Socialism and Communism

We do not here refer to that literature which, in every great modern revolution, has always given voice to the demands of the proletariat, such as the writings of Babeuf and others.

The first direct attempts of the proletariat to attain its own ends, made in times of universal excitement, when feudal society was being overthrown, these attempts necessarily failed, owing to the then undeveloped state of the proletariat, as well as to the absence of the economic conditions for its emancipation, conditions that had yet to be produced, and could be produced by the impending bourgeois epoch alone. The revolutionary literature that accompanied these first movements of the proletariat had necessarily a reactionary character. It inculcated universal asceticism and social levelling in its crudest form.

The socialist and communist systems, properly so called, those of Saint-Simon, Fourier, Owen and others, spring into existence in the early undeveloped period, described above, of the struggle between proletariat and bourgeoisie (see Section 1. Bourgeois and Proletarians).

The founders of these systems, see, indeed, the class antagonisms, as well as the action of the decomposing elements in the prevailing form of society. But the proletariat, as yet in its infancy, offers to them the spectacle of a class without any historical initiative or any independent political movement.

Since the development of class antagonism keeps even pace with the development of industry, the economic situation, as they find it, does not as yet offer to them the material conditions for the emancipation of the proletariat. They therefore search after a new social science, after new social laws, that are to create these conditions.

Historical action is to yield to their personal inventive action; historically created conditions of emancipation to phantastic ones; and the gradual, spontaneous class organisation of the proletariat to an organisation of society especially contrived by these inventors. Future history resolves itself, in their eyes, into the propaganda and the practical carrying out of their social plans.

In the formation of their plans they are conscious of caring chiefly for the interests of the working class, as being the most suffering class. Only from the point of view of being the most suffering class does the proletariat exist for them.

The undeveloped state of the class struggle, as well as their own surroundings, causes Socialists of this kind to consider themselves far superior to all class antagonisms. They want to improve the condition of every member of society, even that of the most favoured. Hence, they habitually appeal to society at large, without distinction of class; nay, by preference, to the ruling class. For how can people, when once they understand their system, fail to see in it the best possible plan of the best possible state of society?

Hence, they reject all political, and especially all revolutionary action; they wish to attain their ends by peaceful means, and endeavour, by small experiments, necessarily doomed to failure, and by the force of example, to pave the way for the new social gospel.

Such phantastic pictures of future society, painted at a time when the proletariat is still in a very undeveloped state and has but a phantastic conception of its own position, correspond with the first instinctive yearnings of that class for a general reconstruction of society.

But these socialist and communist publications contain also a critical element. They attack every principle of existing society. Hence they are full of the most valuable materials for the enlightenment of the working class. The practical measures proposed in them – such as the abolition of the distinction between town and country, of the family, of the carrying on of industries for the account of private individuals, and of the wage system, the proclamation of social harmony, the conversion of the functions of the state into a mere superintendence of production – all these proposals point solely to the disappearance of class antagonisms which were, at that time, only just cropping up, and which, in these publications, are recognised in their earliest, indistinct and undefined forms only. These proposals, therefore, are of a purely utopian character.

The significance of critical-utopian socialism and communism bears an inverse relation to historical development. In proportion as the modern class struggle develops and takes definite shape, this phantastic standing apart from the contest, these phantastic attacks on it, lose all practical value and all theoretical justification. Therefore, although the originators of these systems were, in many respects, revolutionary, their disciples have, in every case, formed mere reactionary sects. They hold fast by the original views of their masters, in opposition to the progressive historical development of the proletariat. They, therefore, endeavour, and that consistently, to deaden the class struggle and to reconcile the class antagonisms. They still dream of experimental realisation of their social utopias, of founding isolated *phalanstères*, of establishing 'Home Colonies,' or setting up a 'Little Icaria' – pocket editions of the New Jerusalem – and to realise all these castles in the air, they are compelled to appeal to the feelings and purses of the bourgeois. By degrees they sink into the category of the reactionary conservative socialists depicted above, differing from these only by more systematic pedantry, and by their fanatical and superstitious belief in the miraculous effects of their social science.

They, therefore, violently oppose all political action on the part of the working class; such action, according to them, can only result from blind unbelief in the new gospel.

The Owenites in England, and the Fourierists in France, respectively, oppose the Chartists and the *Réformistes*.

IV. POSITION OF THE COMMUNISTS IN RELATION TO THE VARIOUS EXISTING OPPOSITION PARTIES

Section II has made clear the relations of the Communists to the existing working class parties, such as the Chartists in England and the Agrarian Reformers in America.

The Communists fight for the attainment of the immediate aims, for the enforcement of the momentary interests of the working class; but in the movement of the present, they also represent and take care of the future of that movement. In France the Communists ally themselves with the Social-Democrats, against the conservative and radical bourgeoisie, reserving, however, the right to take up a critical position in regard to phrases and illusions traditionally handed down from the Great Revolution.

In Switzerland they support the Radicals, without losing sight of the fact that this party consists of antagonistic elements, partly of Democratic Socialists, in the French sense, partly of radical bourgeois.

In Poland they support the party that insists on an agrarian revolution as the prime condition for national emancipation, that party which fomented the insurrection of Cracow in 1846.

In Germany they fight with the bourgeoisie whenever it acts in a revolutionary way, against the absolute monarchy, the feudal squirearchy, and the petty-bourgeoisie.

But they never cease, for a single instant, to instil into the working class the clearest possible recognition of the hostile antagonism between bourgeoisie and proletariat, in order that the German workers may straightway use, as so many weapons against the bourgeoisie, the social and political conditions that the bourgeoisie must necessarily introduce along with its supremacy, and in order that, after the fall of the reactionary classes in Germany, the fight against the bourgeoisie itself may immediately begin.

The Communists turn their attention chiefly to Germany, because that country is on the eve of a bourgeois revolution that is bound to be carried out under more advanced conditions of European civilisation and with a much more developed proletariat than that of England was in the seventeenth, and of France in the eighteenth century, and because the bourgeois revolution in Germany will be but the prelude to an immediately following proletarian revolution.

In short, the Communists everywhere support every revolutionary movement against the existing social and political order of things.

In all these movements they bring to the front, as the leading question in each, the property question, no matter what its degree of development at the time.

Finally, they labour everywhere for the union and agreement of the democratic parties of all countries.

The Communists disdain to conceal their views and aims. They openly declare that their ends can be attained only by the forcible overthrow of all existing social conditions. Let the ruling classes tremble at a communist revolution. The proletarians have nothing to lose but their chains. They have a world to win.

Workingmen of all countries, unite!

Translation by Samuel Moore